Writing Irish

Selected Interviews with Irish Writers
from the *Irish Literary Supplement*

Edited by James P. Myers, Jr.

Syracuse University Press

The paper used in this publication meets the minimum requirements of American National Standard for Information Sciences—Permanence of Paper for Printed Library Materials, ANSI Z39.48-1984. ∞™

Library of Congress Cataloging-in-Publication Data

Writing Irish : selected interviews with Irish writers from the Irish
    literary supplement / edited by James P. Myers, Jr. — 1st ed.
        p.   cm. — (Irish studies)
    Includes bibliographical references (p.   ) and index.
    ISBN 0-8156-0598-6 (pbk. : alk. paper)
    1. English literature—Irish authors—History and criticism—
Theory, etc.   2. English literature—20th century—History and
criticism—Theory, etc.   3. Irish literature—20th century—History
and criticism—Theory, etc.   4. Authors, Irish—20th century—
Interviews.   5. Ireland—Intellectual life—20th century.
6. Ireland—In literature.   7. Authorship.   I. Myers, James P.,
1941–   . II. Irish literary supplement.   III. Series: Irish
studies (Syracuse, N.Y.)
PR8753.W75   1999
820.9′9417—DC21   99-20928

Manufactured in the United States of America

Contents

Preface

THE PRESENT COLLECTION had its genesis in a chance remark to Bob Lowery, editor of the *Irish Literary Supplement*. Concerned that my yellowing and disintegrating newsprint pages of the *ILS* interviews with writers were not holding up well after years of being consulted and photocopied for use in courses, I suggested that he look into the possibility of editing and reprinting the invaluable dialogues in handy, more durable book format. Because *ILS* does not publish books, Bob urged me to locate a publisher for the project, to which he gave both his encouragement and blessing. By the time I succeeded in finding a possible publisher for the proposed selection of interviews, I had also become its editor, a development I had neither intended nor foreseen.

My intention to bring forth this volume involved reprinting the interviews, together with their original headnotes or lead-ins and updating the bibliographic commentary. At the same time, typographic and other errors were to be silently emended. The only real addition involved providing annotations, some updating, and clarifications, these principally for the benefit of undergraduate students (in courses involving contemporary Irish literature) who would find such commentary useful, if not indeed needful. Several individuals who saw parts of the book, however, vigorously suggested that I eliminate most of the annotations. Although I did not identify obvious names and references with which students of Irish literature should have ready acquaintance, it still appeared to some that I was footnoting the texts excessively. Accordingly, I cut back even more.

Notwithstanding this effort, I suspect some will still maintain I should have pruned away more than I did.

Some presentations here differ from the originals in another way: not all the *ILS* interviews were introduced to the reader, or in some instances the lead-ins were unhelpfully short, this for a number of possible reasons. To provide some uniformity in re-presenting the conversations here and to offer useful bibliographic guides to the writers, several new introductions had to be written, the cut-off date being 1997.

I am grateful to the many who helped me prepare this selection by listening to me ramble on about the "genre" of the interview, by answering my questions, by encouraging the effort: to Bob Lowery, Dillon Johnston, and Richard Fallis for encouragement and direction; to my colleagues at Gettysburg College, especially Edward J. Baskerville, Temma F. Berg, and Leonard S. Goldberg (who sometimes had no idea why I was asking the questions I did); to the interlibrary loan staff of the Gettysburg College library, Susan Roach and Nelly Heller, for obtaining on short notice many difficult-to-find titles; to Cara McClintock, who performed much of the early editorial "grunt" work; to several interviewers who did more than merely respond to a few editorial questions by rechecking text for accuracy, giving advice, obtaining photographs, providing additional information from the writers—Deborah Hunter McWilliams, Lucy McDiarmid, Richard Pine, Michael Kenneally, Kevin T. McEneaney, Nancy Means Wright, Dennis J. Hannan, and Kathleen McCracken; to Bruce D. Boling for translating most of the Gaelic terms and phrases. For helping me formulate and formalize my feelings and perceptions on the convention of the interview itself, set forth here in the Introduction, special thanks are due Temma F. Berg, Deborah Hunter McWilliams, and Mary Dalton (whose excellent 1991 *ILS* interview with Paul Durcan unfortunately could not be included).

Special appreciation is also expressed to Gettysburg College for its various kinds of financial support during the past years that made possible the editing of this collection.

The errors, misjudgments, and lapses that may remain, like Prospero's "thing of darkness, I acknowledge mine."

Interviewers

Jacqueline Stahl Aronson, a specialist in Chaucer studies and eighteenth-century prose, teaches at the John Jay College of Criminal Justice, CUNY. She received her Ph.D. from the Graduate Center of CUNY.

Kevin Barry is professor of English literature at University College, Dublin. He is the author of *Language, Music and the Sign* (1987) and editor of *The Irish Review*.

Jennifer Clarke, at the time of the interview, was a doctoral candidate at SUNY, Stony Brook, with an interest in English and Irish literatures.

Michael J. Durkan was librarian at Swarthmore College. He was coeditor (with Ronald Ayling) of *Sean O'Casey: A Bibliography* (1978); editor of *Seamus Heaney: A Checklist for a Bibliography* (1986); and author (with Rand Brandes) of *Seamus Heaney: A Reference Guide* (1996). He died in 1996.

S. F. Gallagher selected and introduced *Selected Plays: Hugh Leonard* (1992). He teaches at Trent University, Peterborough, Ontario, and was president of the Canadian Association for Irish Studies, 1990–93.

Dennis J. Hannan is adjunct associate professor at the SUNY College at New Paltz, New York. As director of Walden Associates, he gives workshops on gender equity in education. He also writes prepublication reviews for *Publishers Weekly*.

Eamonn Hughes is a lecturer at the School of English, Queen's University, Belfast, where he specializes in Irish Literary and cultural studies. He is the author of numerous articles on Irish writing and editor of *Culture and Politics in Northern Ireland, 1960–1990* (1991).

Rüdiger Imhof, professor of English literature and »Irish literature in English at Wuppertal University in Germany, is interested principally in nineteenth- and twentieth-century English literature and twentieth-century Irish fiction and drama. His publications include *John Banville: A Critical Introduction* (1997), *Contemporary Irish Novelists* (1990), *Ireland: Literature, Culture, Politics* (1994), and, with J. Achilles, *Irische Dramatiker der Gegenwerk* (1996).

Dillon Johnston teaches English at Wake Forest University where he founded, and still directs, the press and its series of Irish poetry. A new edition of his *Irish Poetry after Joyce* was published in 1996 by Syracuse University Press.

Michael Kenneally teaches Irish literature at Marianopolis College and Concordia University in Montreal. He is editor of the four-volume series on contemporary Irish literature, *Studies in Contemporary Irish Literature* (1988–) and is current chair of the International Association for the Study of Irish literature.

Eileen Kennedy, after forty-two years of college teaching, has retired as professor of English and director of the master's program in liberal studies at Kean College of New Jersey, which recently designated her *professor emerita* for her many years of service. She has published widely in academic journals and books, such as *The James Joyce Quarterly, New Irish Writing,* and *Contemporary Irish Writing,* and is pursuing research in modern Irish authors.

Kathleen McCracken, lecturer in American studies and English literature at the University of Ulster at Jordanstown, Northern Ireland, is currently preparing a critical study of the poetry of Paul Durcan. She is a Canadian who has published four books of poetry, the most recent of which, *Blue Light, Bay and College* (1991), was nominated for the Governor General's Award for poetry.

Lucy McDiarmid is professor of English at Villanova University and president of the American Conference for Irish Studies (1997–99). Her books include *Saving Civilization: Yeats, Eliot, and Auden Between the Wars* (1984), *Auden's Apologies for Poetry* (1990), and, as coeditor, *Lady Gregory: Selected Writings* (1995) and *High and Low Moderns: Literature and Culture, 1889–1939* (1996).

Kevin T. McEneaney teaches literature and composition at Marist College and St. Thomas Aquinas College. A coeditor of *The Irish Literary Supplement* and associate editor of the *Encyclopedia Americana*, he is the author of the poetic sequence *The Enclosed Garden* (1991) and published his latest sequence, *Longing*, in 1997.

Deborah Hunter McWilliams has held academic appointments at the University of California–Irvine, Chapman College, Orange Coast College, and Irvine Valley College. She has published numerous essays and reviews in books and journals such as *Modern Irish Writers: A Bio-Critical Sourcebook, Éire-Ireland, Irish Studies Review,* the *Irish Literary Supplement, New Hibernia Review, Notes on Modern Irish Literature,* and *Studies.*

James J. Murphy is associate professor of English and director of the Irish Studies Program at Villanova University.

Richard Pine is a critic, lecturer, former secretary of the Irish Writers' Union, and Irish editor of the *Irish Literary Supplement.* He has written on Brian Friel, Oscar Wilde, the Dublin Gate Theatre, and is editor of the essays *Dark Fathers into Light: Brendan Kennelly* (1994).

Nancy Means Wright is adjunct lecturer at Marist College and the author of six books; the latest, a novel, is just out from St. Martin's Press. Her poetry appears in anthologies from Beacon Press, St. Martin's Press, and Ashland Poetry Press.

Introduction

IN THE SIXTEEN DIALOGUES collected here, Irish writers diversely comment upon the traditional themes informing contemporary Irish writing: the significance of place; possible responses to the Troubles; the tyrannical authority that time and, particularly, Irish history exercise upon the present; the importance, or irrelevance, of community; the roles of writers in the world and in Ireland; the interrelationships among writers living and dead—to identify a few of the more evident. Additionally, one learns something of what writers have discovered about the essential drive to write, what they want readers to believe they have discovered, or, indeed, what they have not discovered and what they may choose not to share.

The interviews, moreover, call attention to themselves in several ways, but none is so intriguing and suggestive, perhaps, as the resistance occasionally expressed, occasionally implied, by a writer toward the medium of the interview itself. Striking to the heart of this paradox, two interviewers explored their subjects' reservations concerning the convention. At the conclusion to his interchange with poet John Montague, Michael McEneaney interrogates the dual nature of the interview, its tradition as "an art form" of respectable antiquity, its reputation as "an aspect of society that relates to gossip." Leaving little doubt about his own ambivalence, Montague readily admits to resenting interviews and, notwithstanding this, still giving them. Readers, he fears, oversimplify: "ignorance is invincible." He contends, however, that in this inescapable "media age . . . we should try to use" the interview as another opportunity for explaining our perceptions, "to give a few simple signposts" capable of guiding readers through labyrinthine complexities of poetic vision without at the same moment "cheapening" the endeavor.

Similarly to McEneaney's exchange with Montague, Rüdiger Imhof initiates his 1986 dialogue with novelist John Banville with a challenge: "You are said to be most reluctant to give interviews. Why is that so?" Banville succinctly offers three justifications: they are gossipy; he no longer possesses his earlier certainty that he understands his own work; and he feels that his "business" is his "own."

In one of the most illuminating testimonies to this problem, but in an *Irish Literary Supplement* interview that could not be included here,[1] Mary Dalton describes how she approached her interview with poet Paul Durcan equipped "with questions about influence and inspiration; poetics and writing process; themes political, erotic, religious; matters of performance and collaboration; the poet and pigeonholing -isms." At the same time, she recalls her growing unease, for her careful preparations "seemed a betrayal of my notion of interview as conversation, in which the interviewer acts . . . as an empathetic presence, enabling the writer to speak from deep preoccupations, with little guidance or interference."

Dalton need not have been troubled. After Durcan looked over her prepared questions, he guided the exchange into less formal directions: "Mary, I can't talk about poetry this way." The *ILS* text, but a portion of the original eighty-seven-page transcript and with Mary Dalton's own tentative queries edited out, suggests something closer to a brilliant monologue than a true interview.

A few other writers tacitly, if but occasionally and playfully, register ambivalence for the convention. For example, in an interview remarkable for the tenacity with which the questioner pursues her answers—"that's hardly a fair answer. I don't accept it"—William Trevor, speaking of the fundamental irrationalities that shape lives, cautions those who would probe too deeply with their questions: "We tend to overstudy life," he responds to Jennifer Clarke; "we should leave it alone . . . . There are so many things that we don't know." Indeed, as novelist John Fowles reminds us, mysteries are "energizing."

Similarly, Derek Mahon expresses reservations about those activities that for him interfere with enjoying the Yeatsian "lonely impulse of delight" to be realized in writing. Among the necessary distractions he as poet must endure ("I hate the 'business'") are "those terrible sessions after readings when they have questions too People say, 'Why do you write poetry?'"

Why do people write poetry—or fiction or drama—indeed? It is a provocative question, insisting that writers explore, if not explain, this deepest of impulses, that they confront some of the most irresistible forces lurking within the unconscious. The question also illuminates perhaps one of the basic motives for reading interviews: readers, as well as many writers, want to know more than they do about this essential creative activity. Thus, although one may look to the interview for clarification, for greater appreciation, indeed, for authoritative interpretation of what a writer has set down, one is equally interested in, if not actually more intrigued by, the genesis and process by which writers transmute experience into words on the page. The tension that so frequently exists between those who inquire into the impulse to write and those who heroically undertake the Promethean challenge itself often lies in the difficulty of accounting for an activity whose origin and execution invite curiosity and scrutiny, even as they resist conceptual analysis.

The dynamics between writer and interviewer merit careful study, perhaps as much as that accorded literary dialogue. Although one frequently credits authors' voiced insight into their work, the tension evident in many interviews should remind the reader that, along with all else taken for granted, writers shape their public identity through the responses they choose to provide to the interviewers' carefully selected and focused questions. Sometimes the answers come spontaneously, almost without deliberation; that is one of the tacit expectations readers bring to their experience of reading interviews. More often, the replies represent formulations achieved after careful thought and self-analysis. Occasionally, they have been "added on," that is, emended or even interpolated at the author's insistence, well after the actual exchange. In a few instances, in a kind of esthetic *Jeopardy*, "answers" were used to formulate questions and both later inserted into the text of an interview so that the writer might promote him- or herself in a certain way. Only rarely is the text of an interview a simple transcription. We tend to forget this; we should not.

A literary criticism of the interview has yet to be written. When that time comes, critics will need to examine the disparity between the illusion of spontaneity and the purposeful, thoughtful self-presentation undertaken by the writer. How responsive is an author to the questions? To what degree is he or she imposing, at the time of the interview or before or later, an identity, identities, or direction upon the interviewer's leads, interests, structures? Indeed, how free and spontaneous is the recorded exchange? and, when detectable, how are we to construe the author's shaping of his or her persona? What are we to make of the endeavor?

The yet unformulated esthetic of the interview will also need to assess the degree to which interviewers intervene by editing conversations for publication. The problem here turns more upon practical demands of reducing free-ranging, occasionally rambling dialogue to interesting reading and conveniently publishable size. The real time of many of the interviews here took far longer than the texts intimate. To squeeze them into the columns of the *Irish Literary Supplement*, they had to be shortened. Hours and hours of discussion sometimes became a script readable in twenty or thirty minutes. Mary Dalton, for example, speaks of reducing her eighty-seven-page transcript to a mere portion of the original length.

Providing additional insight into the genesis of the published interview, Deborah H. McWilliams recalled to me that "I never set about to produce interview text for publication. Instead, I set out to engage in a conversation with [the] writers in an effort to understand their work . . . a lot of editing on both sides went into what became the final written version."

Most of the abridged interviews re-present the essential core of the original conversation with digressions and seeming irrelevancies pruned away. In other instances interviewers' own interests and philosophical, even political, urgencies suggested that certain parts of a discussion be retained, emphasized, at the expense of others. Many texts, moreover, also reflect their interviewers' perceived need for structure, even for certain kinds of structure, evident in the way a well-crafted beginning-middle-end reflect literary sensitivity to form, rather than, as is more likely, the original desultory conversation. Again, it bears remembering that an interviewer's textual intervention, although inspired by motives different from those of the writer, needs to be assessed in final appreciations of the interview.

Lest some perceive in these prefatory remarks negative valuations of authorial intent—the writer's desire to represent him- or herself in a certain way, and the interviewer's editing to produce a readable dialogue of printable length and pleasing form and to publicize certain themes or issues rather than others—let me stress that nothing could be further from the truth. Rather, I hope readers will approach these interviews anticipating that they embody, in varying degrees, many attitudes, traditions, conventions appropriate, tacitly or otherwise, to the medium. Although they may lack the immediately recognizable generic features of literary dialogues, they nonetheless share in many of the same impulses. And, importantly, by way of a writer's consulting with the interviewer before and after the event itself, and, thus, contributing to the final editorial shaping, each interview dramatizes how an author wants to present her- or himself to the reader. Allowing that the need or desire to promote a certain identity or role may actually have helped a writer surmount an apparently inherent and traditional, even vocational, distaste for interviews and recognizing the near-universality of this tacit histrionic motive—both should contribute to our greater appreciation of the writer's full persona.

Writing Irish

John McGahern

Interviewed by Eileen Kennedy

[Writing] was always serious or it never was. For me, it was a
way of seeing. You start by playing with words. To some
extent it is always a form of play. Then you find you can see
with words.

—John McGahern

IN ANY RANKING of the contemporary novelists John McGahern would be
either at the top or close to it. Unlike Anthony Burgess, for example,
McGahern uses Ireland for the setting of his novels, and the sense of
place lights up the somber circumstances and grim lives of many of his
protagonists. In his four novels—*The Barracks* (London: Faber and Faber,
1963), *The Dark* (London: Faber and Faber, 1965), *The Leavetaking* (London:
Faber and Faber, 1974), and *The Pornographer* (London: Faber and Faber,
1979) and in his collections of short stories, *Nightlines* (London: Faber and
Faber, 1970) and *Getting Through* (London: Faber and Faber, 1978)—the
author is unsparing but not embittered in his portrayal of Irish life. His
fiction lays bare the often painful emotional life of his characters, but at
the same time it suggests, through the prose rhythms, some untapped
energy, some resiliency of the human imagination. McGahern's first
novel, *The Barracks*, won both the AE Memorial Award and the Macauley
Fellowship Award; his third, *The Leavetaking*, received the Society of Authors Award in 1975.[1]

From *ILS* 3 (spring 1984).

Now nearing fifty, McGahern is a serious man who listens intently and then smiles with warmth. My first meeting with him was in August 1981 when I visited him at his farm overlooking Lough Rowan in Leitrim, and it seemed as though we were continuing our earlier conversation when I interviewed him many months later in his sun-filled apartment at Colgate University on 24 September 1983. [Eileen Kennedy]

EILEEN KENNEDY: How long have you been living on your farm in Ireland? And when did you start teaching at Colgate?

JOHN MCGAHERN: I've been living on and off in Leitrim for almost ten years now. I just like that part of the country, and I liked living in parts of London very much, and Paris. I think of Leitrim as home now. I've been at Colgate off and on since 1969. I was last here in 1980. I have friends. It is a very beautiful part of the country. There is a great openness, a sense of freedom, an absence of that crippling caution I grew up with and have never been quite able to discard. Of course, I come here as a privileged visitor, which may not be the best way to view a country.

KENNEDY: The west of Ireland has played a big part in your own life. You lived with your mother, a school teacher, in small towns in Monaghan and Leitrim until you were about ten while your father lived at the police barracks in Cootehall, Roscommon. How did it happen that your mother moved about so?

MCGAHERN: My mother was a national teacher. It was de Valera's time, the aftermath of the trade war with England, and then the Second World War, the Emergency as it was called.[2] There was a cutback on everything. No new teachers were being employed. So when the numbers fell at a school, the last-line teacher had to move wherever there was a vacancy. It was called the *Panel*, and once you got on the treadmill it was very hard to get off. We seemed to be always on the move.

KENNEDY: Did you use your father, a sergeant in the Garda, in any way for the father in *The Barracks* or *The Dark*?

MCGAHERN: I've been asked that question before, and I don't know. The two characters are certainly very different people. And it *is* fiction. I think aspects of seven or eight people often go into the making of a character, and I suspect part of each character is oneself.

KENNEDY: When your mother died, you went to live with your father in the barracks. How was life different for you there?

McGAHERN: It wasn't that much different. The countryside was much the same, though the Roscommon land is richer than Leitrim. There was no crime, so the police had little to do—stopping people for cycling without lights at night, dog licenses, rows over trespass, raiding the pubs for after-hour drinking. The church was the dominant influence everywhere. People were poor.

In a private sense it was completely different. It was my first experience of the world as a lost world and the actual daily world as not quite real.

KENNEDY: What were your high school years at the Presentation College in Carrick-on-Shannon like?

McGAHERN: We cycled in ten miles. Everybody cycled who didn't live in the town. "Like uncertain flocks of birds on bicycles" was a description of mine. One boy, who had some ailment, rode in on a pony, which was stabled with relatives in the town. I liked the Presentation Brothers. They thought of themselves as a cut above the Christian Brothers. "Remember you are Christian in the sense that you are not pagan, but in no other sense," was a refrain of a Brother Damian.

The only reason they came to Carrick in the first place was that a very courageous woman of that time, a Mrs. Lynch, started a high school, the Rosary High, with all lay teachers. Now, that was subversion in the forties. Before that, the only high schools for boys were the seminaries in the cathedral towns. In our case that was Sligo, thirty miles away. Only the very well-off could send their children there.

I'm sure the Brothers were brought in to run Mrs. Lynch out. Anyhow, they didn't succeed. She must have been a remarkable woman, and Carrick must have been the only town of its size in Ireland at that time with two high schools. They even got on rather well together. In Ireland the personal will mostly win out over any ideology, unless it happens to be factional politics when, in a lovely phrase of Seamus Heaney's, "A hard line is generally pursued with enthusiasm."

KENNEDY: Did you ever think about becoming a priest?

McGAHERN: Of course. It would have been impossible to escape the idea unless you were either mature or thick-skinned. If you were clever or middle-class, and preferably both, there were enormous pressures to enter religion. That the only secondary schools were the seminaries in the cathedral towns tells its own story. Religion was the dominant atmosphere of the schools, and from an early age these priests or brothers looking for vocations passed through like salesmen. "The Recruiting Officer" in *Nightlines* is a description of the pressures even in a national school. And their call was very attractive to the emotions of adolescence: idealism, self-sacrifice, emotional and intellectual security, a sort of poetry and truth. It was approved of as well. A priest in the family was like having money in the bank of this world and the next.

KENNEDY: What did you do after high school?

McGAHERN: I trained as a teacher at St. Patrick's, graduating in 1955, and U.C.D.[3] in 1957. I was one of those teachers who crop up in Flann O'Brien[4]—going into night school at UCD on bicycles.

KENNEDY: When did you start "serious" writing?

McGAHERN: Eileen, it was always serious, or it never was. For me it was a way of seeing. You start by playing with words. To some extent it is always a form of play. Then you find you can see with words.

Isn't reading much the same? First, you read for pleasure, the excitement of the story, the mystery of strange people and places. Then you discover after a time that you are reading about your own life and the lives of others. It is then that the style becomes more important than the material out of which the pattern is shaped.

KENNEDY: Was there anyone who encouraged you in writing?

McGAHERN: There were few books to be found in the countryside. There was no tradition of reading. It was considered a dangerous form of idleness, except to get you on in the world—pass exams. That it was disapproved of made it attractive. Forbidden things somehow have their own attractiveness. The folk tradition had died except for the music. Some sense of the myths lingered on, but as a whisper. The sense of mystery, of luxury, of beauty or terror, all came from the church in its rituals and ceremonies. Against that was also the sharp sense of the more independent country people who suspected that it was all a sham, but conformed. I often heard said, "We had to put up with old Druids once; now this crowd is on our backs."

There was also a Protestant house nearby with a library. A very old man and his middle-aged son lived there, and they gave me the run of their library. Walter Scott, Zane Grey, Dickens, Jeffrey Farnol, Shakespeare—I read them all in much the same way as a boy nowadays might watch television movies, without any direction. If they ever read, old Mr. Moroney and his son, they no longer did so. They were addicted to beekeeping and astrology.

When I went to Dublin, I did meet a person who had a deep, passionate sense of literature, who put many true books in my way, but he was far too intelligent to encourage anybody to write.

KENNEDY: After St. Patrick's, you started to teach school. When did you start to write *The Barracks*?

McGAHERN: I had a pleasant job, teaching very young boys. School finished at two o'clock. I've never written for more than two or three hours a day though it may take several hours to find the energy to write that long.

KENNEDY: Somewhere I read that *The Dark* was the first novel you wrote, but *The Barracks* was the first one published. Is that true?

McGAHERN: I wrote a long first novel which was never published.[5] Then I wrote *The Barracks*. Parts of that first novel were used in *The Dark*. Bits of the first novel were published in a London magazine, now defunct. The first novel was longer, much more gentle.

KENNEDY: Was there much of your mother in the character of Elizabeth?

McGAHERN: I don't think so. Elizabeth was as much a way of looking as a character in her own right. I believe that an author must honor his or her characters, and that extends to allowing them their independent lives once they are down on paper.

KENNEDY: Did you expect the furor that *The Dark* evoked in Ireland?

McGAHERN: No. I just wrote it as I saw or imagined it. I think that's the way most writers work. They're just interested in getting it right. Publishing is different. I look on it as a lottery. Everything or nothing can come of it. *The Dark* was genuinely disliked in Ireland, probably still is.

KENNEDY: As a writer, did you feel you were courageous writing *The Dark* with those scenes of the boy's masturbatory fantasies?

McGAHERN: I certainly didn't feel courageous. As a writer, you deal with

words, and, outside their constraint, there is an illusion of total freedom. I deliberately picked the masturbatory images from the then
most staid newspaper in Ireland, *The Irish Independent*. The boy in the
book uses their black-and-white ads for women's underwear for his
poor excitement. No convent was without the *Independent*. They even
ran an editorial during the furor, stating that they too were used in the
book and in "no savoury circumstances."

KENNEDY: You published *The Dark* and then you had a year's sabbatical,
and it was then—am I right?—that you married in the registry office.
And because of the book and your marriage outside the church, you
lost your teaching position?

McGAHERN: I had been awarded the Macauley Fellowship for *The Barracks*.
One of the conditions of the award was that I had to spend time
abroad, and I was given a year's leave of absence. I was married while
abroad, but that had nothing to do with losing my job. The priest who
fired me told me that the order for my dismissal had come from the
archbishop, John Charles McQuaid,[6] who had a positive obsession
with "impure" books and plays.

It was a strange time. I dislike talking about it even now. Questions were asked in the Dáil.[7] But what was interesting was that it
came out clearly that the Catholic Church had come to enjoy a special
position in the Constitution, contrary to the 1916 Proclamation.[8] This
special position had to be hastily gotten rid of a couple of years afterwards when the Northern Ireland situation blew up.

KENNEDY: Were there people who supported you in your position?

McGAHERN: Yes. The Association of Civil Liberties offered me money to
take the case to the courts. There were some eminent writers who
offered to start a protest petition, which I declined, though I was most
grateful. I was content to make clear what had happened, to let people
make up their own minds, and to bow out. I was amused to read years
afterwards that I had exploited the situation.

KENNEDY: What did you do after you lost your teaching job?

McGAHERN: I moved to London. I did some book reviewing. I had tempo-
rary jobs, relief teaching, work on the buildings with my brothers-in-law.
The usual thing. I grew to love London, but I wasn't able to write. That

was the worst part of the sacking. But maybe I wouldn't have written in those years even if there had been no trouble over *The Dark*.

KENNEDY: Were you surprised by the variety of reviews that *The Pornographer* got? Why do you think the French liked the book?

McGAHERN: As I said, I look on reviews as a lottery. Generally, there's a consensus among the reviewers, but with *The Pornographer* each review seemed to be different. There's a trade journal in California called *Fuckbooks*. They featured it on the cover of the magazine. They said the actual pornography was good soft porn and that the hero or anti-hero was more like a real pornographer, sensitive, intelligent, etc. He was more like them than the poor image the general public had of the trade. I thought he was bad enough. I was just using pornography to show absence of feeling, in the old technique of using shade to show the place of the sun. The French reviewed it as an existential novel. They thought some of it was quite funny.

KENNEDY: I know you've been revising *The Leavetaking* (1974) for the French edition. What changes did you make?

McGAHERN: I had to rewrite the second part from scratch. Generally, one publishes a novel, and it's gone. I found myself working through it again with the French translator, the poet Alain DeLahaye. I saw the second part wasn't right. I had to start it from scratch. What I had been trying to do I hadn't managed. As I say in the preface to the new Faber edition, "The crudity I was attempting to portray, the irredeemable imprisonment of the beloved in reportage, had itself become blatant. I had been too close to the 'Idea,' and the work lacked that distance, that inner formality or calm that all writing, no matter what it is attempting, must possess."

KENNEDY: Is there any form of the novel you want to try and haven't done so yet?—or any subject?

McGAHERN: No. The shape you give the form is intellectual, conscious. It comes over a long period of time. Shape is worked out of the dialogue between the material and the writer. First comes the image, then the rhythm, the rhythms of the prose. At the beginning, one doesn't know whether one's writing is going to be a novel or a shorter work. More often than not, it refuses to turn out the way you first imagined it.

Jennifer Johnston

Interviewed by Michael Kenneally

I think that we have all misunderstood each other, but I also
think we understand each other terribly well. I think that the
two cultures in Ireland cannot live without each other, and
that we have created in the last fifty years a situation which
is hanging by very narrow threads as to how we're going to
go on in the future.

—Jennifer Johnston

JENNIFER JOHNSTON IS THE AUTHOR of six novels, all of which have been
widely acclaimed in both Dublin and London. Although she did not turn
to writing until her late thirties, her first novel, *The Captains and the Kings*
(London: Hamish Hamilton, 1972), received outstanding praise from the
critics and won the Robert Putnum Award and the Yorkshire Post Prize
for the Best First Book of 1972. She retained the setting of Ireland in the
early decades of the twentieth century for *The Gates*, published in 1973
(London: Hamish Hamilton), whereas *How Many Miles to Babylon?* (London: Hamish Hamilton, 1974) is set in the trenches of World War I.
Shadows on Our Skin (London: Hamish Hamilton, 1977), set in Derry in
the 1970s, was short-listed for the Booker Prize, and *The Old Jest* (London: Hamish Hamilton) won the Whitbread Prize for best novel in 1979.
Several critics have singled out her latest novel, *The Christmas Tree* (London: Hamish Hamilton, 1981), as her finest achievement. Three of her

From *ILS* 3 (fall 1984).

novels have been made into television plays, most notably the BBC-TV production of *How Many Miles to Babylon?*, dramatized by the Northern Irish poet Derek Mahon. She has also written two short plays.[1]

Jennifer Johnston is married, has four children, and lives in Derry City. Her father is the dramatist Denis Johnston, and her mother is the actress Shelah Richards. This interview was taped in Montreal during her September 1983 visit to Canada and the United States. [Michael Kenneally]

MICHAEL KENNEALLY: Your first novel was published comparatively late. When did you decide that you wanted to be a writer?

JENNIFER JOHNSTON: Well, that's sort of a silly story. I always wrote—from the time I could write in pencil. I used to write plays, and I used to write stories, and, as I grew into my teens and into some sort of self-consciousness, I just stopped writing. From the time I was eighteen I didn't write for nearly twenty—fifteen years, certainly—didn't even attempt to write. And then, when I was about thirty-five, I started making small nervous attempts, but all purely personal for me, and I spent a lot of time tearing stuff up and throwing it away. Then I wrote a very short novel, and—I don't quite remember why now, I must have met someone—but I sent it to Andre Deutsch, and they read it and asked me to come and see them. They said, this is much too short, and it's not really a novel; it's a long short story, but it has a lot of qualities and we would be very interested to see your next manuscript. I was so heartened by that that I went home and threw all that away, which is sort of silly because I regretted it.

Then I wrote *The Gates*, and I sent it to Andre Deutsch, but they didn't even write me a letter. At this stage I had acquired an agent, and he sent it round to practically all the other London publishers. They all sent it back, but they sent very nice letters with it saying, this is interesting, but we don't really think it will sell terribly well; but whoever has written this is obviously a writer, and we'd be very interested to see anything else she might write. I was more encouraged by that, but at this stage, in any case, I was into *The Captains and the Kings*. Hamish Hamilton took it immediately, and then subsequently published *The Gates*, which I slightly regret because I don't think that it's a good book.

KENNEALLY: It seems to me that there are certain patterns in *The Gates*, certain sets of characters that are developed later. Obviously, you change the setting and the context, but they do appear in various forms in your later novels.

JOHNSTON: Well, only one of my later novels, perhaps two, little bits come into them. There's Nancy in *The Old Jest* who has sort of grown out of me.

KENNEALLY: And there's Uncle Proinseas, who's a preparatory character for Mr. Prendergast in *The Captains and the Kings*.

JOHNSTON: That's right; that is correct to a certain extent. I didn't think that at the time, but looking back I can see that's true.

KENNEALLY: What would you say is the impetus behind your work? What brings you to your desk to write?

JOHNSTON: I couldn't say in rational terms, but what brought me originally to the desk to write was the feeling that I was thirty-five and that there wasn't really very much point in walking around on earth for another thirty-five years without actually making some impression, which is sort of arrogant. Writing seemed to be the natural thing for me to do because of my background and because all I ever knew was books. I mean, I'm totally and utterly uneducated. I went to a school where they didn't make you learn, and the only thing I ever wanted to do was read and write. So I just read and wrote, and everything else was neglected.

KENNEALLY: The central character in your latest novel, *The Christmas Tree*, Constance Keating, as she's facing death, saw the act of writing in terms similar to what you've just described, as a kind of stab at immortality. She gives up and instead opts for the more conventional way of having a child.

JOHNSTON: I've had my children, and I realized that that wasn't much of a stab at immortality.

KENNEALLY: When you start a novel, do you begin with character, some governing idea, or the plotline of a story? How does it come into shape in your mind?

JOHNSTON: It takes quite a long time. I start, usually, with an idea. For example, the idea for *How Many Miles to Babylon?* was growing very much in my mind during the time I was actually writing *The Captains and the Kings*. I wanted to write a book about the First World War. I didn't call it a World War I book, but I wanted it set there. Then, in a curious way, little things happen. Just as you'd live your life, it keeps turning into miraculous happenings. Somebody says in a letter something that fits into a part of the idea in your mind so that it gets a little bigger; then, something else will happen. You're walking down the street and see something, and that, suddenly, fits again, and the idea gets bigger and bigger. It's just a flower growing inside your brain—perhaps a jigsaw puzzle would be a better analogy. All those little seemingly irrelevant things all start building up inside your head, but I'm never finished writing it until I put the last full stop. I can never show anything that I'm writing to anyone because I'm not sure that that's the way it's going to be until that last full stop. So the whole process from the germ of the idea just goes on and on and on in a continuous flow until that last moment.

KENNEALLY: So, many of the details are not necessarily worked out previously. It's an organic process.

JOHNSTON: Absolutely, absolutely.

KENNEALLY: What about the process of revision? Do you work on a chapter and revise it before moving on?

JOHNSTON: No, it doesn't really work like that at all. I really look with admiration on people who can write chapter by chapter and have a perfect thing. Because I'm not really ever sure until the end, I can't do that. Basically, what has always seemed to happen is that you always forget—I mean, it sounds like having a baby: you forget the feelings of having a baby until the next one—the difficulties and problems. Each time it has happened to me, I've been taken unawares. I get about halfway through, and then suddenly, as if somebody has pulled a lot of veils away from the front of my eyes, I see exactly what is happening, right to the end, and I see that an awful lot of what I've done is wrong, so I forget about it, and I go right through to the end. Then I go back and rewrite the first half. I really don't have to touch the second half much. It's very strange, and this has always happened.

I have been having a very bad time with the book I'm writing at the moment. In a way, I had thought that I won't do that anymore; I know what I'm at. I'm a professional writer now, and it won't be like that. But, of course, exactly the same thing happened, and I had a really bad time until I suddenly said, stop being so foolish—this is the pattern; the halfway point will come, and it did—but it was strange, and it was very unpleasant.

KENNEALLY: So, for much of the time, you write to discover the direction you're going and what it is you want to do?

JOHNSTON: That's right, and I'm sure this can't be right. I'm sure if I were a more organized person, I would be able to sort that out some other way. It's really quite painful when you're doing that because you feel, why am I sitting here doing this? It's going nowhere. And yet something inside you says, you've got to finish this book. And you know it's not right. And then suddenly this extraordinary thing happens, and you feel fifty years younger.

KENNEALLY: If we could switch now to your image of yourself as an Irish writer, if you have that perception of yourself. John Banville, in an interview, makes the statement that Irish writers after Joyce can do things in the novel but not to the novel. As a post-Joycean Irish writer, do you feel that you have come out from under his overcoat? Or were you ever under the overcoat?

JOHNSTON: I don't think I was particularly under his overcoat. I would think, though, that I'm not an innovative sort of writer, so I would never be able to do anything to the novel anyway. I'm always working with fairly strict, rather old-fashioned terms of what the novel means to me. And I'm working on a very, very small canvas. I would not have ever felt under the shadow of Joyce at all because my own way of looking at my work and looking at what I'm trying to say was so minuscule. I would look at myself much more in terms of somebody like E. M. Forster or Jane Austen, writing my novel of manners but yet in my own rather stylized milieu.

KENNEALLY: The focus in several of your novels, particularly the first three, is on that world of the Anglo-Irish, Big House society. Do you see yourself, in a way, almost leapfrogging past Joyce to the nineteenth-century Irish novels, the Big House novels of, say, Somerville and Ross or even further back to Maria Edgeworth?[2]

JOHNSTON: No, I don't really. Certainly, not consciously at all. I see my canvas as very small because I am focusing on a dwindling way of thinking about Ireland. I also would like to feel, in a way, that there's a bridge being built there because I think that there are such fantastic misunderstandings. One of my few points would be that we have to stop and consider each phrase, each sentence, each reason why somebody says something.

KENNEALLY: I think that what you're saying would be true of the majority of the people in the South today. Do you think that they have perhaps misunderstood the inheritance or the legacy of the Anglo-Irish?

JOHNSTON: I think that we have all misunderstood each other, but I also think we understand each other terribly well. I think that the two cultures in Ireland cannot live without each other and that we have created in the last fifty years a situation that is hanging by very narrow threads as to how we're going to go in the future. We have to . . . we have to put our hands out to each other. We have to understand. We have to realize how much we gain from each other and from the past and the suffering. And we seem to be finding it very difficult to do so.

KENNEALLY: Do you think that sense of understanding each other was closer before 1916?[3]

JOHNSTON: I think there was a great moment then, immense excitement, which generated a generosity all round. We've lost that generosity now, for some strange reason, and I don't quite know why. There is a sort of terrible provincialism taking over, which I think is not right for the country. I don't like to see it narrowing, looking in on itself like that.

KENNEALLY: Do you think that Catholics in the South tend to associate Protestantism and Protestants with the North, ignoring the minority in the South as an integral and ongoing part of their social fabric?

JOHNSTON: Well, I think whatever has happened to the Protestants in the South, they have brought it upon themselves because, since 1922,[4] those who found what happened then distasteful left the country. Those who felt Irish stayed in the country, but they kept their heads down in a very curious way, and they didn't really participate in the political and community life in a way that they should have. They're starting to now, and it's great because there's a whole new generation of young and very committed Irish Protestant people growing up who want nothing but the best for their own country. They're starting to speak, but they almost left it too late. I'm hoping they haven't because what they have to say is well worth listening to.

KENNEALLY: In *How Many Miles to Babylon?* there is a scene where Alexander looks at the house before he leaves to go to the front and says, "I love these granite stones, this house, and this land." Do you think, perhaps, that that was the weakness in those Protestants who chose to remain?— that their affection was to the land, and it wasn't transferred to the people outside the walls? In that novel, and in *The Gates*, you have a sense of the native Irish being outside. Now, there are characters like Minnie and Mr. Prendergast who do bridge and attempt to reach out. Do you think that the Protestants, at least the landed Protestants, looked at themselves as Irish only in terms of their love and commitment to the land rather than in their involvement in the social milieu around them?

JOHNSTON: I don't think so, totally . . . possibly. I think there might have been an element of that with a certain number of people. But by and large their commitment was to a nation. They quite genuinely felt, don't let's make things difficult for ourselves. We're here. Let's be thankful nobody's taken anything away from us; nobody's been nasty to us. Let us just keep very, very quiet and see what happens. And I think that that was a pity. But I don't think that meant they weren't committed to the people; I think they were just rather amazed and wondering what was going to happen and were waiting to see. And they waited too long.

KENNEALLY: Of course, immediately after 1922 even the majority shared that sense of tentativeness, an uncertainty over what was evolving and how committed they should be.

    While we are talking about that sense of reaching out, of making contact, it seems that many of the characters in your novels, and not just the Anglo-Irish figures, have this desire to break out of the self, to communicate with others. Several of these are writers, whether of very private poetry or merely personal jottings. Do you see that as a prime motivating impulse in your characters, this desire to attempt to form individual bonds with those around them?

JOHNSTON: Oh, yes, I think so. I think so because then basically I'm writing about myself the whole time and that is really all I know quite a lot about. So a lot of the impulses in my books are my own impulses, which I am trying to examine.

KENNEALLY: Another pattern I see recurring in your novels is the presentation of characters who are either at the threshold of life, at the stage of initiation, who are about to come face to face with a world of betrayal, violence, or the witnessing of death, or, on the other hand, those characters who are at the other end of the continuum for whom death is imminent. Did you choose these specific times at heightened moments of awareness as good instances when the human condition might be examined?

JOHNSTON: Very much so. Between the young person who is just walking into life filled with a magnificent innocence and the old person who has passed through it all, there's a terrible gray area where everything, all one's most beautiful and magical thoughts, is always being messed about by people. We don't have courage. All the time, we have things being heaped on our backs which stop us from doing the things that we really would like to do, say the things we really would like to say, and be the people that we have in our dreaming hearts. When you're finished with all that, then it seems to me to be one of the justifications for old age, that you can start all that again and be somebody new.

KENNEALLY: In *The Old Jest* Aunt Mary says to Nancy that young people are afraid of all those impulses, and she advises her to make an effort not to be afraid to do, to be, to respond fully to life. Because when one looks at all your novels, those middle years are curiously absent. They are present for Constance, in *The Christmas Tree*, but she's dying and so is not really an exception to the pattern.

JOHNSTON: Well, I'm writing a middle-years novel at the moment.

KENNEALLY: The reason I'm interested in this is that another feature of your writing—and I'm not sure it's typical of contemporary Irish fiction, but it's certainly there in much of John McGahern's[5] work and in Bernard MacLaverty's *Lamb*[6]—is the absence of a strong matriarchal figure. We think of the female figures in O'Casey, and there is almost a cliché image of Irish mothers, and yet they are curiously absent from so much of contemporary Irish writing. Very few of the characters in your novels are mothers.

JOHNSTON: There's a very instant psychological reason for that: I have a very, very strong, dominating and powerful mother. She and my father were divorced when I was at seven. Other people point out these things, that there are horrible mothers in my books or no mothers or people looking for their fathers. And presumably this is a psychological thing, which I don't understand because I never lived with my father, and I really know him very little. I feel that Nancy searching for her father comes out of something inside me, but I can't write about mothers, couldn't even begin to. I did a terrible thing—I wrote this one-act play which was about an old, failed actress who was an alcoholic, and she lives in the top of this hall in the country.

KENNEALLY: This is *The Nightingale and Not the Lark?*[7]—

JOHNSTON: Yes; and she is lonely and dying, and she has this ghost, the ghost of her husband who left. And he keeps coming and talking to her, and they have these terrible rows. It was produced at the Abbey four or five years ago at the lunchtime theater festival. I wasn't at any of the rehearsals, but I went to the dress rehearsal and realized that this play was about my mother. It couldn't have been more unlike her in position in life or background. But yet it was my mother. It was such a terrible shock to me. I mean, I nearly died when I saw this figure on the stage. So there's just no way I could write about somebody of that age. That really frightened me.

KENNEALLY: If we could return again to your first three novels: World War I is presented as the pivotal event in the characters' lives, particularly the landed gentry. Could you describe your fascination with that subject?

JOHNSTON: Well, it's not really just the landed gentry. It's the effect the war had on Ireland and on Europe. It was the pivotal happening of the century, apart from the Russian Revolution, and that was part of the whole thing. It seemed to me to be useless slaughter. People were not yet used to thinking for themselves and went like sheep to be slaughtered. The play I wrote is about the aftermath of that war, too, because it takes place in 1920 in Ireland, the time of the war against the British. The effect that World War I had—the massacre of a whole generation of young men—embittered a large number of people who remained. In Ireland it was the beginnings of the troubles that we are now in. I'm not denigrating what happened in 1916 because I think it was a piece of magnificent romantic nonsense. It could never have happened, but it was magnificent, and it, in fact, probably is the reason why Ireland is in the terrible situation it is in now. I think that, had the uprising not happened, come 1918, we would have had Home Rule. There would have been no problems about the North because the British wouldn't have allowed there to be problems, and we would have moved on from there in some cumbersome but logical way to being a republic. Once that happened, something cracked in us and we suddenly saw ourselves as people with freedom dangling in front of us, and we couldn't wait any longer. Therefore, that war has had an extraordinary effect on the country.

KENNEALLY: I'm just wondering why you chose to deal with Ireland through the consequences of World War I for the Anglo-Irish rather than the people who were busy with the nationalist struggle.

JOHNSTON: I think I've used it as a metaphor for what is presently happening. I was trying to write about human relationships with the undercurrent of violence. I've just always had this obsession with that terrible, terrible war, such outrageous, unnecessary slaughter. All my life, older people told you stories about it. All the songs that people used to sing when I was growing up—"It's a Long Way to Tipperary"—and all those things were there in the back of my mind. I knew nothing about the Civil War.

KENNEALLY: Why didn't World War II impinge on your consciousness as much? Was it because of de Valera's neutrality policy?[8]

JOHNSTON: Yes, it was because of the neutrality. We listened to the radio and read the newspapers—my father was a war correspondent—but it somehow seemed to be happening elsewhere. Whereas, the First

World War seemed to be happening on everyone's back door, in spite of the fact that they weren't there. Every single person in Ireland must have lost someone in that war. In people's kitchens in the West of Ireland there were photographs of the Connaught Rangers. They were there in the back of people's minds.

I think a rather sad thing has happened in Ireland about that war. Those men and what they did, without understanding what was happening at all, have now been turned into some sort of treachery. When they were making the film *How Many Miles to Babylon?* they had a hundred Irish soldiers marching around county Wicklow, dressed up in British uniforms, looking like all the photographs you've seen of those kids going out to the Somme.[9] I was talking to some of them, and I asked if any of their grandfathers fought in World War I. There was a very long silence while they all looked at me, and then one of them said, "Yes, my grandfather was a Connaught Ranger." Another said, "I had a great uncle," and somebody else said he had somebody in it. Suddenly, you realized that they wouldn't admit it to each other. Of course, they all had connections with the Great War. It didn't mean that their grandfathers were better or worse Irish men. It meant that they were, in their own way, small heroes.

KENNEALLY: In terms of the characters in your later books, do you see the war as a metaphor, something which ushered in the modern sensibility, the sense of alienation and lack of ability, not merely to understand but to make implicit bonds with each other?

JOHNSTON: Oh, yes, I think so very much. And I think you can see this in the North of Ireland, too.

KENNEALLY: For your fourth novel, *Shadows on Our Skin*, you turned to the situation in the North. Could you give some of the background to the decision to confront that issue?

JOHNSTON: Well, I haven't really confronted it very well. I decided to because I had, at that stage, been living in Derry a couple of years. I had found it an amazingly beautiful place to be living. That sounds like a silly word, but that was, and is still, the way I feel about it. I felt I wanted to write a book about the heart of the city.

I'm not a Northern writer, and while I admire and am very aware of the aspects of the Northern character that are different from the Southern, I actually wasn't able to fit myself into that. So I wrote a photographic book rather than a real book. Nothing was, in effect, totally true, except the feeling of the city itself. The little boy was a little boy, but he wasn't specifically a Derry little boy; he could have been found anywhere. I lost a large amount there.

Basically, what I should have confronted was not the little boy. It would have been a different book, but it would have been the right book for me had I taken time and courage to write it. The character in that book I should have been looking at was Brendan because he is the most interesting person. It turned out to be quite a charming story about a little boy, but it is a totally unimportant book. It's ironic and stupid, where the British all say this is brilliant, and this is Derry city as it really is. That's not true. They don't know what they are talking about. So I feel a bit embarrassed. As the years go by, I feel more embarrassed about that book because I realize I shouldn't have done it, that I should have taken ·that story and set it somewhere else. It was a sentimental gesture.

KENNEALLY: What aspects of the North do you feel you failed to capture?

JOHNSTON: I don't think I attempted to capture why people were the way they were. That is why I say I should have written the book about Brendan, and then I would have been absolutely forced to write some truth. Looking back at it, I can say that to write about a little boy was an easy thing to do, though it wasn't at the time. I was looking at the book through his eyes, and, therefore, I was able to take a fairly simplistic view of the situation. It was a view, as I say, that outsiders thought was lovely—outsiders not just in Britain but in the Republic. They thought it was absolutely lovely, and that's the sort of view they wanted. And that made me feel a bit disgusted with myself. I really didn't intend to do that at all. I didn't actually think everybody would like it, and I suddenly was shocked with what I'd done because it was such a petty sort of a thing in the end.

KENNEALLY: What truth do you think you would have been able to strive for with your double perspective as a Republican and a Southern Protestant?

JOHNSTON: I don't know if it's because I have a double perspective or not, but I do find that it's very easy for people to talk to me because both sides believe I'm on their side. By the time that they discover that I may not be totally and utterly on their side, they don't mind; they go on talking to me, and I hear a lot of things that, were I a Southern Catholic, I mightn't hear, and were I a Northern Protestant, I certainly wouldn't hear. So I have an enormous amount of information, ideas— useless, useful, exciting, boring—all inside my head and a sort of permanent shifting process going on a large amount of the time.

I have a very open mind about all the activities that are going on there. I mean by that—and everybody knows, and I make no bones about it: I'm a pacifist—I know why people are killing each other. The period of the hunger strikes[10] was the most horrific six months I ever lived through because the pain inside my head was almost unbearable. The whole province was filled with the weight of it. It was inconceivable that across the water they couldn't understand what was happening. That was terrible, and that is something I couldn't possibly write about.

KENNEALLY: I was just going to ask you whether you felt the writer could deal with such experiences.

JOHNSTON: In ten years perhaps. Certainly not then and certainly not yet; I couldn't.

KENNEALLY: Do you think, then, that you will turn to the issue of the North again in your writing?

JOHNSTON: Oh, yes, I think I will have to. But it won't be for a very long time. Ben Kiely tried, and he wrote a dreadful book called *Proxopera*,[11] which was hailed by England as something that was absolutely marvelous. But it was a hysterical scream, and it was not true. It was a load of romantic rubbish. O.K., the story was great and all that. It was taken in a very big way in England and, indeed, in Dublin, too. All the critics said that this is the great book about the North, and everybody agreed that it was absolutely brilliant and truthful. It wasn't. And he's never attempted another one like that, so I think he knows in his own heart that it was wrong. It was a bad thing. It was a worse thing to do than *Shadows* because it was very shrill and a lie from start to finish.

KENNEALLY: What writers have, in your view, dealt with the issues of the North in a positive manner?

JOHNSTON: I think that the poets have really responded much more positively than the novelists. Brian Friel, of course, in *Translations*[12] has broadened it out in Irish terms. And you have to look at it in Irish terms; you can't just isolate it and say "the North"—it's actually the whole country. That's something again we keep forgetting about.

KENNEALLY: How would you explain the prevalence of so many successful poets from the North in recent years?—the sense of a whole generation of writers discovering their voice in a way that has not happened before?

JOHNSTON: Well, I suppose it's a whole explosion of people coming out of the postwar heightening of British education. These were people who were being very highly educated by the state; they were coming out and going into the universities. They created the Civil Rights Movement,[13] and they created these amazing writers. I'm sure it had something to do with that energy of people who say, "Right, now we have to find a place for ourselves because we know there is one." They had a confidence and still have.

This is a very interesting thing about the North: that the Catholic people of the North have now got a place and a confidence that they never had before. The Protestants have got nothing because the British Empire has disappeared; they don't have that behind them. They refuse, adamantly refuse, to take their place in Ireland. The Catholics in the North not only have a place in Ireland but now, with this current pope,[14] they also have an international place, whereas the Protestants have their own curious brand of Unionism that means nothing, but, yet, they have their poets, too: Derek Mahon and Michael Longley[15] speak loud and clear and magnificently.

KENNEALLY: That brings us to the role of the writer in society: in an interview, two Northern poets, John Montague and John Hewitt, a Protestant,[16] were talking about their audience, about who, in fact, was listening to them. Eventually, they questioned whether anyone was.

JOHNSTON: Oh, yes, they are being read by young people, school children, but they are probably being forced upon them. But whether they are being digested, I don't know. But who was it who said, "Hang the poets; they're the people to get rid of"? In England artists have always been "don't let's rock the boat." They have been speaking with the

English voice, and it may have been splendid, but it has very seldom been dangerous. In Ireland the poet's role has been the agitator. And in a way they haven't got dangerous again, not dangerous enough. It's considered at the moment a very good thing to be a writer. And I think there's something wrong there. I think you've got to be the conscience of the people as opposed to the voice of the people. I certainly will never be that. I'm much too frightened and have not really enough confidence to be the conscience of anybody. I'm just my own conscience and only ticking over,[17] but I do believe that this is the great role of the artist. Brian Friel and the whole Field Day concept[18] is working in this direction. But it doesn't look to me as if it's going to work because they are only speaking to a very few people.

I think if you are going to be the conscience of the people, you've got to undermine the whole system so that all the people know what you're saying. There's no point in just intellectuals reading and agreeing and disagreeing. You've got to be much more fundamental than that—like the Russian dissident poets and the fact that they were and are still in those gulags. The people in Moscow and Leningrad know their poetry by heart and say them to each other in streets and in cellars. That poetry is not the story of poetry we have. We've never had that tradition.

KENNEALLY: Do you think that the role of poet as subversive was subsumed into that of patriot fighting for the cause of Cathleen Ní Houlihan?[19] that when the goal was ostensibly achieved, there was a failure of the writer to switch with the same intensity to social concerns?

JOHNSTON: Yes, you may be right. We're not what you call socially concerned.

KENNEALLY: I would like to conclude by asking if you think you've left the Ireland of the 1920s in your writing, or will you return to it? In *The Christmas Tree* you have moved along the continuum we spoke of—Constance Keating is of a later generation than your other characters.

JOHNSTON: My current book is contemporary also.[20] Again, it's about a woman, and the North comes into it peripherally, the whole violence of the country in general. I don't know what I'll do next. Then, I'd like to write another play.[21]

John Montague

Interviewed by Kevin T. McEneaney

I'm partly American, loving and loathing the place, but with
the added irony that I see it from outside most of the time.
And, of course, my central loyalty, or disloyalty, is to Ireland.

—John Montague

JOHN MONTAGUE WAS BORN on 28 February 1929 in Brooklyn, New York,
but at the age of four his parents sent him to be raised by his aunts in
Garvaghey, County Tyrone. As a poet, he has self-consciously tried to
combine both Irish and American strains in his work: his approach to line
and sound is influenced by William Carlos Williams while his subject
matter has centered upon Ireland or his own biography. Montague attended both University College, Dublin, and Yale (where he studied under Robert Penn Warren). He experienced the now-legendary Dublin
pub scene in the fifties and published his first book, *Forms of Exile* (Dublin:
Dolmen Press) in 1958 with the Dolmen Press.

In *The Rough Field* (Dublin: Dolmen Press, 1972) Montague followed and
surpassed Williams's historical epic, *Paterson*, giving a rural, Goldsmithian
vision of Ireland and the Tyrone locale in which he grew up. Influenced
by his stay in California during the heyday of the San Francisco poetry
movement, he developed a historical vision that also contained resonant
contemporary commentary. In addition to other volumes of poetry inves-

From *ILS* 4 (spring 1985).

27

tigating romance and society Montague has also published short stories and a notable novella, *The Lost Notebook* (Cork: Mercier Press, 1987).

At the time of the interview I was both bookseller and apprentice poet, and Montague, a distinguished professor at University College, Cork, was working on his poetic sequence *The Dead Kingdom* (Mountrath, Ireland: Dolmen Press; Winston-Salem, N. C.: Wake Forest University Press, 1984),[1] a work melding family history and the Northern Troubles. While a graduate student, I had studied Elizabethan epyllion at Columbia University; we had some lively poetic and philosophic discussions when Montague stayed at my apartment in Manhattan Valley, overlooking Central Park. I recall being fascinated by Montague's probing sense of musical composition, in terms of how poems were arranged to form epyllion sequence. The upshot was a little interview with him (conducted in my basement bookshop off Fifth Avenue) for Bob Callahan's short-lived *Callahan's Irish Quarterly*, but the publication folded before the piece could appear. I showed the interview to Robert Lowery and asked if he was interested in running it in *The Irish Literary Supplement*. Robert said, "Yes, but it's too short. Can you get him to expand it?" I wrote Montague, and he graciously agreed to redo it. [Kevin T. McEneaney]

KEVIN McENEANEY: In your recent poem "Process" from *The Dead Kingdom* you speak of everyone and the world "closed" in their dream of history, race, memory, and sense. Do you think that the present period is afflicted with a narcissistic *Zeitgeist*? Is the present an essentially confused period?

JOHN MONTAGUE: Of course. A global brain is growing, both in the crude sense of communications and the spiritual growth described by de Chardin.[2] But the other point of the gyre is a narrowing:[3] things have never been nastier, in Belfast or Beirut, Afghanistan or Central America. The old instincts of religion and race are fighting a rearguard action against centralization, which is both necessary and, if done for the wrong reasons, narcissistic. My solution would be both an intense attention to your home area and a sympathy for the endangered world—my old and doubtless boring cry of global regionalism.

McNEANEY: The tradition of Irish poetry has been a second nature in your poetry—from early nature poetry, medieval heroic poetry, to W. B. Yeats. Yet you are completely a man of the modern world. How is such a synthesis or marriage possible?

MONTAGUE: Because of my American birth, I suppose. I mean, New York, even Depression Brooklyn, was the most modern city in the world, just as Ulster was nearly as backward as you could get, outside Donegal. That tension has kept me going. Though I am not proud of my Irish, I seem to have access to the literature. I'd love to put the Fenian cycle[4] together, but . . . A bilingual version of Michael Comyn's *Pursuit of Diarmuid and Grainne* was in Garvaghey and that was the book that set off Yeats *and* Clarke.[5] I loved it, especially Niamh of the Golden Hair; I'm still enchanted by her.

MCNEANEY: Most people who know the poem "All Legendary Obstacles" acclaim it as one of the great love poems of the century; yet it does not appear in American anthologies. Ironically, the poem is set in America, actually in California. Why do you think Americans have tended to neglect or ignore this poem?

MONTAGUE: There's a lot of typecasting around as if people couldn't face complexity of reaction. Of course, I'm partly American, loving and loathing the place, but with the added irony that I see it from outside most of the time. And, of course, my central loyalty, or disloyalty, is to Ireland. But I would like to gather my good American poems.

Sometimes I think the American poets and critics are more insular than they like to think though the "Roots" racket has a good side in that you need not be ashamed of being Irish-American, as John O'Hara[6] was. There was an awful lot of snobbery in American writers of Irish background, like F. Scott Fitzgerald. So I went to Yale as well as University College, Dublin. James Joyce seems a richer master than the few writers who survived New Haven! Still, I wish someone would put me in an American anthology for a change. I would think a real love poem is international—Cavafy[7] or Auden's "Lay Your Sleeping Head." The poem you speak of, though, has a specifically western landscape, and I don't remember that of many American love poems—so, yes, they should adopt it.

McNEANEY: The Celtic revival of the late nineteenth century produced some great Celticists, two poets in particular—W. B. Yeats and Robert Graves. Some of your poems seem to be part of that revival. The little poem about Cernnunos, "The Split Lyre," is in that tradition but also in the tradition of Shelley's "Ode to the West Wind" and Francis Thompson's lesser poem "Ode to the Setting Sun"—Thompson's poem being Christian and Aristotelian; Shelley's being atheistic and Democritean; yours being pantheistic, or in terms of philosophy, Platonic. Like Plato, you have a way of integrating mythology into your aesthetics that is unobtrusive and instructive, integral and psychologically illuminating. Yet unlike Yeats's *Vision* or Graves's *White Goddess*, your poems don't need a coda or guide book. It seems that your poems are pretty much accessible to anyone. They have a simplicity although they retain an intellectual depth. How do you manage this?

MONTAGUE: God knows. I have great sympathy with the Celtic thing as a kind of nature religion, but I am prepared to argue for classical order if I feel it. I like Vivaldi's "La estro harmonico" *and* Bruckner's *Eighth*,[8] which I have just discovered—a marvelous monster! And good jazz sends me wild, controlled elation, *duende*.[9] I tried to do a double degree at college with philosophy as well as English, but I now agree with Beckett: *que c'est de la merde*.[10] Kant is a wonderful mental construct, but Pascal hurts.[11] *The Critique of Pure Reason* is like Bach's *Art of the Fugue*,[12] a wonderful exercise, the mathematics of our head. But Plato was a great writer who could dramatize our dilemma.

McNEANEY: In the poem "Deities" you use both Greek and Irish mythology as if it were a part of a single continuum. This tradition is both international and classical as well as part of the native Irish poetic tradition: I am thinking of the profusion of Greek mythology in Middle Irish poetry and even in later folk songs such as "The Limerick Rake." Celtic mythology was certainly an Indo-European mythology and could not have been very far removed from Greek mythology. I think that Joyce knew this. In the poem "Deities" the distinction between gods and heroes is blurred. This strikes me as very Celtic or early Greek, anarchically and pantheistically so.

MONTAGUE: Why not? The gods have fled from Greece, except maybe Delphi, and the tourists climb like ants over the sacred places. Some of Ireland still has presence as Mexico had when I visited it years ago. Greek is at the root of what we call "Western Civilization," and its pantheon has great psychological power. Many complexes are identified through Greek names—Oedipus, Electra, and even fair Psyche herself.[13] The Irish pantheon doesn't have the same currency, but if you use them together, you will see that Lugh and Apollo, for instance, are not that different.[14] Patrick Kavanagh loved Homer as if he were a local writer, and we were all taught that we were partly divine.

MCNEANEY: Your poems have great variety: imagism, free verse, rhymes, internal rhymes, prose poems, litanies (as in "For the Mother"), mythopoetic poems (as in "Mount Eagle" and "The Well Dreams"), and even concrete poems. You pointed out that "A Graveyard in Queens" is a concrete poem with the lines arranged on the page like rows of tombstones which the reader's eyes "walk" between. Do you think that the twentieth century is a collage of forms, an assembly in a kaleidoscopic time warp? Or do you think that the style of the century lies in imagistic concision and spoken voice?

MONTAGUE: The modern movement began with imagism—Pound, Eliot, Hulme—and it enlisted the verse of Lawrence and later Williams.[15] The spoken word, as opposed to the written word only, was an attempt to reinvigorate poetic language, rediscover natural rhythms. The French developed the prose form as well: early Ponge is marvelous, as was Baudelaire.[16] Now we have inherited all that and can do whatever we, or the poem, wants. We have a renewed sense of tradition as well as an armory of techniques to wrestle or woo raw experience.

MCNEANEY: The literary epic is a tricky thing. Most of them are failures—the *Aeneid* and *Paradise Lost*. Even *Paterson*[17] has, I think, its weak moments. *The Rough Field* is an epic that is personal, historical, and communal, and it is all of a piece. The choice of topic is important in such matters. Milton agonized over this problem for years. When Berryman and Merrill[18] came to the epic, they drifted into a solipsistic mode. What do you think are the pitfalls of the enterprise?

MONTAGUE: The long poem is a fascinating task. I say that, and yet I only drifted into my two efforts, and I wouldn't like to get a whopper on my line again for a while for the problems are ferocious. Biographically, it might be of some interest that as a student I made a special study of Milton although I haven't read him since. And I loved Langland.[19] The supreme long poem of the West is *La Divina Comedia*,[20] and I have just begun to get a sense of, say, *Paradiso*, which is pure poetry, poetry of vision. But most people prefer the harsh facts of *Inferno* and don't understand that the greatest poetry redeems suffering, like Beethoven's *Ninth*. I find your list odd.

MCNEANEY: Well, it's pretty arbitrary. There's Allingham, Ariosto, and Ashbery.[21]

MONTAGUE: There is the classical epic, from the *Iliad* to the *Aeneid*, and then maybe the religious epic, Dante and Milton and du Bartas.[22] *The Faerie Queene* fails for me because of the ludicrous schema, but I haven't read Ariosto, so I can't judge the genre, romantic epic. Then there is the personal, Wordsworth's *Prelude* more than the labored *Excursion*.

MCNEANEY: The earlier version of the *Prelude*, the 1805 version, is more spontaneous and flowing, more like a personal letter to Coleridge or the reader, less monumental symbolism. But Wordsworth hardly has the scope of somebody like Homer.

MONTAGUE: The older epic summed up a civilization, but you still must have a pressure of community, the unexpressed feelings of an area seeking outlet. I hope that is obvious in both *The Rough Field* and *The Dead Kingdom*. But first one must be readable as I hope they also are. Give me Chaucer and Byron over Spenser every time; he was a great poet, but he had no momentum, no central thrust.

MCNEANEY: What of the modern effort?

MONTAGUE: The modern long poem is quite a problem. The canny Eliot settled for the very eighteenth-century shape of the Augustan essay poem. If *Paterson*, which I got published in England, doesn't work entirely, it is less indulgent than Olson's *Maximus* or Dorn's *Gunslinger*,[23] the lunatic notion of "open form." It is like the symphony: I can follow

Beethoven through Brahms and Bruckner to Mahler,[24] but when Messiaen[25] adds bird calls, I say why not catcalls?

McNEANEY: But there are some successful efforts.

MONTAGUE: There are poets like MacDiarmuid and David Jones,[26] who recall dying cultures, or the fabulous Neruda,[27] a volcano of good and bad. We are a bit less ambitious, I think. Kinnell's *Book of Nightmares* is less rhetorical than "The Bridge"[28] under which I was born. Whitman's influence may be releasing for South Americans but dangerous for us Irish. He wrote arias like Verdi and Victor Hugo, the warm blast of amplitude. Lord knows, I loved Berryman, but the *Dream Songs* needs to be dramatized, perhaps, to work. God has shrunk to a ouija board, which I presume is Merrill's point.

McNEANEY: What do you think of Paul Muldoon's "Immran?"[29]

MONTAGUE: Good stuff. A bit smart-ass, but he joins a glimpse of the old with a *literary* version of American culture. You folks deserve it after flooding us with good and bad. "Immran" is very witty, mock-Gaelic, a new genre perhaps, and proof of how far we have come. I think he is wittier than his English contemporaries, but as with Pope, there is the question of how you let the emotions into a cool style. Miles Davis[30] could, but the Modern Jazz Quartet tinkled easy. Those who actually endure the North day-by-day—I almost said "die-by-die"—are bound to develop a macabre wit of survival, a sting.

McNEANEY: Do you have anything to say about the young poets growing up in Cork? There's Tom McCarthy and Sean Dunne.[31] Are there others?

MONTAGUE: Theo Dorgan, Greg Delanty, Gerry Murphy, John Bourke—we could nearly put a team in the field. Tom is the most accomplished and may be the best poet of his generation, book-for-book, so far in the south. Tom won the Patrick Kavanagh award, and Greg has just done the same. No matter how they grow, they are a way-open group. All have a passion for poetry, which is very heartening. They love the stanza, and I like to think that bringing Graves and MacDiarmuid over in the '70s gave them an example.

MCNEANEY: Your poetry seems to have kept pace with life. Unlike many poets, you don't let art become an idol in your poetry. You keep to the bone and muscle, don't get lost in a wash of colors or begin placing a self-importance before your work. You are not distracted by flattery or fame. This is not easy. It is easier to succumb to these temptations.

MONTAGUE: All this is very flattering—will I succumb? I live in remote Cork, which is bad for my career, but good for my character. I partly believe in Keats's "negative capability"—to let things speak through you. I am continually an apprentice before life, but now nearing my mid-fifties, I feel I can, should, risk a few Yeatsian generalizations. My career has been slow, though steady, so I have only occasionally had to wrestle with the kind of public acclaim you describe, which is always partly an accident. If it were to come, it shouldn't distract me from the central thrust: to express what is essentially mine. I imagine that to be dishonest would be even more painful, but, to be certain, I listen to even the cat cries of the envious as remedies against self-deception. I think that Yeats handled fame by using it to keep others. He practically invented the Abbey and Synge. I would like to see more of that generosity around.

MCNEANEY: You said that this is the "age of the interview." Do you think that the interview is, at its best, an art form, a kind of Platonic or Erasmian[32] dialogue? Or do you think that, at its worst, it is merely an aspect of society that relates to gossip?—I mean, that here is a part of society that has a jealous fear of artists and wants to cannibalize their every thought and act, to take from them the sources of their powers, and even to take away their very lives as was done to Orpheus?

MONTAGUE: I resent interviews, and yet I give them. It can be justified, perhaps, if you have just published a book that people otherwise wouldn't read, or so seems the practice. I have given two long ones—to *The Literary Review*, another to *NER/BLQ*[33]—and a handful of lesser ones, the last to *The Cork Examiner*, my local paper. They usually turn out well enough but are unnecessary in the sense that the information *should* be in the work, but if you are a poet, you can't be sure that they have read it. *The Rough Field*, of course, always crops up, notably in *The*

Crane Bag's[34] joint interview with John Hewitt. But my views on Irish, and indeed world history, are both so intimate and so detached that people must simplify them. Was my father a mad Republican dog? Does "The Wild Dog Rose" equal Mother Island? Perhaps ignorance is invincible, but one yields, with interest and shame, to yet another chance to explain, hoping, especially if it is to a friend, that it will not be a cheapening process. It is also connected with McLuhan's[35] vision of the global village. How many interviews did Joyce give? This is a media age, and we cannot escape it; we should try to use it. Any real poem is both simple and infinitely complicated, so perhaps it is fair to give a few simple signposts, as Joyce himself did.

William Trevor

Interviewed by Jacqueline Stahl Aronson

> We tend to overstudy life. We should leave it alone. . . .
> There are so many things that we don't know. If one knew
> the answers, life would be very dull, so you keep coming
> back to a sense of curiosity. . . . I was meant to be very
> pessimistic, but I think I've become optimistic.
>
> —William Trevor

WHEN I MET THE ANGLO-IRISH WRITER William Trevor, there was nothing in his appearance that matched the photographs and drawings on the jackets of his recent books. I expected to encounter a man of medium build whose face was distinguished by a furrowed brow and down-turned eyes. Instead, I extended my hand to a tall, tweed-and-ascotted gentleman of elegant appearance. There was something unexpected as well about Trevor's description of himself. Early in our conversation, Trevor spoke of himself as a person "who was meant to be a pessimist, but wasn't."

Born William Trevor Cox in County Cork [in 1928], Trevor has for many years lived in Devon. Some of his stories are directly concerned with the Irish Troubles, and all of his work suggests the steadfastness of his Irish identity. When he writes about violence and alienation, we feel his anger. But the greater number of Trevor's stories are about the quiet lives of

From *ILS* 5 (spring 1986).

everyday people—the married and the never married, children who are loved and who are not. When he writes about these, the tone of his narrative voice is compassionate.

Trevor says that he thinks that human beings are irrational and that our lives are determined primarily by chance. Despite his apparently fatalistic view of human life and the resulting bleakness of the lives of so many of his characters some of his people attain a degree of peace. What often distinguishes these characters from those who are defeated is their imagination, and this Trevor especially values. But even the struggles of the least promising of Trevor's characters—the despised, the isolated— have significance.

In an early story, "An Evening with John Joe Dempsey," Trevor described the struggles of a fifteen-year-old boy to survive with his sense of self more or less intact. Of late, writing about young people has become particularly appealing to Trevor—a preoccupation that enriches his forthcoming collection of stories, *The News from Ireland* (London: Bodley Head, 1986). Like Joyce and O'Connor, Trevor contrasts the hypocrisy and self-deception of the adult world with the adolescent imperative to survive by secrecy.

The following interview reveals a man who is a master of restraint in person and in his stories. Readers of the *Irish Literary Supplement*, having enjoyed his urbanity, wit, and understatement, will find the same qualities in his wry conversation. We sat and talked on a spring afternoon in Devon while a choir rehearsed in the cathedral nearby.

William Trevor and I meet for tea at a small hotel. We step around workmen busy renovating the hotel's old-fashioned interior as we walk to the dining room. Once seated, I ask Trevor how he conceives his fictional characters. He tells me that his figures do not stand before him full-blown initially but evolve as he writes. As I turn on my tape recorder, I hear the sandblasting just outside. I notice that Trevor is eavesdropping on the conversation of a couple at a corner table behind us. Suddenly aware of the presence of other people in the room, I realize that it must be very hard for Trevor to hear what they are saying. Noticing that I have observed him, he says that listening is second nature to him, that he would rather listen than speak.[1] [Jacqueline Stahl Aronson]

TREVOR: I think if you write fiction you have to be a good listener. That doesn't mean that writing is the natural outcome of listening, but it's one of the many implements you've got. The desire and urge to listen is one of the tools of your trade. There are lots and lots of others.

ARONSON: Such as?

TREVOR: Well, you have to be able to do certain things with the written word. You have to be able to tell a story; you have to be able to communicate your characters to other people so that other people understand them. Also, it's no good being able just to write good dialogue. If you just write good dialogue, it'll just sit on the page being good dialogue. It's all these tools and pieces that have got to be put together which make the fiction writer. It is very difficult to pick one out from this felicity and say that it all comes from that because I think it might be misleading. But listening is important. It is something I share with other writers of fiction. I mean, we're tempted to listen whether we like it or not and wonder who these people are. Curiosity is very important because it seems to me one couldn't really write about people without being curious about the real people in the real world. That is a very personal statement, but I suspect it might be true of writers in a general way. I don't know.

ARONSON: I'm interested in your notion of fantasy and reality, especially women's fantasies. In the title story, "The Ballroom of Romance,"[2] Bridey at thirty-six has a fantasy about marrying Dano Ryan. She thinks to herself, "If you couldn't have love, the next best thing was surely a decent man." She imagines Dano living with her, helping her one-legged father on their farm; she envisions evenings at home with him, what they would be like. And then, when she realizes that Dano has become attached to his landlady, in her mind she accepts Bowser Egan, who is lazy and who drinks, and she imagines, realistically, what life with him would be like. Do you think that men have such explicit fantasies?

TREVOR: I think they do. Actually, I think the word *fantasy* is a little grand for what we are talking about.

ARONSON: Imaginings?

TREVOR: I think *imaginings* is much better because I think that people simply imagine things. I mean, you have to imagine things if you're a human being: since imagination has been given to you, you use it. I think *fantasy* is a more modern concept, which I don't like; I think it's a dressed-up expression. Everybody imagines, and somebody as isolated as Bridey certainly would have no difficulty imagining. I would say that's approximately how she would imagine, and people sometimes don't—don't imagine enough. They don't use that side of their minds: I've written a bit about it recently. That's an interesting thing, too.

ARONSON: What have you written about it?

TREVOR: I've portrayed an unimaginative person.

ARONSON: Who?

TREVOR: There are some newish stories, and there's one in particular called "Her Mother's Daughter," which you wouldn't have read because it hasn't come out in America. It's coming out in a magazine called *Grand Street*.[3] There is a study of such a person in that—Helena's mother.

ARONSON: Mr. Trevor, do you have a favorite piece of writing, a favorite child, so to speak, early, late? "In Isfahan," an early story from the *Angels at the Ritz*[4] collection, is one I especially like.

TREVOR: The last one that you have written is the recent favorite.

ARONSON: I was afraid you would say, "Either the last or the next"; that's hardly a fair answer. I don't accept it.

TREVOR: I don't really have a favorite though there are stories which I like. I like the one you mentioned, "In Isfahan." I like that story, but it's not a great favorite. "Death in Jerusalem" is one I like, but in fact . . . really, no, there aren't favorites. These, in the paperback collection of my short stories, are just all the stories that they've got, and they put it in one book. I'm collecting them together in a hardback.[5] I am sort of selecting, as it were, and I can either include all the stories in the paperback or I can leave some out. But you see, you don't think about them when you've done with them. You're too glad to get rid of them.

ARONSON: I know exactly what you mean. But what about themes in your fictions? Do you feel you have a recurring theme or several?

TREVOR: Hundreds of little ones, but in fact, to be quite honest, you sometimes aren't even aware of them, but afterward you have the misfortune of having to read what you've written.

ARONSON: In your latest novel, *Fools of Fortune*, set in the midst of the Troubles,[6] did you start with certain themes in mind—mutilation, violence, revenge? or did they, like your characters, evolve as you wrote?

TREVOR: Actually, I have been rereading *Fools of Fortune* recently, and I see themes that I didn't know existed.

ARONSON: What themes?

TREVOR: Let me think. I think there is in *Fools of Fortune* the theme of the resilience of the young that comes into it because Willie and Marianne are quite young in the book—they might be a bit younger, I think—and that is simply emphasizing and underlining the theme; the idea of youth's resilience runs through the first quarter of *Fools of Fortune*. Willie can recover from such an awful experience as the fire, whereas his mother can't, and she hasn't really lost more than he has lost. She has lost two daughters and a husband, and Willie has lost two sisters of whom he was very fond and a beloved father. And what interests me is that human beings are made like that. Willie has the resilience and the toughness, as anyone, I think, of that age would—he is about eleven at the time of the fire—react with such resilience. As I get older, I find that I like to write about young people.

ARONSON: May we go back to the subject of some themes that seem to recur in your fictions? Your fictions often seem to suggest the possibility of compassion as well as the possibility, to use E. M. Forster's term, of *connecting*.[7] But, to move for a moment from idea to image, that is, from theme to plot, several of your fictions concern themselves with marital infidelity, frequently with a married man who dallies with a young, unmarried woman. What can you tell me about the image of the predatory male in your work?

TREVOR: Well, are there many predatory males?

ARONSON: In your books and stories there are.

TREVOR: Well, there's Francis in *Other People's Worlds*, but he is more than predatory: he's a criminal.

ARONSON: Yes, but in some of the other cases, predatory may be too strong a word. The women in these stories, for example, Angela in "Office Romance," cooperate eagerly in giving themselves to relationships that appear to offer the chance to see themselves as desirable but actually deny their already tenuous sense of their own identities. On the other hand, there's the story of the poor but resourceful lovers who discover a bathtub "big enough for two" in the public bathroom of a nearby hotel—the man in that story is sincere.

TREVOR: That's "Lovers of Their Time," yes.

ARONSON: Those lovers connect emotionally, not just physically. But the man, Norman Britt, is an exception: he leaves his wife to live with his Marie, unlike other married men in fiction, and, I suspect, in life, most of whom stay married. Yet their love is beaten down by their poverty until at last he returns to his wife, and Marie marries "a man in a brewery." But in many of your other stories of marital infidelity the men feel less and are less honest, and the women are duped by their own romantic illusions. Are these situations a metaphor for illusion, betrayal, something of that sort?

TREVOR: I don't think so. I don't think they are meant to be metaphoric. I'm not that sort of a writer, really, who uses metaphor. It's just something observed, I think. It's just—you have to write about something—and I think often the stories start off with some little shred of reality, and they take off from that. I suppose "The Mark-2 Wife" is one of those.

ARONSON: I can certainly imagine your getting the idea for that story from something you witnessed. But that tale also is different from most of your other stories about infidelity. First, its focus is on the feelings of the wife, rather than on those of the man or of the other woman. Second, although you've left it ambiguous, the wife in this story too may be abandoned, just as, in her worst fantasies she had imagined she would be.

But since we've disposed of metaphor, let's talk about chance—about the chanciness of fate in your fictional worlds. In *Fools of Fortune* Willie Quinton is lucky not only in his youthful resilience in coping with the first tragedy but also because, until the fire, he had a very solid life, suffused with love and affection. But the second tragedy, his mother's death, impels him to the revenge that forces him into exile. Again, in "A Choice of Butchers," it's chance that brings the apprentice, Henry Dukelow, into the little boy's life for six months and during that time gives the child a standard of decency, warmth, and understanding. And in your novel *The Children of Dynmouth* it's only chance that Timothy Gedge has the bad luck, from the moment of his birth, to be humiliated and unloved and that he is so warped by his ill-treatment that we can't know how he'll turn out. As you suggest, Timothy's youth is in his favor; also, his troubles have brought him the concern of the young minister and his wife. This good luck may straighten Timothy out, but we can't know how much of the early damage will be undone.

TREVOR: Yes, yes. I think Timothy would have recovered. But I don't think his story, *The Children of Dynmouth*, has to do with that. I think he would have recovered from his appalling experiences because I believe that *at that age* most people would recover. I don't think that people are as easily damaged as we make out. They are damaged in other ways, but a child can go through what Timothy or Willie went through and can be perfectly normal. But in the case of Willie, the whole point of the novel *Fools of Fortune* is that there is a moment when you push the thing too far, and chance is too hard on you. Willie walked into the room and found his mother dead; that was too much. After his mother takes her life, his need for vengeance must have become impossible to ignore. After that, he just couldn't *live* a normal life, and it seems to me to be understandable that he couldn't—there's a sort of guilt and a dreadful shame that he would have felt. After he kills the man responsible for the massacre, he goes into exile for fifty years, and that changes everything.

ARONSON: His mother had suggested it over and over. Even when they talked about other things, she would suddenly break in and ask, "Why does nobody kill that man?"

TREVOR: Yes, his mother always pressed for retribution.

ARONSON: When she takes Willie to tea at the Victoria Hotel, even then, she speaks the murderer's name.

TREVOR: That's right, yes, yes. So that when he finds himself so alone again after she dies—although he does actually say, "What a nuisance she was," he doesn't really mean that—he's terribly upset. His mother's death is just too much; that's the point, I think. It's too much for him to take. That was just chance. That was not anyone being evil or wicked; it was simply fortune. And then he was in the same boat as his mother had been, thinking the way she had thought, obsessively wanting revenge at any cost, but he was in a position to do something about it, while she wasn't. And he did what he had to do. I think that *Fools of Fortune* was entirely about *chance.*

ARONSON: So many of your stories are concerned with chance, but coincidence also figures in many of them, and modern people have learned to distrust coincidence.

TREVOR: Yes.

ARONSON: What would you say about the place of coincidence in your work?

TREVOR: Well, of course, chance is different from coincidence. There is an element of chance in coincidence, but it is a slightly different thing. In *Fools of Fortune* chance—fortune, really—placed all the characters where they were at that particular time. It was just bad luck in many ways that so many things happened. It was the merest chance that the traitor Doyle was hanged on the Quinton's land and then that Sergeant Rudkin took revenge by setting fire to their house. You know, all this was sort of very chancy stuff, but that's the way life is.

ARONSON: Yet your fictions don't suggest that chance alone determines fate. A theme of "Being Stolen From" seems to be that character is also fate. Brigid, whose story it is, reflects that fate "began with the kind of person you were," then poignantly demonstrates this by relinquishing the child she loves. But can you say more about fortune's randomness?

TREVOR: What can I say? I don't think one has any sort of feeling of controlling one's destiny. Nobody's in charge of anything; you're doled out time, from beginning to end. That's your given. Now, when you think of what happened to Willie Quinton's family, when you think of that particular family, that particular house, you have to remember that they were people who were traitors to their class and traitors to their background—that's what one set of people would have said, although I wouldn't say that. Nevertheless, it's chance that placed them there at that particular time. Had Michael Collins not been in their home, had Willie's father not written a check to help his guest's revolutionary cause . . . it was just bad fortune . . . or call it fate. And it was chance as well that Marianne became pregnant after her one tryst with Willie. She might not have become pregnant, but she did, and that created the second half of the book. There would be no book if that had not happened, and, again, it was just fate.

ARONSON: Immediate conception seems to occur in fiction with some frequency, but this brings me to a question I have about the child, Imelda, that Marianne bears. Imelda is a sort of blessed innocent, a medieval conception of blessed: "possessing special powers." Certainly, the people of Kilneagh believe in Imelda's power to heal. Similarly, in your novel *The Love Department* Lady Delores has perfect faith that Edward Blakeston-Smith, another apparently mad innocent, will be able to track down and deliver that elusive lover, Septimus Tuam, to her. And Edward, in spite of his incredible ineptness—by his own admission, it's all he can do "to butter his bread'—not only fulfills the greater part of his mission but, in the course of his pursuit, finds what we would call sanity.

TREVOR: I think that frequently people like Imelda and Edward, who are called mad because they are innocent, are thought to be imbued with special powers. In Imelda's case you have to imagine a very beautiful girl, a very beautiful *woman*, who is also very *gentle*; she has the qualities of a saint. And you have to imagine the local people: they don't know anything very much about the state of mind called *madness*—what they do know is the story of the house, what's happened there that has by now become a legend. They all have this feeling for the family because it is a family of heroes and heroines to the local people, and they would begin to say that Imelda is a sort of a saint.

ARONSON: Touched with divine power.

TREVOR: That's the opinion of the local people. It's not necessarily my opinion. So that it's very likely that a presence like Imelda's, her smiling beauty, in such a house—burnt out, ugly, melancholy with the background of what had happened—all contributed to the family becoming a legend. There was the extraordinary series of stories: Anna Quinton in the nineteenth century who fed the poor during the time of the Famine.

ARONSON: She also persuaded her husband to give all of his money away.

TREVOR: Yes, and long before that, the Quintons had turned British soldiers away from their door because they had killed people in the local village. All this would begin to merge into a single legend about the family. From the legend would then emerge the saintly figure of Imelda.

ARONSON: Granted that Imelda's apparent madness, like Edward Blakeston-Smith's, does seem divinely inspired, what about ordinary human irrationality? Do you consider human behavior irrational?

TREVOR: Well, it *is* irrational. I'll absolutely stand by that. Human behavior is very rarely rational.

ARONSON: Well, Freud said something to that effect. He suggested that when one has to make a choice, one should make two lists, pro and con, except in matters of marriage and career, love and work, because those will be decided by the unconscious anyway. Do you feel that?

TREVOR: I think so, yes. I think that's really true. You know, we tend to overstudy life. We should leave it alone, as Thurber[8] would say, "Leave your mind alone." There are so many things that we don't know. If one knew the answers, life would be very dull, so you keep coming back to a sense of curiosity.

ARONSON: That's a wonderfully optimistic view. Are you an optimistic person?

TREVOR: I was meant to be very pessimistic, but I think I've become optimistic.

ARONSON: I would like to talk some more about the relations between men and women in your fictions.

TREVOR: They rather vary as far as I can remember. Sometimes men and women get on very badly, but sometimes they get on really rather well. I think there is some amount of humor in the relationships between men and women in my books.

ARONSON: Yes, in your novel *The Old Boys* the dialogues between the Jarabys are very funny, unlike any I've ever read except perhaps in Restoration comedy. *The Old Boys* was done for British television, wasn't it?

TREVOR: A long time ago; it was rather better on the radio.

ARONSON: I'm not surprised; what matters are the words—and the timing. Mrs. Jaraby is so quick-witted, full of surprises: she gets the better of her husband every time. She's a better arguer than he is. There's usually nothing left for him to do but to retreat by withdrawing.

TREVOR: Michael Redgrave was Jaraby when it was done on the stage. It wasn't a very good production—he was very ill. The best I think *was* probably the radio one. It was very funny, very amusing.

ARONSON: Yes, some of these bitter dialogues between husband and wife are extremely funny. Moreover, although Mrs. Jaraby has always had the last word, when her husband learns that he has been defeated in his club's election, she rallies to her husband by asking his advice at last. She says, "We're together again, Mr. Jaraby; this is an occasion for celebration, and you must do the talking." Although their preceding exchanges were suffused with spite, Mrs. Jaraby's words, which close the novel, are suffused with spirit and optimism: "Come now," she asks, "how shall we prove we are not dead?"

TREVOR: Oh, yes, yes, their battles keep them going. The exchanges are fairly terrible, but the pair are companions, you know. That's the thing that people didn't realize. They are companions, and they will continue to be because, you see, he has lost his companionship with all those silly old men, and he will turn more and more toward his wife. It's a very fragile companionship, yet it's very real. They argue and bicker, but there is no silence between them, which I think is what the book is meant to be saying. They don't sit there silently. They always talk. Everything she says and everything he says is replied to.

ARONSON: The Jarabys quarrel fiercely, but, to use popular jargon, they communicate. Their relationship is actually very stable; they just go about things in a certain way. On the other hand, take the chilling story "Grass Widow" in which the newlyweds are heard through the wall by the husband's former headmaster and his wife: When the bride of one day begs her husband to take her away from the inn, from the presence of the headmaster and his frightening wife, her husband ignores her, pleading misery. He proceeds to explain that it's not practical to leave: the room is paid for; they don't have reservations elsewhere. But he isn't rude to her as Mr. Jaraby is to Mrs. Jaraby.

TREVOR: No, no, the young couple's marriage is going to be different from the Jarabys'; very likely, it will be like that of the headmaster and his wife. There will be great silences; there will be great, long sitting-at-home-by-the-fire sorts of things, not saying anything or whatever, which is much, much worse than the quarreling and the bickering and everything else. Because that's more like birds or dogs yapping, it's perfectly healthy. What is awful is this heavy emptiness, the terrible vacuum, in which no effort is made to communicate, and that is appalling. And I don't think that's in *The Old Boys*. I think it's a cheerful book; I always think it's one of my most cheerful books.

ARONSON: Is it hard to write cheerful books these days?

TREVOR: It is.

ARONSON: *The Love Department* is a cheerful book and a wonderfully funny one, but it was published eighteen years ago. Rereading it recently, I found myself laughing out loud. It seems to me very fresh, and I admire the way one of its themes, the impact and evolution of the "blessed innocent," is worked out. For example, when Edward Blakeston-Smith simultaneously completes his mission and is restored to sanity, his diction changes: it becomes more realistic, more everyday, less holy. Then, no longer so vulnerable, no longer menaced, for example, by the huge advertising posters he sees in the Tube, he is able to function in the world that surrounds him, but he retires from it. Will anything be done with *The Love Department?* I think it would make a fine movie, splendidly comic and zany: the dwarfish Lady Delores running her finger wildly through her hair, washing down her chocolate cake with Scotch, screaming out orders to her bemused subordinates.

TREVOR: Well, that was bought by Twentieth-Century Fox, and they sat on it for a long time. Silvio Narizzano,[9] who directed *Georgy Girl,* was to have directed it. But then he made a film called *Blue,* which wasn't successful. It was a western, and he overspent very savagely; he also overspent on the scripting of *The Love Department,* and they fell out with him, and it was all shelved. I think, possibly, it has reverted to me because that must be, as you say, it's eighteen years ago . . . is it eighteen years ago?

ARONSON: Yes.

TREVOR: Because I reckon it would all come back to me. It was going to be done with the English couple—they were very funny—Peter Cook and Dudley Moore. They were a kind of a duo: they were going to do the two parts, the inept pursuer and the slippery pursued. It would have been very good.

ARONSON: I keep seeing references to movies in your fictions. I don't know whether you were just doing your homework and filling in the period pieces or whether you love movies. Are you an avid moviegoer?

TREVOR: Yes. I get to them a lot. Do you?

ARONSON: Yes, all the good ones. I'd like to see *The Love Department.* One last question: Do you keep a journal?

TREVOR: No, no.

ARONSON: Have you ever?

TREVOR: Not that I can remember. I think once I did, before I wrote, but nothing any further.

Michael Longley

Interviewed by Dillon Johnston

I like to believe that in this very dangerous trade—and
poetry is very dangerous—silence is part of the impulse, and
one must wait for the muse. I do believe in the old-fashioned
notion of inspiration. I don't think I've ever written anything
without impulsive excitement, a sense of exploration, and the
chill of psychological risk.

—Michael Longley

FOR POETS, SAID LOUIS MacNEICE, the middle stretch was the most difficult. Michael Longley recalls this advice in his 1986 interview. Undergo-
ing his own personal transitions, Michael Longley came to Boston in May
to give a major poetry reading at the national conference of the American Committee for Irish Studies (ACIS).[1] In 1985 he observed the publication of his collected poems,[2] and he anticipates in 1987 a popular
edition of the same work by Penguin and Wake Forest University Press.
While major anthologies—*The Penguin Book of Contemporary British Poetry*
(Harmondsworth: Penguin, 1982) and *The Faber Contemporary Irish Poetry*
(London: Faber and Faber, 1986)—honored him with copious selections
and assertions that he was one of the major Ulster poets in whose
shadow English poetry etiolated, he suffered a four-year period of poetic
barrenness. Having begun a year-long sabbatical in January, he has already conceived a new series of poems based on a sojourn in a cottage in

From *ILS* 5 (spring 1986).

51

Mayo. Consequently, the May visit to Boston offered a special focus on an important literary career at midpoint.

Born in Belfast to transplanted English parents in 1939, Michael Longley and his twin brother, now a merchant mariner, attended school with working-class students in southern Belfast. He enrolled in the Royal Belfast Academical Institute before reading classics at Trinity College where he met his wife-to-be, Edna, and the poet Derek Mahon. After graduation, he taught in London and Dublin before taking up residence in Belfast where he exchanged early poems with Seamus Heaney, Mahon, and, occasionally, members of Philip Hobsbaum's weekly circle of readers.[3] While Edna Longley lectured at Queen's University and developed a series of probing essays,[4] Michael was serving as associate director of the Arts Council of Northern Ireland and writing five volumes of poetry: *No Continuing City* (London: Gill and Macmillan; Chester Springs, Pa.: Dufour Editions, 1969, *An Exploded View* (London: Gollancz, 1973), *Man Lying on a Wall* (London: Gollancz, 1976), *The Echo Gate* (London: Secker and Warburg, 1979), and *Selected Poems, 1963–1980* (Winston-Salem, N.C.: Wake Forest University Press, 1981).[5]

After the ACIS conference, Longley came to Winston-Salem, North Carolina, to help celebrate the tenth anniversary of Wake Forest University Press. On a temperate Saturday afternoon, above the sound of lawn mowers and arias, he engaged in the following conversation. [Dillon Johnston]

DILLON JOHNSTON: May I ask you about your poem "Wounds" and the ending to "Wounds," particularly, because I think it has to do with audience?—the lines that read "shot through the head / By a shivering boy . . . / . . . / to the children, to a bewildered wife,/ I think 'Sorry, Missus,' was what he said."

MICHAEL LONGLEY: Well, I think it means "it is rumored," and also "I hope," and it's looking for some glimpse of humanity amid the brutality of that particular circumstance. But, of course, "I think" is more neutral than either of those and is intended to be.

JOHNSTON: But it's a kind of scrupulousness, a kind of attempt to be honest.

LONGLEY: Yes, it's saying that if there is anything to be optimistic about out of this mess, I'm not going to overstress it.

JOHNSTON: The poem has sympathy for a number of people, including the "shivering boy."

LONGLEY: Yes, it has. That was before the IRA campaign became even more brutalized. We are inclined to forget that a lot of people involved who are under twenty-five and even teenagers haven't known any other political circumstances except civil unrest. So it seems important to me to try and think oneself into their shoes, as it were, and to imagine how one can be so brainwashed or so angry or, in a sense, perhaps even so innocent that one can drive in a car and go into somebody's house and shoot that person stone dead. It seems important to imagine that.

JOHNSTON: Let's get to another subject of sympathy in the poem. The Ulster Division at the Somme,[6] the trenches, the life that you imagine for your father's stories, the tales of the First World War?—what about that war? You've written about it a number of times.

LONGLEY: Well, it was important to me to realize as a young man that my father was a representative of a generation, the remnants of a generation, that survived that nightmare. I suppose Europe is still recovering from the First World War. When you think of it, it was just the tatters of a generation that ruled Britain, France, Germany for many years— the Attlees, the Macmillans.[7] Looked at from the next century, we will be thinking in terms of the fifty or sixty years war that began in 1914: there was a respite; it picked up again in 1939; then there was Korea and Vietnam. It's been a long struggle, and the Edwardian dream ended in 1914; mechanized slaughter became the norm, and the world has never been the same since.

JOHNSTON: When you imagine yourself into your father's situation, to what extent do you have a sympathy for the English side of yourself, your English background?

LONGLEY: That's unavoidable. From an early age, I think I was quite schizoid. In order to survive in the street I had to develop a Belfast accent, a rather severe one. When I went home, this would be modified for my parents, who retained their English accents and didn't find the Belfast accent very attractive. So, from quite an early age, I was recreating myself twice a day or more. I mean, I'm Irish, inasmuch as Ireland has provided me with most of the data out of which I make sense of experience, and I feel most at home in Ireland. But, of course, I was brought up by English parents. Part of the way I see things is bound to be of an English tinge. And, as I've said elsewhere, the result of being brought up by English parents in Ireland is that I feel slightly ill at ease on both islands. I'm neither English nor Irish completely, and I like to think that is a healthy condition. It's out of such splits, out of such tensions, that I write, perhaps.

JOHNSTON: There are other people who feel that same sort of division, Catholic and republican and people in the South who exercise another version of that.

LONGLEY: No, I don't see how they would. I didn't enjoy the familial hinterland of a Seamus Heaney or a Derek Mahon. There were no aunts or uncles living around the corner. The family ended at the front door and was contained within that home.

JOHNSTON: Were there grandparents in England?

LONGLEY: Yes, but I never met my father's parents; my Grandpa George was the only relative who crossed the Irish Sea to visit us in Belfast. He was a marvelously Dickensian cockney who taught ballroom dancing and was quite an exciting mix of vulgarity and refinement. He introduced me to things like pheasant and hare and tripe, and at the same time he had the coarse confidences of the master of ceremonies in a ballroom. But he was so different from any of my friends' grandparents. I was continually reminded, I suppose, that I was not quite the same as my playmates. I remember one of my friends who came from a strict Presbyterian household: when he came to play with me, he noticed the crate of empty Guinness bottles outside the back door and said, "Ach, the English."

JOHNSTON: Let me ask you about living in Belfast itself. Some of your best friends are poets or are connected with the arts generally. The community there cuts across any kind of line or forms a kind of model for a mixed society living more or less peacefully, aside from the row now and then at the Eglantine Inn.[8]

LONGLEY: Yes, I think the artists of Belfast have imagined an ideal Belfast. Art does cross all the barriers and the frontiers, and it doesn't admit of borders. This has made life very rich for me in Belfast. Do you want to pursue that?

I think it was de Valera[9] who said somewhat mischievously that Belfast is the most Irish of cities. In a way, that's not true inasmuch as Belfast is a creation of the Industrial Revolution and has more in common with Glasgow and Liverpool than with Dublin. But because of its tribal mix, it's the place where the antique European religious struggle is guttering out, we hope; it's the fag end of that religious war. And if that is so, and I believe that is the case, I would ask, who knows Ireland who does not Belfast know?

JOHNSTON: The community around Wellington Park Bar[10] earlier and the Eglantine Inn, as I witnessed it anyway, includes a number of very good friends interested in poetry and art. What about the absence from that group of Paul Muldoon, who left in February for Dingle?[11]

LONGLEY: Of course, his leaving leaves a big gap in my life. My two closest friends in Belfast are the critic Michael Allen and Paul Muldoon. It's not exactly a café culture in Belfast; there's no real literary pub like, say, McDaid's used to be in Dublin. I think that's because being reticent "Northerners" we all prefer the *tête-à-tête* to the group showoff around the table. Even with my two closest friends, we would meet in twos rather than a threesome. When I've seen Paul recently in Dingle, it reminded me of how much I was missing him in Belfast and how I used to enjoy very much the gradual conversational exploration with the help of alcohol down through the layers of the psyche until round about midnight you had reached the basement. [*Laughter.*]

JOHNSTON: It's called "soundings."

LONGLEY: Soundings, indeed.

JOHNSTON: Would either Paul or Michael be readers of poems in draft?—not speaking of draft beer this time.

LONGLEY: Yes, but the first critic of a poem that I write would be my wife, Edna, and she's quite hard to please; so I feel more confident about showing it to Michael Allen and Paul Muldoon. If those two like it and Edna likes it, I don't really care what anyone else says. Heaney and Derek Mahon used to be in that immediate circle of readers. I would send them poems through the post, but by that time the poems would have had the Good Housekeeping seal of approval from Edna, Michael, and Paul, and there would be less urgency. I mean, I'm talking about those circumstances where you order the pints, and you sit down, and you nervously take a folded bit of paper out of your pocket.

JOHNSTON: At what point does your secret scratching in the den or wherever become something you share with Edna? When do you know that a poem is fairly finished?

LONGLEY: In the early days I'd show it to her when I thought it might be finished rather than when I knew it was finished. She would say, "Well, yes, I like that, but that line's not right" or "that word's not right." And, of course, I would see that she was right; she has what I would call a very good ear.

It's agreed between Edna and me that she won't write about my work. Somehow or other, I think that would be improper. To quote Oscar Wilde, it would be like washing your clean linen in public although, naturally, I hope that my poetry has influenced her critical stance a little.

JOHNSTON: Is that reciprocal? Can we assume that you don't write your love poetry about her?

LONGLEY: That's an interesting question. I suppose that my love poetry is addressed to what I grandiosely call the female principle, to the Gravesian notion of the muse.[12] It's written out of my experience of womankind, and, of course, Edna makes a big contribution to that experience. But when I read my love poems in public, I don't feel that

I'm "undressing" Edna for others to look at. It would be bad love poetry if that were the case. If the artifact has any validity at all, it acquires an impersonal authority of its own. If I were a painter and I couldn't afford a model, I should feel free to paint my wife in the nude without people who came to look at the picture, rubbing their hands and thinking they were having a glimpse of my wife in the nude. They would simply be looking at a painting, and I hope the same thing applies to my poems.

JOHNSTON: Are there poems of yours that couldn't have been written by a woman?

LONGLEY: I don't know the answer to that question, but I think that I am a very feminine man. I think that I see the world through the woman part of me. I feel the world through the woman part of me more than most men. If that is true, I suppose there must be some poems which one wouldn't be surprised to have discovered written by a woman.

JOHNSTON: Are there any poems of yours that couldn't be understood by women?

LONGLEY: No; if that were the case, I think that they would be bad poems, and I would throw them out.

JOHNSTON: You're the combined arts director of the Arts Council of Northern Ireland. To what extent did those heavy responsibilities contribute to the period of silence from which you've just emerged?

LONGLEY: I think it did contribute. There were other factors, of course, but to do that kind of job—and it's a very privileged job, really—to do that kind of job well, you do it creatively. But I also think of my vision of how I wanted the arts to develop in Northern Ireland: In my innocence, I thought I could rush that vision through. So there was a certain amount of tension in the job as I came up against—well, "vested interests" is putting it too strongly. Let's say that power gravitates toward the center, and in the arts world that tends to mean middle brow, middle class, middle age, middle of the road. I've been interested in a more profound involvement with the community than the Arts Council can manage at the moment. Therefore, my frustration took up too much energy.

Having said that, though, my job in the Arts Council is exciting, and I meet lots of interesting people. The silence was brought about by much more than just that. It might have been the male menopause. As Louis MacNeice said, the middle stretch is bad for poets. It might have been that I had nothing to say, and I think I do also move in manic-depressive cycles which last for long periods. I was in a depressive trough, but I've had silences before. I had a very long silence about 1968–70. I do feel, Dillon, that most poets write and publish too much, and surviving the silence—I should say the silences—separates the men from the boys. After twenty-five years of practice, one has acquired quite a lot of technique, and it would be very easy to produce forgeries that would fool other people and perhaps even fool one's self. I like to believe that in this very dangerous trade—and poetry is very dangerous—silence is part of the impulse, and one must wait for the muse. I do believe in the old-fashioned notion of inspiration. I don't think I've ever written anything without impulsive excitement, a sense of exploration, and the chill of psychological risk.

JOHNSTON: There must have been points when this kind of wisdom left you and at some discomfort from not writing.

LONGLEY: Yes, it's a commonplace to say that every poet thinks of the most recent poem as possibly the last. That's only partially true because you know in the back of your mind when you've struck a vein. There's this enormous sense of confidence and, indeed, insouciance, which is an essential part of the enterprise. But it's when the block is prolonged that there's a loss of confidence which is very damaging, not just to the writer but in all other aspects of life as well. It's like having an itch and not being able to scratch.

JOHNSTON: Or a period of impotence.

LONGLEY: Yes, it's exactly like impotence.

JOHNSTON: Not that we would know about that. [*Laughter.*]

LONGLEY: Having the equipment and not being able to do anything with it—yeah. Part of me had to say, sooner or later, fuck off to form. I got my sabbatical and then went to this cottage in Mayo for four or five weeks and lived entirely on my own. For the first ten days, I was trying too hard. Then I said, well, I'm just here to enjoy myself. Once I said that, the lines started to come, and in a sense what I'm saying through those more relaxed long lines is, "I'm just here to enjoy my-self" within the shape of the poem.

JOHNSTON: There are clear signs that you have emerged from the period of silence, Michael. How long was it? Is that dangerous?

LONGLEY: It was three or four years. I wrote one or two poems. I didn't have the appetite for it, and, as I said, I didn't have the confidence. The usual formal preoccupations were knocking me off balance, whereas in fact they are normally a part of balance and poise.

JOHNSTON: Can you describe what those formal preoccupations are?

LONGLEY: Producing an organic form, a shape, which makes emotional, spiritual, and linguistic sense. Finding within the confinements of a shape the pulse of life, valid rhythms. I think that rhythm is what poetry is all about. When rhythm fails, the poem fails.

JOHNSTON: We're listening to a National Public Radio broadcast of *Madame Butterfly*. Among your new poems is a lovely tribute to her. When you recited the poem earlier, in anticipation of a Puccini afternoon, it sounded as if it was much longer than a six-line poem. I suppose that with pauses in the lines there are ways in which it is both six lines and something more extensive.

LONGLEY: How can I say this without sounding presumptuous? Yes, I think that's one of the bigger poems I've written. I hate the confusion of miniature with minor, and I hope I have said extensive things within a small compass. I'm complimented to think that you're surprised that it's only six lines long.

JOHNSTON: You speak about these poems as if they're unbuttoned, and there is something a bit wild about the imagery and lovely turns. Is that related to the formal qualities of the poem, or the less trammeled formal quality?

LONGLEY: I once said that if prose is a river and poetry's a fountain, then the shape of the poem and the form of the poem are like the nozzle that forces under pressure the water into a shape that is recognizable as a shape but is free-flowing and alive. The trouble in the past for me has been that the shape has become increasingly defined, perfected, so that at certain points in my formal explorations there's been nowhere to go. I've often thought sympathetically of the American painter Rothko,[13] who as you know painted icons of color, three bands of color, and explored that. Even with the nearly infinite potential of that idea, the paintings got darker and darker until he reached the blank wall of a nearly black canvas. And he shot himself. But that's part of the risk of poetry. I do think that poetry is more complicated, more dangerous, than high-wire walking. Most people who call themselves poets would be dead if they were high-wire walkers; they'd have fallen off the wire. So technical facility seems to me of importance, but one can get to a certain stage where one becomes almost too capable, and I think that when you become too capable the darker parts of your psyche resist the facility and the result is silence. One has to go back to the beginning at certain stages in what one hopes is a long career and, as it were, learn all over again.

JOHNSTON: Where all the ladders start?[14]

LONGLEY: Where all the ladders start, yes.

JOHNSTON: Thomas Kinsella and John Montague[15] have both described a feeling of being boxed in and have found some relief in American models. Kinsella mentions William Carlos Williams as someone who blew some fog away for him. Do you read American poetry? and have you found poets here that you're particularly attracted to?

LONGLEY: Yes, I read quite a lot of American poetry, and most of it I find is chopped prose.

JOHNSTON: Sounds like a delicatessen choice.

LONGLEY: "Chopped prose." Yes, I like some of Williams, but I find it thin on my ear, not rich enough. I don't see how somebody living in a small island where the landscape changes at every turn in the road and where the fields are small and where the sky is low could write the same way as someone who lives on the prairies where the vista is unchanged for hundreds of miles. I'm against any notion of an international style. In the 1960s, the abstract expressionists' international style depressed me inasmuch as it was impossible to tell whether the painter was Italian or American or British. So I think that what I can learn from American models is limited. But I would very much hope that one day I'll be able to write some distinguished free verse like the great psalms of Theodore Roethke in the North American Sequence.

JOHNSTON: What about English poetry? Are there models and would you consider yourself equally separated from, or distinguished from, the English poet in this avoidance of international style?

LONGLEY: Separated more in matters of tone of voice. With American poetry, it's more in matters of form. I've never really thought in terms of models. I know what you mean—glimpses of possible ways forward. In my early twenties the three books that made me enormously excited and were, in a sense, enabling, facilitating at one or two removes, were *The Less Deceived* by Philip Larkin, *Lupercal* by Ted Hughes, and *For the Unfallen* by Geoffrey Hill. They seem to me still to be the best English poets.

JOHNSTON: There's enough variety there to escape from any kind of restricted verse.

LONGLEY: Well, you occasionally despair when you've read the umpteenth boring poem in the *New Statesman* or *TLS*. And then you think, well, a tradition that's still throwing up poets like Larkin, Hill, and Hughes must be doing all right. The other enabling influences? It was important certainly for Mahon and me to pick up the works of Louis MacNeice when we were in our early twenties and, to a lesser extent for him and me than for Heaney, Patrick Kavanagh. It was very important to read those two poets writing about one's own experiences. And then Graves, Robert Graves, remains a much-loved poet as far as I'm concerned.

JOHNSTON: What about earlier poets, dead poets? Who matters to you?

LONGLEY: Quite a few. Wilfrid Owen, Edward Thomas, Keats, John Clare, George Herbert,[16] and then from the classical world, Catullus, Propertius, Tibullus,[17] the Roman love elegists.

JOHNSTON: What have you learned from your university studies in Latin and Greek generally, or from Latin and Greek poets?

LONGLEY: From Latin and Greek studies one learns that our civilization is about seven-eighths, or at least six-eighths, Graeco-Roman, our institutions and language and culture. From reading the Latin poets I was alerted to the possibilities of syntax, which is the muscle of poetry. I get bored by so much poetry which is written in short, jerky sentences. I love stretching out over a stanza a sentence and playing the pauses of meaning against the line endings and trying to make the sentence, the grammatical unit, coincide with the stanzaic unit—using the rush of syntax in a way that plays off the constriction of the stanzaic shape and results in a linguistic energy which is like pushing water through a dynamo, the principles of hydroelectricity—the tensions between the freedom of a long sentence playing against the tight form.

JOHNSTON: Whom do you address in the poem? What sense of audience do you have when you write the poem? Are you thinking of any particular kind of reader?

LONGLEY: No, not really. I write first of all to satisfy myself and secondly [*laughter*] for the world, I suppose, for anyone who wants to read it. But I don't have a sense of an audience in the way, say, Seamus Heaney has. I mean, he's rather like Frost inasmuch as he addresses poetry lovers and people who don't normally read poetry and succeeds in getting through to both. For better or worse, I'm not that kind of poet. Coming to the States, I realized that there were certain references in my poems to birds and flowers that need to be explained to an American audience. I think it would be very dangerous for me if I was distracted by that. All the words I use have to be used as if by second nature.

JOHNSTON: Michael, we've talked about parents and about Edna. Would you just name your children?

LONGLEY: Well, there's Rebecca, who's eighteen, and shaping up to be a modern linguist. She hopes to go to London University next autumn— [*with a drawl and laughter*] next fall—and study French and German. Then there's Daniel, fifteen, and very mathematical and scientific. He's a very good footballer. And there's Sarah, who's eleven, and is the artistic one of the trio, already producing drawings and paintings that excite me. The extraordinary thing about children is that one wonders until one has had them whether one is capable, whether one's doing it right.

JOHNSTON: Then you're in for the long haul.

LONGLEY: Then you're in for the long haul. In a sense, it's a life sentence, of course, but I would say that the profoundest thing that's happened to me in my life is being a father.

JOHNSTON: That does get into your poetry.

LONGLEY: It does, but perhaps not enough. It's hard to write about children without being trite. A poet is no different from anyone else in being potentially very boring on the topic of his or her children.

JOHNSTON: Those are beautiful names: Rebecca, Daniel, and Sarah. They're all Old Testament names.

LONGLEY: Edna and I would have liked to have selected Irish names for the children, but they sounded so phony against my very Anglo-Saxon surname; so since my grandmother, my mother's mother, was Jewish, we opted for the Old Testament names, which are very hard to beat.

JOHNSTON: I thought "long lea" was Irish.

LONGLEY: No, it's an Anglo-Saxon, locative, surname, meaning the "long field" or the "long clearing." And there's a lot of them around Sussex. I remember going to visit Derek Mahon and his family when they were in Sussex and going down to the local pub for a few drinks, and the landlord was called Jack Longley. That was the first Longley in my life that I've ever met who wasn't a relative. Then I went for a stroll around the village and found a number of shopowners were called Longley. I had this very confusing feeling—and I liked the landscape; it made some kind of sense to me although I was new to it—I had this strange feeling that this might be home. And I remember saying to myself: No, this isn't home; Sussex isn't home; Belfast is home. We could end on that, couldn't we?

John Banville
Interviewed by Rüdiger Imhof

Causation . . . is no more and no less than what the
physicists would call a thought experiment; it is, like
mathematics and theology, a thing invented by men in order
to explain and, therefore, make habitable a chaotic, hostile,
and impassive world. I foresee a time, not at all far off, when
physics will produce a new theory of reality which will be as
revolutionary as the theory of relativity. In the new schema
chance will play a large, perhaps a central, part.

—John Banville

JOHN BANVILLE IS ONE of *the* most outstanding Irish novelists to have
emerged since 1960. To date, he has published seven books. The first,
Long Lankin (London: Secker and Warburg, 1970), consisted of nine stories, which show the influence of Joyce's *Dubliners*, and a novella that
would seem to be indebted to Dostoevsky's *The Possessed*. The second
book, *Nightspawn* (London: Secker and Warburg; New York: W. W. Norton, 1971), is a parodic novel with the metafictional intention of laying
bare the conventions of fiction writing. With *Birchwood* (London: Secker
and Warburg; New York: W. W. Norton, 1973), frequently mistaken for a
straight Big House novel, Banville turned to the theme of how the artistic
imagination tries to come to terms with reality—a theme that has preoccupied him ever since. Next followed a series of four fictions devoted to
prime representatives of what a character in one of them called "those

From *ILS* 6 (spring 1987).

high cold heroes who renounced the world and human happiness to pursue the big game of the intellect": *Doctor Copernicus* (New York: W. W. Norton, 1976), *Kepler* (London: Secker and Warburg, 1981), *The Newton Letter* (London: Secker and Warburg, 1982), and most recently, *Mefisto* (London: Secker and Warburg, 1986). Perhaps the most salient thematic feature of the tetralogy is concerned with how the scientific imagination strives to account for the world by weaving supreme fictions about it. As Banville sees it, the scientific imagination operates along lines comparable to those of the artistic imagination.

All of his books show him to be a highly conscientious artist who takes great pains in matching the form of his books to the subject matter. His work is highly significant for contemporary Irish fiction, not least because it represents one of the very rare cases where an attempt is made to open up a somewhat parochial area of literary expression and to link the Irish novel to the European tradition.[1]

The interview was conducted in Wuppertal, Germany, in November 1986. [Rüdiger Imhof]

RÜDIGER IMHOF: You are said to be most reluctant to give interviews. Why is that so?

JOHN BANVILLE: First, because I feel there is always too much gossip about "bookchat." Second, because I no longer believe that I know what I'm talking about. I used to be a great one for explaining my own work; now I think I don't understand it myself. Age brings not wisdom, but confusion. And third, because I think my business is my own.

IMHOF: With the appearance of *Mefisto*, your tetralogy is complete. Looking back on the venture, are you satisfied?

BANVILLE: I can't believe that any one is ever satisfied with his past work; if he were, he wouldn't need to try again. I confess to some deep reservations about the tetralogy. The first two books, *Doctor Copernicus* and *Kepler*, misled a lot of people into thinking that I had decided to become a "historical novelist" and others that I engaged in an effort to trace the history of scientific ideas from the sixteenth century to the present. These readers can be forgiven their misapprehension, for, after all, *Copernicus* and *Kepler* were indeed set in the past, but then what novel is not? And there was in both a certain "scientific" content although I doubt that a scientist would agree. However, these astronomers were merely a means for me to speak of certain ideas and to speak of them *in certain ways*. They also, of course, supplied ready-made plots, which was handy.

IMHOF: Quite a few of your books are based on, or at least refer to, literary works by other writers. The *Newton Letter* is a case in point, and so is *Mefisto*, with its numerous references to Goethe's *Faust*, Dante's *Inferno*, and others. What entices you to adopt this strategy?

BANVILLE: We're part of a tradition, a *European* tradition: Why not acknowledge it? And then, books are to a large extent made out of other books: Why not acknowledge that, too? Also, I find that the incorporation of references to other works, and even quotations from those works, gives the text a peculiar and interesting resonance, which is registered even when the reader does not realize that something is being quoted.

IMHOF: Most of the reviews of *Mefisto* published so far would seem to make apparent that their authors were helplessly at sea. One question that should be asked in connection with your most recent book—although it is one that, curiously enough, not many reviewers have cared to tackle—is how it fits into the series. Could you throw some light on the matter?

BANVILLE: This is a large and difficult question. *Mefisto*, in ways which even I find odd and obscure, seems to me not to *answer* the questions raised by the previous three books but to reformulate them, which, in art, is as near as one ever comes to an answer. I can't really elaborate on this; it's for others to explain.

IMHOF: Gabriel Swan, the main character in *Mefisto*, equals Copernicus, Kepler, and the fictional writer of the Newton letter in that he, too, is in search of an all-embracing, unifying system. His system is based on numbers, pure numbers. Would it be appropriate to call *him a Pythagorean?*

BANVILLE: Yes.

IMHOF: The many references to Greek writers in *Mefisto* would seem to aim at a revival of classical ideas, perhaps in a way that is comparable to what Goethe tried to achieve by *Faust II*.

BANVILLE: This hadn't occurred to me, but since you mention it I suppose it is a possible reading of the book . . . "Greece Preserv'd"—yes, I like it.

IMHOF: Would it be acceptable to suggest that by means of offering a Pythagorean character and likening his experiences to Greek mythology and motifs from Goethe's *Faust II*, you have brought your investigation of "those cold heroes,"[2] whose works represent paradigms of how the scientific imagination endeavors to come to terms with the world, full circle? For, after all, it was a member of the Pythagorean brotherhood who contended that the sun is at the center of the universe.

BANVILLE: I have now finished with science and scientists, and with "history," forever and ever, thank the Lord. Gabriel Swan is more of an *artist*, whatever that may mean, than a *scientist*, whatever *that* may mean. A hidden theme of the series is the similarity between the workings of the artistic mind and the scientific mind; indeed, I sometimes feel that one could substitute the word *identity* for *similarity*.

IMHOF: You have also brought full circle another aspect of your work to date. *Mefisto* would, at least as far as part 1 is concerned, seem to go back to *Birchwood*, the book you published before you turned to the tetralogy.

BANVILLE: Yes, *Mefisto* makes many overt and covert allusions to *Birchwood*. I wanted to signal—to myself, mainly—the fact that I was returning to what one might call the realm of pure imagination out of which *Birchwood* was produced. No more history, no more facts!

IMHOF: Can it be said that the two parts of *Mefisto*—part 1 being all naturalistic, as it were, and part 2 all hallucinatory, otherworldly— mimic the two essentially different parts of *Faust*?

BANVILLE: I would not want the *Faust* analogy to be taken too literally. As Joyce said when someone asked him why he had used the Homeric extension in *Ulysses*, it was simply my way of working—by which I take him to have meant that one has to have a scaffolding, a base, so that one can then go on and do things more interesting. It should be noted that Gabriel is *not* Faust, but merely an attendant lord. He is invited to sell his soul, to become a Faust in the next *ewige Wiederkunft*,[3] but, although he spends a *saison d'enfer*,[4] I don't think he damns himself. Mind you, I don't know that he is redeemed, either.

IMHOF: It appears to me that one of the principal strategies governing *Mefisto* is that of reversal. In quite a few cases you seem to have evoked particular literary models in order to effect a reversal. Aunt Philomena and Uncle Ambrose are a case in point. Those two seem to echo, in a contrapuntal fashion, Philemon and Baucis:[5] they are not rewarded but punished.

BANVILLE: One should remember what happens to Philemon and Baucis in *Faustus II*.[6] *Reversal?*—*reflection*, rather, I would have said.

IMHOF: Why the introduction of Mephistophelian machinations into Gabriel Swan's "Greek" world?

BANVILLE: Is Gabriel Swan's a Greek world? Surely, even Greece had its Felixes, its Mephistos. Look at Kleist's[7] version of the classical world. Or Sophocles's, for that matter.

IMHOF: What does Gabriel mean by chance?

BANVILLE: A difficult question. By way of an attempt at an answer let's look briefly at the notion of causation. To speak of an *event* and a *cause* of that event is to pretend that individual things—*monads*, if you like—can be isolated from everything else, can be held aloft in a pure space, as it were, and scrutinized by philosopher-scientists. However, as we know very well if we think about it for a moment, there is no such thing as an event and no such thing as a cause: there is only, as Nietzsche points out, a continuum. Causation, then, is no more and no less than what the physicists would call a thought experiment; it is, like mathematics and theology, a thing invented by men in order to explain and, therefore, make habitable a chaotic, hostile, and impassive world. I foresee a time, not at all far off, when physics will produce a new theory of reality which will be as revolutionary as the theory of relativity. In the new schema chance will play a large, perhaps a central, part. I realize that this merely brings us back to the beginning: what is chance? A difficult question.

IMHOF: The book refers to a die *ewige Wiederkunft*, which reference may also make one immediately think of Nietzsche.[8] Could you also have had in mind Democritus and his atomistic world picture?[9]

BANVILLE: I must have had, mustn't I?

IMHOF: When you were still working on *Mefisto*, you told me that the Gabriel of part 1 did not appear in part 2. Now, in the finished book, there is a Gabriel in part 2. Is he the same Gabriel as the one in part 1? If not, is the fact that his name is also Gabriel and that he, too, meets a man called Felix yet another instance of chance?

BANVILLE: I had always thought of the Gabriel of part 1 being somehow supplanted by his dead twin in part 2. Certainly, something mysterious happened in the space between the two parts. At the beginning of part 2, in the "birth scene" in the hospital, Gabriel II remarks that "something had sheared away, when I pulled through"; perhaps it was Gabriel I who died in part 2? I don't know.

IMHOF: Could it be possible that there is some influence of Thomas Mann[10]—-I am thinking of *Doktor Faustus*—on *Mefisto*?

BANVILLE: Of course; *Doktor Faustus* is a presence behind all four books in the series. The title *Doctor Copernicus* is an open acknowledgment of that debt.

IMHOF: What significance should be assigned to Professor Kosok and his computer?

BANVILLE: He's a version of poor old Faust, isn't he?—working away to prove that nothing can be proved. Surely, the world of computers is teeming with Fausts.

IMHOF: Are you aware that a real Professor Kosok[11] does exist, who is an eminent scholar of Irish literature?

BANVILLE: Yes, and I hope he does not mind my using his splendid palindromic name.[12]

IMHOF: Is it correct that the two parts of *Mefisto* are symmetrical as well as mirror-symmetrical? The first sentences in the book find their counterpart in the last sentences.

BANVILLE: You tell me.

IMHOF: Does Heisenberg's "uncertainty principle"[13] have any bearings on *Mefisto*?

BANVILLE: Yes. I have always been fascinated by that principle, which is very beautiful, very simple, very elegant, and very anarchic—just like *Mefisto*, eh?

IMHOF: Why the drug-taking as well as the sex in the chapel?

BANVILLE: Well, everyone says that the world of the drug addict is a kind of hell, and sex in the chapel is certainly a blasphemous notion—not in classical Greece, though. And part 2 of *Mefisto* is set in some sort of infernal region.

IMHOF: You are quoted in the *Sunday Tribune* as saying that *Mefisto* marks your farewell to science. What will you turn to next?

BANVILLE: I have started a new book, a murder story.[14]

Benedict Kiely

Interviewed by Jennifer Clarke

I don't believe in a god or in an Irish republic or any of those
things, but I do believe in my neighborhood. I say that if you
don't believe in your neighborhood and that your neighbor's
life is sacred, there is no point in shouting about believing in
God or in anybody else's God—which seems to me to be
perfectly reasonable.

—Benedict Kiely

BENEDICT KIELY, journalist, broadcaster, critic, scholar, novelist, and short-
story writer is one of Ireland's leading literary figures although he is not
as well known in the United States as he deserves to be. He has published eighteen books, both fiction and nonfiction. His nonfiction books
include *Poor Scholar* (London: Sheed and Ward, 1947), a study of William
Carleton, and *Modern Irish Fiction: A Critique* (Dublin: Golden Eagle, 1950).
However, it is as a short-story writer that he has drawn the highest critical acclaim.

Benedict Kiely was born in Dromore, near Omagh in County Tyrone, on
15 August 1919. He grew up in Omagh where he was educated at the
Christian Brothers school. In 1937, after a brief stint in the British post
office, Kiely entered the Jesuit novitiate in County Laois, but this religious life was terminated by spinal tuberculosis and a long convalescence
in a hospital that supplied the setting for his 1968 novel *Dogs Enjoy the*

From *ILS* 6 (spring 1987).

Morning (London: Gollancz). In good health again, Kiely entered the National University in Dublin, graduating with a B.A. in 1943. During his years at the university he worked part-time as a journalist for the *Standard*, and he continued his journalistic career until 1964 at the *Irish Independent* and the *Irish Press*. At the same time, he published a number of short stories and his first seven novels, beginning with *Land Without Stars* (London: Christopher Johnson, 1947); an updated version of a folktale, *The Cards of the Gambler* (London: Methuen, 1953); and one of his finest novels *The Captain with the Whiskers* (Swords, Ireland: Poolbeg Press; London: Methuen, 1960), a fascinating study of evil. The years 1964–68 were spent in the United States as a writer-in-residence and creative writing instructor at colleges in Virginia, Oregon, and Georgia.

Since his return to Dublin in 1968, Kiely has been a full-time writer, but he has also lectured at University College, Dublin, and worked and written for the press, radio, and television.

With *Proxopera* (London: Gollancz, 1977), a novella included in his collection of stories *The State of Ireland* (Boston: D. R. Godine, 1980; Harmondsworth, Eng.: Penguin, 1982), Kiely returned to a Six-Counties setting. The theme of *Proxopera*, already anticipated in "Bluebell Meadow," is that of the Troubles. Outspoken in its attack on terrorism in the North, *Proxopera* marked a radical change in Kiely's fiction, a change that he sustained in the ironically titled *Nothing Happens in Carmincross* (London: Gollancz, 1985).

On 11 July 1986 Kiely was granted the degree of Doctor of Literature *honoris causa* by Queen's University, Belfast. The speaker, introducing Kiely, said of *Proxopera* and *Nothing Happens in Carmincross*. "In both works he treats fictionally but seriously the perennial problem which he sought to describe in his very first work . . . *Counties of Contention* ([Cork: Mercier Press], 1945). In the forward to that essay he says of it: 'It does not offer any foolproof remedy for its present ills. The finding of that remedy and its proper application will be the task of the new generation in Ireland.' Forty years on, he might perhaps be inclined to endorse that early statement." From the following interview it might be inferred that Kiely wishes the present generation would take up "the task."[1]

This interview took place on 7 July 1986 at Kiely's home in Dublin. [Jennifer Clarke]

JENNIFER CLARKE: You were born and brought up in Omagh. How long did you live there?

BENEDICT KIELY: No, I was born a little outside Omagh, but I grew up in Omagh town, and I spent my boyhood and youth there.

CLARKE: The town comes up over and over again in your work.

KIELY: It literally was a good town.

CLARKE: From your books it seems that Catholics and Protestants in Omagh in those days not only tolerated one another but were even friendly with one another.

KIELY: That was quite certain.

CLARKE: But at the same time, how did Catholics feel? Were they discriminated against?

KIELY: Not specifically in Omagh town. The first instance of discrimination there came from the Stormont government[2] in Belfast—which you could only call a *government* out of courtesy—when they decided to gerrymander the local wards. Two of the most reputable men in Omagh town, Protestants, a Mr. MacMillan and a Mr. Bloomfield (they were big drapers), publicly protested against the gerrymandering. That's the sort of town it was; there was never any bigotry. Gradually, however, the Stormont government influence began to be felt.

Before I decided to be a Jesuit, I worked for seven months in the British post office as a sorting clerk and telegraphist. The rank of sorting clerk and telegraphist is now extinct; so I'm a dodo! When I went into the post office around 1936, the arrangement was one Catholic, one Protestant, and a Protestant schoolteacher's son went in with me. But when I left, they put a Protestant in my place. The Stormont influence was beginning to make itself felt in the British post office, which, until then, had been above that sort of thing. This kind of interference was a continual process. The Stormont government interfered with everything east of the River Bann. They destroyed the railway to Derry; they destroyed Derry city; they wouldn't spend a ha'penny on it.

CLARKE: They?

KIELY: They—the Orange caucus, the Orangemen. "What we have, we hold," they said. And I prefer to call things by their own names— there's no point in saying the *Loyalists*. I mean, what the hell are they *loyal* to when they attack the Royal Ulster Constabulary in the streets?

CLARKE: So, growing up there in the twenties and thirties, there wasn't tension between Catholic and Protestant?

KIELY: Not only not between Catholic and Protestant—but remember, Omagh was a garrison town. We had the Royal Irish and the Royal Inniskillins there, and most of my boyhood was spent quite happily hanging around the military barracks. It wasn't just because my father had been in the British army in his time; they were lovely people, and the barracks was a great place. The huge soldiers' home was a playground, and no one bothered.

CLARKE: How were the British regarded?

KIELY: Well, the actual fact about the Royal Irish and the Royal Inniskillins was that they were nearly all Irish.

CLARKE: Yes, but they were put there by the British government, presumably.

KIELY: Ah, yes, there was the odd fanatic over by Dungannon or some remote place like that who might get really worked up about the Republic, and there were a few old-style Irish republicans in Omagh, including my dear and good brother, but they didn't foam at the mouth about it.

CLARKE: What did they want?

KIELY: What they wanted—what my brother wanted—was an Ireland peaceably united where people would speak to each other.

CLARKE: And the British out?

KIELY: It didn't necessarily imply the immediate *out* of the British. It was an assumption that the Home Rule business that had been aborted in 1911 or 1912 by the English high Tories would be concluded.

CLARKE: When did you first know you wanted to be a writer?

KIELY: Oh, I was always scribbling since I was the age of God-knows-what. I even composed a little album of my own in which, when I was short of a rhyme, I mostly used a dirty word. My brother, I regret to say, still preserves a copy. But I was sort of scribbling all the time.

CLARKE: When did it become possible for you to become a writer?

KIELY: My first actual published piece was an obituary for a schoolfellow, one Thomas Tummon. The funeral ceremony, I remember, was held in a country church in Fermanagh, and the poor little priest said a few words over the coffin. When the piece appeared in the *Ulster Herald* afterward, there were all sorts of flowery phrases that he purportedly used. I often wonder if the poor man ever read it.

CLARKE: And after the post office?

KIELY: After the post office, I was in the Jesuit novitiate for a bit, and then I had eighteen months in hospital with an injury to my spine, which had developed tuberculosis. From my hospital bed, I wrote a letter to a weekly paper called the *Standard*, edited by Peadar O'Currie, about something in the North of Ireland. A copy of that letter must be fun to read, but it was printed anyway.

After then, after I came out of hospital, I met this friar, a Father Senan, who said to me, "If you're going home to Tyrone, write a long article for me about Tyrone." So I cycled across Tyrone, and I wrote this article for Senan, and that was the first long thing I ever had printed.

CLARKE: After that spell in the hospital, there was no returning to the Jesuits?

KIELY: No, although I learned about method and order from the Jesuits. The Jesuits live a very orderly life. To the fact that I was a Jesuit novice and that my father was in the British army I account the fact that I'm the best dishwasher in Ireland. To see me washing dishes is an instructor's sight. *Ordo est dux ad deum et omnia a deo ordinata sint*—that's St. Augustine.[3]

Then I came up to college here in Dublin, and in my first term I read a paper on G. K. Chesterton. The chairman of the meeting was the same Peadar O'Currie—the man, incidentally, who wrote about and befriended Patrick Kavanagh—and he came up to me afterward and said, "What are you going to do?" "Take a degree and teach, I suppose," said I. And Peader asked, "Do you want a job?"—and this was 1940! "A job," I said, "like j.o.b. = *job?*" "Yes," he said, "come down to me tomorrow and you'll have one."

So I became a newspaperman, and I worked part-time all the way through college. And I have a feeling I was richer then than I've ever been since. I had about £5.10s. from Peader and £2 a week from Senan whether I did anything or not. With £7.10s. a week in 1940, about $30 then, I was rich!

I worked for Peadar until I was offered a job as leader writer on the *Irish Independent.* That was a complete sinecure. I didn't go in until seven in the evening, and I left about eleven, and my day was free. I also did theater for them, and I was there for four or five years. I left because there was some trouble with censorship. My novel *In the Harbour Green*[4] had been banned, and the *Independent* was, in those days, a terribly conservative paper. However, at that time, I was very friendly with both the great R. M. Smyllie,[5] the man who altered the course of the *Irish Times,* and with M. J. MacManus,[6] who was literary editor of the *Irish Press.* Both men offered me jobs, but as M. J. actually had more money to offer me, R. M. said I should go where the money was. So I went to the *Irish Press* as M. J. MacManus's assistant. I was there about a year when M. J. regrettably dropped dead, so I took over from him, and I was there until 1964, when I went to the States, to Hollins College in Virginia.

CLARKE: And all this time you were writing?

KIELY: I wrote, of course, yes. Literary editing, you know, didn't exactly kill you. At the same time, with my friend Sean White I did a daily column. It was a sort of rural column under the name of Patrick Lagan. That was marvelous—we'd vanish down the country for three or four days at a time. It was a good way of getting around Ireland.

CLARKE: How do you write? Do you have a specified time set aside for it?

KIELY: I sort of work all the time. I'm an early riser, and I work at this desk here if I'm writing fiction, and I have a chest of drawers on the side at which I'm working on my memoirs and other matters. That means I can stand up. It's quite simple, you know; you don't have to sit down the whole time. And my voluminous international correspondence is conducted from the kitchen table! I keep moving about according to a time pattern so that I'm not too long stuck in the same place.

What I do at this desk is read a bit of something decent in the morning. At the moment, I am rereading Gibbon[7] from start to finish because I never read Gibbon that way. It sort of clears out your mind from the general pollution of the world if you read something decent in the morning. Then I work for as long as I can sit here and about a similar length of time at the chest of drawers, or more perhaps, for any journalism is done there, and then a few letters at the kitchen table. And then I work backward, and so on.

CLARKE: And you give yourself a break, say, at lunchtime?

KIELY: Oh, I do! I give myself two million breaks. I walk out into the main street of this great town of Donnybrook, and if you really wish to waste time, you can always find someone in Donnybrook to waste time with you. Donnybrook has preserved to this day a curious village atmosphere, and I think the spirit of Donnybrook Fair is still here. So, if you want to get away from work, it's very easy to do.

CLARKE: How does a novel or story start with you? What comes first: a memory or a concept or an idea?

KIELY: It doesn't work according to any pattern all the time.

CLARKE: Say, *Proxopera*, for example.

KIELY: Well now, *Proxopera*. . . . I began to write *Proxopera* in Delaware of all places. The *Irish Times* kindly sent me their paper every day, and I read this story about a man in Kesh in County Fermanagh who had been stopped in the road by gunmen. They put bombs into his car and told him to drive them into Kesh. Well, he drove up the road for about fifty yards, and then he swung around and went straight for the gunmen—complete with bombs. And the gunmen took off in a fashion described by that pleasant Irish phrase—used by Mr. Joyce, slightly altered, in *Ulysses*—"like shit off a shovel," and they didn't stop running till they got to Bundoran in County Donegal.[8] Then the man abandoned his car and ran for his life and let it blow up. This incident brought an element of the Keystone cops into an abominable situation, and I began to laugh at it in Delaware, and I thought, there's the beginning of something. Then I remembered M. J. Curry, who's a part of Mr. Binchey, a very formidable and impressive man who taught me Latin and English literature in high school, and it began to come together from that. The lake is Lough Muck, the lake of the Black Pig, which is quite close to my own hometown. The comic ballad was written by my brother-in-law. The book grew out of these things.

CLARKE: Is it true, as you say in the beginning of *Proxopera*, that the lake will never be the same again?

KIELY: The lake . . . well, I read about that man's murder. I had met this man in a pub in the little village of Trillick, and I was horrified to read about his dead body being found, not in Lough Muck but in a lake in County Fermanagh.

CLARKE: You speak of a connection between the violence and the land itself.

KIELY: The violence must leave a certain pollution behind. But what part of the world is clean now? Except the top of Mount Everest or, perhaps, the Greenland cap. Something violent has happened everywhere. Although you must not allow your memory and imagination to be too much affected, I feel that if you were intimate with the landscape, you must remember that these things happened there.

CLARKE: *Then the fact that they happened affects the land itself?—or people's memories?*

KIELY: People's memories are long, you see, even for the trivialities that go on in the North. I said recently to John Banville,[9] who is a man of short and sharp words, "John, we're not as bad as Lebanon." And he said, "Not yet." Two words and rather shaky. John does not waste words.

CLARKE: What is the most difficult part of a book for you to write?

KIELY: I feel when you are about two-thirds of the way toward the end— something like that. You're getting a bit tired for one thing. You can always see the end—the end is okay—but there are bits in between which are still cloudy when you get two-thirds of the way through.

CLARKE: Do you have the whole story mapped out before you begin, or does it grow almost organically?

KIELY: Well, Brendan Behan used to say that every cripple has his own way of walking. I have a rough summary, and I work from that on rough copy paper. Then I scribble it out as I go.

CLARKE: How many drafts do you write?

KIELY: I make several of those rough drafts until I get it somewhat clear, and then I write out what might be called a clean copy—but not all the way through, just insofar as it goes. It seems to me that if I stop, it gives me time to rethink. And then I rewrite that again, and so on, until I get a final draft. It might take three or four attempts, but I get a final draft eventually.

CLARKE: That you're willing to let someone else look at?

KIELY: I've a friend here who looks at drafts, and if they pass muster that's okay, but I have to go on and finish it according to what I think myself in the end.

CLARKE: How do you know when it's really right?

KIELY: It's intuition, I think. I know it's right.

CLARKE: You've done many kinds of writing—newspaper articles, novels, short stories, etc. Is there a form that you prefer?

KIELY: Not really; perhaps I prefer writing fiction. The short stories, maybe. It depends on what's in your head. You see, the idea creates the length and the form ultimately.

CLARKE: As you probably know, Irish studies are "big business" in America, especially the Joyce and Yeats industries. What is your opinion of all this Irish-centered literary activity in the States?

KIELY: I think it's a very, very good thing because it was the American critics—and I'm talking of men like Richard Ellmann[10]—who really gave James Joyce his proper due and paid proper attention to him. After all, when you think of the attitude of the Bloomsbury people, Virginia Woolf, for example, talking of the educated language of a workingman and things like that, the American scholars, men like Ellmann and Hugh Kenner, deserve all due credit for the great work they've done. However, it's inevitable that when something becomes fashionable there will be, perhaps, too many people writing on the same subject, and I suspect this is going to happen with Flann O'Brien.[11]

CLARKE: Do you ever read criticism of your work?

KIELY: Not much; I don't bother, to tell you God's truth. You know, I wouldn't go from here to the newsagents to read a review of myself.

CLARKE: It doesn't affect your work in any way?

KIELY: No, not in the least, I'm afraid. I must be terribly arrogant or something. However, I am always glad to get the good word. Maurice Brown, the man who used to work for the BBC, said that we all affect to despise reviews but that we all like good ones. I always like a good review. I remember when I was very young, I had a review by Hugh l'Anson Fawcett in the *Manchester Guardian*—I forget for which novel. It wasn't what you'd call a favorable review, but he gave the book considerable space, and he considered me as a serious person. He also knew what I was trying to do. I'll never forget reading that; It really pleased me. It was better than if he'd just buttered me up.

CLARKE: Would it in any way affect your writing?

KIELY: No. There's no one who can teach you how to write, ultimately.

CLARKE: No one can teach you how to write? I ask that because in America creative writing is taught.

KIELY: Ah well, that's gone a bit crazy, that. You can help people, though. A friend of mine went to some of Frank O'Connor's classes, and he said that O'Connor could tell you things *not* to do, and that was a great help. That saves a lot of time. But nobody can really teach you. You pick it up for yourself. Way back in the early forties, I remember reading Graham Greene and getting fascinated by the sheer technique in a good book like *England Made Me*. That was a revelation to me.

CLARKE: So Graham Greene was an influence.

KIELY: Oh, the narrative technique of that man is astounding.

CLARKE: Is there anyone else who had an influence on you?

KIELY: Ah well, you read Joyce; that was a national duty, but great. And William Saroyan;[12] he sort of lifted you up in jubilation. And William Faulkner, of course.

CLARKE: In the introduction to *The State of Ireland* Tom Flanagan draws a parallel between Faulkner's Yoknapotawpha County and your Omagh.

KIELY: Well, that was no deliberate imitation. But I did spend about two-and-one-half days once talking and drinking with Allen Tate[13] in Virginia, and I said something about my cousin Joe Gormley of Claramore. And Allen Tate said that that was southern talk: you never mention a man's name without mentioning his locality. So, some of the Faulkner thing came naturally. My cousin was Joe Gormley of Claramore, and nobody ever called him just Joe Gormley. It is as simple as that. And that goes on all over Ireland—identifying the man with his locality. It's a kind of fingerprinting.

CLARKE: Do you ever consider who your readers are when you are writing?

KIELY: No, I wouldn't honestly say so. If I think about a reader at all, I begin to think about him from where I am sitting, as a listener to me or something like that. I just tell the story and hope that someone out there is listening.

CLARKE: In much of your work you deal with the connection between Ireland and America—the Irish-American returning to Ireland, for example.

KIELY: That is because all my aunts and uncles lived most of their lives in America. My godmother, my Aunt Rose, lived most of her life in Philadelphia. My Aunt Bridget was in New York. It comes from nothing more complicated than that.

CLARKE: Many critics talk of your habit of incorporating into your prose lines from and allusions to other writers—Shelley, Yeats, and Eliot, for example. Would you care to comment?

KIELY: I wouldn't say that it was exactly deliberate. I don't wish to confuse the reader by over-reference, but the mind does go on like that, always connecting. And I always say that everything in Ireland reminds me of something else. Both Joyce and Eliot suffered from the same disease, you know. Most minds do work like that. The only problem in any sort of prose narrative is to restrain it so that it makes sense.

CLARKE: You don't lose me with Eliot, Joyce, or Yeats, but you certainly lose me with the music hall songs.

KIELY: Ah well. Some of those are post-Eliot and post-Joyce. Remember what Joyce said to Yeats? You're too old for me to help you.

CLARKE: With *Proxopera* and *Nothing Happens in Carmincross,* and even earlier in a short story like "Bluebell Meadow," your work changes and you begin to write about the Troubles in Northern Ireland.

KIELY: Well, that's obvious enough although some of "Bluebell Meadow" came from a hint in a letter from a lady in South Bend, Indiana—the lady in "Down Then by Derry." But the Troubles . . . things began to get nasty at the end of the sixties. When I came back from the States in 1968, matters had not gone too badly, mainly because the civil rights movement was beginning then. But after that, the nastiness began and the idiots began to plant the bombs. And it became obvious to me that one must have some concern for the place and for the lives of the people there—*they* are important. So "Bluebell Meadow" came out of that period, and then *Proxopera.*

CLARKE: Other than telling the story, what are you trying to do with works like *Proxopera* and *Nothing Happens in Carmincross?*

KIELY: There is no deliberate message whatsoever. Stephen Crane said that the only thing a writer should do—and I presume he meant with fiction—was to mirror his own society, and if you mirror your own society, that should convey a message. But I'm not *telling* anyone to do anything. I'm only trying to write it down as it was and as it is, and readers can come to their own conclusions from that.

I suppose I'm some sort of an agnostic, or to put it less grandly, an ignoramus. I don't believe in a god or in an Irish republic or any of those things, but I do believe in my neighborhood. I say that if you don't believe in your neighborhood and that your neighbor's life is sacred, there is no point in shouting about believing in God or in anybody else's god—which seems to me to be perfectly reasonable. And after all, I believe if you search in the New Testament, you'll find something like that.

CLARKE: In both *Proxopera* and *Nothing Happens in Carmincross* you juxtapose past and present, and the past always comes out more favorably.

KIELY: That's pretty obvious, you know, if you are living in a society in which people are murdering one another.

CLARKE: In both of the above works and in many of the short stories there is this tremendous sense of nostalgia for a world that is lost, a world that seemed to be very superior to the world we have now. Is this really the case?

KIELY: I think it is quite a simple thing. I am a man remembering his boyhood and youth with a certain amount of pleasure and nostalgia— that's all. It's inevitable. Mr. Yeats has it, you know, when he talks about climbing Ben Bulben's back with rod and line when he had the livelong summer day to spend.

I think, however, that in many ways the world in which I am now living is perhaps a better world than the world I grew up in. I grew up in a town that had no evidence of poverty, but there were other towns, Derry city at that time, that had every evidence of poverty. I had a very happy boyhood, and I look back to a town that was doing rather well; the nostalgia may be accounted for by that. But I am not saying that there are things in this world that I can't and won't grapple with. I mean, how many Irish writers have said that there are murderers in our midst? I have done so, and I think it necessary to do so. Although I have had letters from some very strange people telling me to keep my voice down, I say that if I am writing at all, and if there is murder going on in the country in which I live, I am going to say it's going on.

CLARKE: The narrator in *Nothing Happens in Carmincross* seems to be a composite character.

KIELY: Well, he had to be, you see. At the time the incident happened in Killeter (which is "Carmincross"), I was writing a coffee-table history, and I gave up on it. I explained to the publishers that this was no time for coffee-table books. What I wanted to write about was how the situation in Northern Ireland had reached this point; how, in a village like "Carmincross," or Killeter, where nothing had ever happened to warrant such an incident, a girl could be blown up posting her wedding invitations.

CLARKE: So why does the narrator have to be a composite character?

KIELY: He had to be half-Irish, half-American, and he had to have his head rattling with a sort of learning because I wanted him to do a historic tour before I got him to Carmincross. It was partly a writing of Irish history of a sort.

How had it come to pass that in a village where nothing had happened that a girl could be killed in such a way? This was what I intended to do, and yet I had to keep it off the ground a bit because if I had begun by telling people that this was a book about a girl being blown up, they wouldn't have gone any further with it. So I had to let it run. And at one stage, I had to stop and go back; I literally had to write it backward.

CLARKE: How long did it take you to write *Nothing Happens in Carmincross*?

KIELY: Ah, I was a long time with it; it was simmering in my mind for a long time. It was a painful topic and very hard to write. I'd a darn sight have written another *In a Harbour Green* than that.

CLARKE: But you had to write it.

KIELY: *Somebody* had to. Whether I would willingly do it again, I don't know, but I had to put it down. I mean, it is what Stephen Crane says: It is my society, and I have to mirror it. Otherwise, I'd be false to whatever vocation, God help us, I might have.

CLARKE: Is it possible to be optimistic about the future in Ireland?

KIELY: Well, I would royally hope so. I mean we must never abandon hope, and I just wish that the bombers would restrain their hands and let things in peace so that reason might come finally. All we want is peace, and that London, Dublin, Belfast, and whoever might be responsible for anything up there in the North will sit down and talk about some condition of peace. Britain and Ireland are two small islands in a very shrinking world, and they have to live together in peace. There is no good and no reason that can come out of indiscriminate murder and slaughter.

CLARKE: What are you writing at the moment? I know you are writing your autobiography.

KIELY: No, my memoirs.[14] I'm not in it. It's about other people. I knew a lot of nice people, and I want to write about them, not about me. I have about sixty-five thousand words written; that's more or less the first volume, which brings us to a kind of closing date in history when I was back from hospital and I was watching the fusiliers marching to France in 1940. They were very sour-faced, reluctant men; they'd been everywhere, and they thought their soldiering days were over. But they were in the reserve, and they had to go.

And I've just finished a longish short story for a new collection. It's a comic story told by a man writing to his girlfriend on Peachtree Street in Atlanta, telling her of the funny things that happen in Ireland. It is the only time I have collaborated with a dead man; I am reworking a brief passage from his journal to fit into my own memories of the event and then reconstructing these into a long story. The effort is extraordinary, but some good things come into it. It will be called "A Letter to Peachtree."[15]

CLARKE: To finish, let me ask you this: Of all the Irish writers working today, whom do you admire the most?

KIELY: That's a tricky sort of question. I prefer not to mention names— you're always going to leave somebody out. But there's a lot of good writing being done in this country at the moment. Patrick Kavanagh always said that at any given moment there was in Dublin a standing army of one thousand young poets! Sean O'Faolain is the greatest figure in this country now, far and away the greatest person. He is the man who, after Mr. Yeats himself, is the most civilizing influence this country has ever had.

Paul Muldoon
Interviewed by Kevin Barry

Nobody gives a damn what I do or where I live. I have no
sense of an audience; nobody much reads me, and I think
that's wonderful because it means that I don't have a sense of
having to fulfill anyone's notion, including my own, of what I
might do next—and it's that freedom I want.

—Paul Muldoon

BORN IN 1951 IN COUNTY ARMAGH, Paul Muldoon attended Queen's
University, Belfast. After a career as radio producer for BBC Northern
Ireland, he resigned the year before Kevin Barry interviewed him, to re-
side in Dingle. Since then, Muldoon has moved to the United States.
Currently, he teaches at Princeton University.

Recognizing the dangers inhering in all generalizations, one may see Paul
Muldoon's poetry distinguished by its multitiered, gamesome complexity.
Often relying upon Irish and American myth and history for background, on
the motif of the quest/search for structure, and on punning and other varieties of wordplay for greater reader engagement, he creates poetic inquiries
into the issues confronting contemporary poets in general and Northern Irish
poets in particular: violence and the Troubles; degrees of personal and public
involvement; beginnings/origins, of self, of family, of race, and of nation;
debates between stability and stasis, arbitrariness andflux. He examines lan-

From *ILS* 6 (fall 1987).

guage as public discourse and private communication for the ways in which it both betrays and destroys individuals and nations.

Reinforcing these concerns, Muldoon frequently explores the paradoxes that derive from and impinge upon the understanding of boundaries, frontiers, and limits. The result is a poetry at times reminiscent of Shakespeare and Nabokov in its verbal "slipperiness" and combination of playfulness and seriousness. Ultimately, as boundaries collapse, limits give way, and identities become blurred, Muldoon creates for himself and, perhaps, his readers opportunities for experiencing, albeit momentarily, the freedom that inspires much of his poetic motive.

His principal collections include *New Weather* (London: Faber and Faber 1973), *Mules* (London: Faber and Faber; Winston-Salem, N.C.: Wake Forest University Press, 1977), *Why Brownlee Left* (London: Faber and Faber; Winston-Salem, N.C.: Wake Forest University Press, 1980), *Quoof* (London: Faber and Faber; Winston-Salem, N.C.: Wake Forest University Press, 1983), *Meeting the British* (London: Faber and Faber; Winston-Salem, N.C.: Wake Forest University Press, 1987), *Selected Poems, 1968–1983* (London: Faber and Faber, 1986), *Madoc: A Mystery* (London: Faber and Faber, 1990), and *The Annals of Chile* (New York: Farrar, Straus, Giroux, 1994). In 1986 he edited and published *The Faber Book of Contemporary Irish Poetry* (London: Faber and Faber). [Kevin Barry]

KEVIN BARRY: You have taken up your bags and walked away from a steady job in Belfast at BBC and now—Dingle, Cambridge, New York—all in twelve months. Why has Brownlee left?[1]

PAUL MULDOON: Well, I suppose that the notion of staying or going is one that occupies anybody who lives in Northern Ireland. We're a nation of voyagers. I enjoyed very much living in Belfast, and I had a job which was challenging and rewarding for the most part, but I've been doing it for almost thirteen years, and I couldn't see myself staying until retirement age—if ever I see retirement age. Also, the climate within BBC had changed considerably. When I joined BBC, there were notions of public-service broadcasting, and those notions are still bandied about, but I don't really think that anyone who runs the show believes very much in them. I covered the arts, and a lot of my time, a lot of my energy—far too much of it—was spent fighting management figures within BBC Northern Ireland who professed an interest in the arts but frankly didn't give a damn about them. I decided that I was getting too long in the tooth for that.

Much as I like Belfast—I spent all my life there—I got to the stage where I decided that I didn't really want to reach the age of sixty and say to myself, you know, perhaps there was something else that you should have done. Perhaps you should have given this other thing a whirl. I've no illusions about being a full-time writer. In fact, that's the last thing I want to be since I'm only really interested in the poems, which you can't do full time. I'm not interested in hacking about doing anything else. I'd much sooner sweep the streets.

BARRY: So, for different reasons, you didn't want to go on being an insider in Belfast?

MULDOON: Yes. There were other things, too. I've no connections there any longer. My father died a couple of years ago, and that had been one of the reasons I stayed around for so long. Not that I saw him as often as I should, but he was still in the country, and I'd go down and see him. I'm still attached to the place—it's my home; it's where I'm from—but I don't have the same attachment as I did when my parents, my father specifically, were alive.

BARRY: You want to feel a sense of being in places where you're positively not at home?

MULDOON: I didn't feel an outsider in Dingle. Naturally, I felt an outsider in the same way my family were outsiders in Collegelands in County Armagh where they moved when I was four or five, almost thirty years ago. It was really only when my parents were buried there that we even remotely belonged. To belong in a place like Dingle one would have to have several close relatives buried in the vicinity. In that sense I felt I was an outsider, a blow-in. But I enjoyed it there very much. It's a marvelous spot for a town that size, partly because it is to a large extent a tourist town, though one would have found that difficult to believe during the bad summer. It has a very good bookshop. There are a lot of people, a lot of foreigners, so being an outsider is not strange to the folk of Dingle. Many of the people who reside there are Germans or come from Cork, which is almost the same thing.

BARRY: Edna Longley's new book, *Poetry in the Wars*,[2] presents you in approximately these terms: "Muldoon's writing is anti-tribal. The manner in which he writes is that of an escaped prisoner of war, of a secret agent, of a double agent, of a saboteur."

MULDOON: I didn't know about that. I am the last person in the world equipped to comment on my things. I don't like knowing too much about what I'm doing. That's not to say that I don't try to be circumspect, but I don't want to be able to categorize myself. Those words may have a certain coloring in the Irish context.

BARRY: Which they do have.

MULDOON: Well, they do; they have coloring in any context. I think a writer's job is to be an outsider, to belong to no groups, no tribes, no clubs. So far as any of us can, it's to be a free agent, within the state of oneself, or roaming through the different states of oneself.

BARRY: Is the pressure of that description—with the kind of coloring it has in an Irish situation—as limiting as if one had a fixed political allegiance?

MULDOON: Yes, intellectually it's part of the same thing. I don't go around thinking of myself from day to day as being an outsider. There's no tribe in Ireland for which I would feel comfortable as a spokesman. I wonder who would, who does, who is? I think Seamus Heaney flirted—I think *flirted* is the word—with the idea of it for a while. Seamus is so well-known, is a public figure, that these are concerns that impinge more on him. He did become associated, for example, with the Northern Catholic nationalist position. I was brought up in that society with a similar background as Seamus. But things have changed a bit in the ten or fifteen years between us. Ireland has changed; well, certainly, it *had* changed. But I don't think even Seamus flirts with that now. From what I can work out from his recent poems I think Seamus is now much more interested in the idea of the free agent, arguing very much for the supremacy and separateness of art.

You see, there's a lot of nonsense about this. At moments like these, one would almost be tempted to believe that the writer has some status in Ireland, which we know perfectly well is not the case at all, or that anyone pays attention to what writers say, which they don't. It's at times like these when constructs are placed on writers' positions in a critical or journalistic way. That's all very fine and well, but actually it's somewhat beside the point. Nobody gives a damn what I do or where I live. I have no sense of an audience; nobody much reads me, and I think that's wonderful because it means that I don't have a sense of having to fulfill anyone's notion, including my own, of what I might do next—and it's that freedom I want.

BARRY: You say that the critical and journalistic way of looking at writers in Ireland tends to draw writers back into the idea of writing for a community, writing as a part of a community, that a community is their audience, and this actually doesn't happen from day to day in terms of the business of writing?

MULDOON: Absolutely not. There's a lot of lip service paid to even a figure like Seamus Heaney. A lot of people have read him, but a lot of people who have talked about him still haven't read him simply as the man who wrote the poems about frogs and flax dams properly, which he's moved away from considerably. So a certain amount of lip service is paid to that notion. A country can only entertain one writer at a time, and Seamus is the man, quite rightly. I think Seamus is a brilliant poet, but there *are* a few others. Unfortunately, internationally, that's also the case. The same is true of England. There can only be one poet for England. It's hilarious to watch the scramble at the moment, not so much among the writers as among the critics' fainthearted attempts to, for example, canonize Fenton[3] as the new Auden, which is a lot of nonsense. Fenton's very good at his best, but he's not the new Auden.

BARRY: In recent poetry readings you have read again and again the poem "Anseo." There are two people, particularly, in that poem, in that schoolroom: there's Paul Muldoon and Joseph Mary Plunkett Ward.

MULDOON: I don't think Paul Muldoon's in that poem.

BARRY: Okay. Apart from the Ward figure, who becomes a Provo, what happened to the other people in your class at school?

MULDOON: They represent a cross section of any parish in Ireland, North or South. One of them is involved in computers at some high level, but most of them are on the dole or working in factories, if they're lucky enough to have jobs, and some of them are working on the land.

BARRY: So they were never going to become part of what you're writing about? Do they stop there?—Do they stop in that room? Or are they the people who ten, fifteen years later in their lives populate your poetry?

MULDOON: Very few of them are in the poems because they're not the people I know. I didn't know them terribly well, having left that primary school. I didn't mix with them because I was stuck in most of the time doing my homework or writing poems. But are you suggesting that in some way I might have responsibility to know more about them? I don't think I have a responsibility to anything at all.

BARRY: But in that poem, and maybe in other poems like that, there is a sense of people living in a particular place at a certain time and, in the case of Joseph Mary Plunkett Ward, being a creature of circumstance.

MULDOON: To some extent he wishes the circumstances upon himself.

BARRY: In the later poems about Belfast people appear in a less concretely realized world. They move in and out of the poems in a sort of edgy, surreal, sudden set of movements where they're here and then they're gone.

MULDOON: One of the things about those "area" poems is that while they draw on physically very viable locations and psychologically very viable reactions and responses to situations, they are almost completely fictionalized. The figures who appear are characters of fiction. The landscapes are often little shorthand, thumbnail sketches to establish characters.

As it occurs in the poems, my family is from the earliest invented, invented brothers and sisters and mothers and fathers. The father who appears with, for some people, distressing regularity in these poems is a fictitious character or characters. Sometimes he's illiterate and sometimes he's extremely literate, allusive, and speaks in a way that the real "father" would never have done. I often use that as a little shorthand, just to establish a notion of a world with everything more or less in order in which something slightly extraordinary happens. What am I trying to say? I'm trying to say that the figures who inhabit the earlier poems are no more or less shadowy or real than those of the later poems—except, I suppose, historically I wrote a lot of poems about that place or imagined place.

BARRY: Take one of the invented fathers: "I imagined him sitting outside a hacienda / Somewhere in the Argentine. / He would peer for hours /

Into the vastness of the pampas. / Or he might be pointing out the constellations / Of the Southern hemisphere / To the open-mouthed child at his elbow. / He sleeps with a loaded pistol under his pillow."[4] Now, the open-mouthed child at his elbow—this child isn't a Patrick Kavanagh child; he's much more a Stephen Spielberg child who meets with extraterrestrials that Patrick Kavanagh's child didn't meet.

MULDOON: I was brought up on television and the frost on a puddle or someone playing the melodeon. When people came into our house to play a melodeon, my father and mother got out the tape recorder, the Philips tape recorder, to record them. That's a measure of the society I was brought up in. It was also the society in which mother had bought a piano at vast expense, and each of us in turn, the three kids, were sent off to piano lessons and to elocution lessons and all the rest of it. Each of us failed miserably on the piano. The piano was finally sold, and a tape recorder was bought.

BARRY: There seems to be a simple, direct connection between this wide-eyed child and a much older figure in the poems who wishes to see things clearly.

MULDOON: Yes, that's the aim. We've all got to open our eyes and try to be surprised by the fabric of that brick over there or by the gooselamp. To see them again, that's one of the things that writing is all about.

BARRY: It is, but there's also a feeling that in contrast to a lot of writing at the moment, which is nostalgic, holding things in place, you enjoy dislocating things. You have recently completed a long poem about, among others, W. H. Auden, in which there is a strong sense of constant dislocation.[5]

MULDOON: Yes, although perversely it's about a very specific place and a specific time, Thanksgiving Day, 1940, 7 Middagh Street, and is a series of monologues with Gipsy Rose Lee, Benjamin Britten, Chester Kallman, Carson McCullers, Salvador Dali, and Louis MacNeice, but at a crucial time and a crucial place. That allows for all kinds of invention, inventions that are, I hope, if not in character then not out of character. In a way, it gets back to what I was trying to say earlier: with the strict descriptions of places in some of the earlier poems, those areas of the canvas are carefully colored so that the areas where nothing is said, or where things are implied, where other logics are operating, become more persuasive. One could say roughly that the central preoccupation or thrust of it has to do with the notion of responsibility, the relationship between the artist and the world and his or her time. It sounds pretty crude, but that's what it's about.

BARRY: As an afterward to writing it?

MULDOON: The word *responsibility* was in my mind, but what kept me going was just the cast list and the fact that in reality all these people, with the exception of Dali, were in that room on that date or some time around then.

BARRY: You have recently edited *The Faber Book of Contemporary Irish Poetry*. Derek Mahon said that he hopes you will live to regret it. Have you lived to regret it?

MULDOON: Well, I have a good idea of what Derek was up to in that *Irish Times* review, but I don't know if it's appropriate to say it. Anthologies, as you know, are minefields. The reviews of every anthology, by and large, comprise alternate anthologies that the reviewer would produce. That's good because one of the things that people choose to forget is that anthologies are actually monomania and fascism. People dress them up in all sorts of moral disguises. They write very fancy introductions, but basically they are saying, "These are a few of my favorite things," with some kind of intellectual exploitation. It was almost what I didn't want to do that determined what I did in the end. I did not want to produce another anthology of Irish poetry. There are many of them, including Derek Mahon's.[6]

BARRY: But did you want simply to select the poets who were dearest to you?

MULDOON: Or the poems—there are many poems. I would argue against myself, against the procedures of that book, by saying that I don't believe in poets—*poems* are what matter. There are poems by poets who were not included as good as the best by some of the poets who were included. The poets who were included managed to write a considerable number of very good poems, which is a different matter. If people want to devise arguments against the book, there are real arguments that I'm surprised no one in the fury of composition of reviews at three o'clock in the morning hit on. One, for example, is that most of the work available in the anthology is *readily* available elsewhere. Now, if anyone wants a strong argument against the book, that is the strongest one. But there's been a certain amount of hassle over it. It's a way to lose friends and influence people. Some of the complaints, though, are quite extraordinary: that there's a Northern bias because I'm a Northerner. There was the implication that I hadn't read Austin Clarke and that I think Clarke's a bore. Derek had a very snide remark in his *Irish Times* review about Irish-language poets—that I ought to know what these people are writing in Irish—as if he did and I didn't.

BARRY: In "Quoof," you write of a "shy beast . . . that has yet to enter the language." Does your poetry aim to realize gentleness more than intelligence or scepticism?

MULDOON: Possibly. I would not be able to divine this, and I wouldn't want to. Perhaps one of the things is the tone: there's a range of tones. There is that jokey thing, perhaps too much. But there is that sweet, inveigling voice, and the speaker quite often says, "Come on in. Please come in, and sit down and make yourself at home." Usually, what happens then is that the next thing you know, you get a punch in the nose. In fact, you know there's been some shift, some change, some dislocation. The voice is a soft, soapy sort of voice quite often—in that sense, not particularly attractive. It seems to me that one of the things that one's trying to do is to discover something, is to *be* disturbed. It's not about assurance.

BARRY: It seems that the emphasis is on what happens at a level of privacy or intimacy between two or three people, but never at a level of community nor of the louder voice speaking in a public forum.

MULDOON: That's right. I hope that there are many things happening. I don't set out to do different things for the sake of doing different things. I want to be able to approach anything and to be able to approach it in the tone of voice or the attitude that will best reflect it or the language that floats around it. The tone is not buttonholing the public in a rhetorical way but to buttonhole them perhaps in another way. You see, I don't have anything to say to mankind. I have nothing to say to a mass audience. I'm suspicious of people who do.

Nuala Ní Dhomhnaill

Interviewed by Lucy McDiarmid
and Michael J. Durkan

Here you have a white aborigine who rejoices in being a
white aborigine, who loves the sense I get of undermining all
of us. The willful, unholy glee should never be
underestimated. And I know—it's in my roots—I'm
something they don't want to be reminded of, that I am well-
fleshed and red-haired and high-cheekboned. In the
establishment in the south of Ireland they hate me because I
remind them of their tinker ancestry. And I play it up no end.

—Nuala Ní Dhomhnaill

reminder

NUALA NÍ DHOMHNAILL SWEPT UP AND DOWN the east coast of the
United States this past winter like a force of nature; to call her a breath
of fresh air would be understatement. She was more like a gale-force
wind, not a destructive wind but a creative one, the true animating spirit.
In the three weeks of her first American tour Ní Dhomhnaill read her
poems in Irish and in English translations at Harvard, Oneonta, Queens,
Villanova, and other universities, delighting her audiences and giving herself bronchitis.

One of Ireland's foremost Irish-language poets, Nuala Ní Dhomhnaill began winning national awards as soon as her first volume appeared. *An
Dealg Droighin* (Cork: Mercier, 1981) shared Duais Sheáin Uí Ríordáin in

From *ILS* 6 (fall 1987).

99

the Oireachtas competition in 1982 and was awarded the Arts Council Prize for Irish poetry as the best collection published in the years 1980–82. Her second volume, *Féar Suaithinseach* (Maigh Nuad: An Sagart, 1984), won both Duais an Ríordánaigh and the special "Gradam an Oireachtais" for work of exceptional merit.

A great part of Ní Dhomhnaill's vitality comes from her contact with other cultures. Born in 1952 in Lancashire of west Kerry parentage, she returned to Ireland at the age of five and grew up in the Dingle Gaeltacht and in Nenagh, County Tipperary. As an undergraduate at University College, Cork, she was an active member of the student drama movement in Irish—acting, writing, translating, and producing plays. After graduation, she moved with her Turkish husband to Holland for a year and then lived for five years in Turkey where two of her three children were born. She has lived in Ireland since 1980.

Ní Dhomhnaill, who also writes children's plays, is well-known to Irish television audiences through the program "Im Aonar Seal" and to the audience of Radio na Gaeltachta. Her poems have appeared in several anthologies and in translations by Michael Harnett. She is currently working on two new collections of poems, *An Mháthair Dhorcha* (*The dark mother*) and *An Leannán Sí* (*The demon lover*).[1]

Toward the end of her recent tour, after a reading at Villanova, Nuala Ní Dhomhnaill joined Lucy McDiarmid and Michael Durkan for dinner in Philadelphia and talked with them into the wee hours of a March morning.[Lucy McDiarmid]

LUCY McDIARMID & MICHAEL DURKAN: Why do you write in Irish?

NUALA NÍ DHOMHNAILL: Because I'm a physical and psychological throwback. I'm the dead spit of my great-grandmother to look at. I feel my creativity is like this island inside of me, in the subconscious, that emerges. It's like the demon lover in my parthenogenesis poem:[2] it's a merman, an energy from underneath the subconscious, and obviously I need to get that in the native language. The creative impulse is all unconscious, and it's in Irish. I have no interest whatsoever in ever writing in English though at some stage I would like to develop enough of a discursive voice to do some kind of popularization, to show people what they're missing by not having Irish.

McDIARMID & DURKAN: A book of your own poems?

NÍ DHOMHNAILL: No, the whole length and breadth of the language and everything that's available so you could know that this is all there. I could develop that much of a voice in English, but I would never be a creative person in English.

McDIARMID & DURKAN: Was the first poem you ever wrote in Irish?

NÍ DHOMHNAILL: No, my first poems were in English. I was in school at the time. They were okay, but there was something wrong. And suddenly one day in the study, when I was sixteen, it dawned on me that I was writing Irish poems in English—that's what was wrong with them! All the rhythms were Irish metrical rhythms, and I was doing them in English. I thought to myself: this is ridiculous; why don't you leave them in the language they belong in in the first place? I had been working on this kind of rhythm in my head, and I just switched over and wrote this poem. It is the first one in my first collection. It is juvenilia, really, but I left it in just for the sake of this, that it was the first Irish poem I ever wrote. It was much better than some poems I'd been writing in English. I sent it to the *Irish Times*, and it won a prize and got published. I was all of seventeen, and it was "heavy stuff."

McDIARMID & DURKAN: What was that first poem about?

NÍ DHOMHNAILL: I was down in the garden in school and there was an old nuns' graveyard and there were primroses and it was the juxtaposition of the primroses and November.

McDIARMID & DURKAN: What poetry in Irish had you read at that point?

NÍ DHOMHNAILL: I had a very good Irish teacher and there was a well-stocked library and it was an A school where we did everything through Irish. I actually was one of the few pupils in my time who learned poetry that wasn't on the course. I was very interested, and I learned all the Aodhagán Ó Rathaille and all the Eoghan Rua Ó Súilleabháin.[3] They weren't on the course, but I did that out of interest, and my teacher encouraged me.

McDIARMID & DURKAN: How did your Irish begin? You were born in England; did you have contact with the Irish language there?

Ní DHOMHNAILL: My parents spoke Irish between themselves. I distinctly remember being in a cot at the bottom of the double bed and not being able to see over the bottom of the bed but hearing my parents say the rosary in Irish. But they didn't speak Irish to me because they didn't know about the psychology of language acquisition. When I was five, my father decided we might come back to Ireland, and what were they going to do with this child who spoke no Irish? So they dumped me unceremoniously on my aunts. I had a Lancashire accent in English, and they had a Kerry accent in English, and we just couldn't understand each other. So I started learning Irish. Mind you, I distinctly remember a period of protest when I knew certain words and I wouldn't use them.

McDIARMID & DURKAN: You knew them in Irish?

Ní DHOMHNAILL: Yes, and then one day at the table I was thirsty. I wanted milk, and I knew the word for it. In the end I gave in and said the word for milk, *bainne*. The milk appeared in front of me, and I decided, this thing works. Before that, in England, I only knew my name in Irish, and then if anyone asked me, *"An bfhuil Gaeilge agat,"*[4] I would say, *"Tá am baist"* ("on my baptism"), and that would shut them up. It's a very Kerry swearword and intimidated outsiders.

McDIARMID & DURKAN: Where did you live in Kerry?

Ní DHOMHNAILL: I lived in my aunt's house in a small village called Cahiratrant, in the parish of Ventry.[5] There was no running water; there was no electricity; there was no radio even. I remember distinctly we were down in the *geata beag*,[6] where we used to play, racing snails one day. That's not as slow a process as you might think.

McDIARMID & DURKAN: You each had your snail, and you lined them up?

Ní DHOMHNAILL: Yes, we each had one and we lined them up and we raced them. We were racing snails, and I remember trying to tell the others what a television was, that there was this box, you see, and there were people in it and men on white horses, *fir ar chapail bhána.* They didn't believe a word I said. Ah no, they said, you couldn't have horses in a box. So we went back to our snails.

McDIARMID & DURKAN: What Irish did you get from your parents?

Ní DHOMHNAILL: Once we moved to Ireland, it was all Irish. Even up in north Tipperary, my father would come in from work and hear us speaking English among ourselves and immediately go, *"Tá an iomarca Béarla ar siul sa tigh seo"* ("There is too much English going on in this house"). And we would switch over to Irish. My father used to sing us *sean-nós* songs.[7]

I remember when I was eleven or so being on a school bus going out to a picnic to Spanish Point. Everyone on the bus did a party piece, and when it came to me the only things I knew how to sing were "Bean Dubh an Ghleanna" and "Róisín Dubh." I was embarrassed by this sort of stuff, but when it came down to brass tacks and singing in public, this was the level that was most vivid.

McDIARMID & DURKAN: When I[8] was going to school in Ireland, our music teacher felt we were deprived because we didn't know any songs. We knew a lot of local songs, ballads, and "come-all-ye"s, but those were not considered good, so they'd teach us Thomas Moore.[9] If you were called upon to sing a song, Moore was respectable.

Ní DHOMHNAILL: There was a Republican spirit in our house, and Moore would not be allowed to be sung. Moore was a West Briton.[10]

McDIARMID & DURKAN: Who is your audience?

Ní DHOMHNAILL: When I started off my first poems, I had an audience of five or six who knew what I was at. Then someone told me that Máire Mhac an tSaoi was crazy about them, and I said, "Well, that's two more" because she had probably read them out to Conor Cruise O'Brien.[11] So I had an audience of seven. Then when I was twenty-nine, my first book came out, and within six months it had sold out of one thousand copies. I thought, I must be good! Poetry in Irish! And it was a badly produced book—there was no hype, no launching. I went to Writers' Week in 1981 to find my own book on sale; I didn't even know it was out! I bought a copy of my own book and went into a corner and cried.

McDIARMID & DURKAN: In six months you sold one thousand copies? Who bought them?

NÍ DHOMHNAILL: I don't know—people up and down the country. That is my audience. You're in a pub, say, in Limerick, and someone says, "Are you Nuala Ní Dhomhnaill?" And I'll say, "Yes." And they'll say, "Are you the one that wrote that poem?" They wouldn't mean the book so much as *this* poem. I'll say, "Yes," and they'll say, "That's great." And sometimes they'll know it by heart, which is more than I do. It was surprising, and nobody was more surprised than me. That is my real audience: some totally unknown person coming up to me in a pub and telling me they like this poem. That's what makes it all worthwhile.

McDIARMID & DURKAN: So it's not at all an academic, "literary," university audience?

NÍ DHOMHNAILL: No, this is the real thing. It's grass roots, something I really appreciate. That's what keeps me going.

McDIARMID & DURKAN: Does it bother you that a lot of people who read your work don't know your own words? Do you feel anything can be gotten in the translation?

NÍ DHOMHNAILL: I would like people to realize that what they are reading is only a translation and that there are qualities in Irish which you can only approximate in translation. But at some level I am very pleased that people will realize that there is this poetry and it's not so bad and it is actually going on in Irish and it's real and it's alive and it's now. Maybe their attitude to Irish might change a little because of this.

McDIARMID & DURKAN: Do you mean the attitude of Irish people as well as Americans and English?

NÍ DHOMHNAILL: Yes. I went through a school system in which the teachers used Irish as an instrument of power. I had much better Irish than most of the teachers, but there were other children who were victimized. Frank McGuinness[12] tackled me with that recently. "Oh, go on," he says, "you know as well as I do that Irish is the language of our humiliation and our pain," and he's right.

McDIARMID & DURKAN: Why is it the language of humiliation and pain?—because the teachers use it that way?

NÍ DHOMHNAILL: Yes, I have seen this happen. You see, you might have some smart, witty kids, irrepressible and impossible to keep down, and the teacher couldn't handle them. He'd have a go at them in Irish; they couldn't hit back with it and were silenced.

McDIARMID & DURKAN: It's also seen as the language of the underprivileged. It's the language of the poor areas.

NÍ DHOMHNAILL: It's seen as two things: the language of the small farmers and of fishermen, and of poverty and hunger. But it's also the language of civil servants, school inspectors, the bureaucracy, the *culchees*[13] who come up from the country and go into the civil service and are out to get the rest of the population.

McDIARMID & DURKAN: In the Gaeltacht areas they are thinking of it as the deontas.[14] You get grants for speaking Irish, and so you only speak it when there's an inspector around. Special grants are made for house building and so forth, just to keep the language alive.

NÍ DHOMHNAILL: Oh yes—"How much can you blather for?" Myles Na Gopalleen is wonderful on that in *An Beal Bocht*.[15] You see, there are all these pigs, and they're all grunting away in Irish. And the inspector comes around, and he says, "God, I can't understand a word. They must have great Irish." By the time my generation came along, it was as if a very conservative, middle-class, middle-aged, almost geriatric class of people had taken it upon themselves to monopolize Irish and be associated with it. It should be taken back from them quick. But to do that you have to put your head in the lion's mouth, and sometimes it goes CHOMP! I feel the teeth all around me.

McDIARMID & DURKAN: As I was growing up in Ireland, Irish was a requirement for state exams. Lots of kids had trouble with Irish, and failing that meant failing the whole examination. It created a lot of anxiety and gave them a lot of animosity toward the language.

NÍ DHOMHNAILL: I sometimes teach a creative writing class for the Vocational Education Committee. It's usually a two-hour block. In the first hour I do "The Personal Voice." Generally they like me, and I have them eating out of my hand. In the second hour I try to push them a little, and I bring up the subject of Irish. As soon as I mention the word, oh dear, they are wriggling in their seats and going on about how they hate Irish. But no matter how bad their school Irish, I insist that they write a certain thing in Irish.

McDIARMID & DURKAN: So for them, it would be like writing poetry in Latin?

NÍ DHOMHNAILL: Worse, because there's a whole ethos attached to the language. One wonderful paper came out of this. It was like a set of ten commandments: "*Ná caith tobac, ná fead, ná glaoigh*," etc.: "Don't do this, don't do that, don't smoke, don't play foreign games." He wrote it in very simple Irish, but it had this incantatory quality. He wrote it out of sheer rage that I had managed to touch something.

McDIARMID & DURKAN: There are a lot of themes that have been locked out of Irish poetry for so long.

NÍ DHOMHNAILL: It's explosive. I know I'm mucking around in very brackish water.

McDIARMID & DURKAN: Do you ever feel your audience is limited because of your writing in Irish? What do you feel like, depending on your translators to put you before the English-speaking world?

NÍ DHOMHNAILL: What can I do? At my age, it's good enough to be heard at all. If I had really been interested in succeeding in English, I would have written in English years ago. And I would, by hook or by crook, have kicked my English into some form of poetry by now.

McDIARMID & DURKAN: But would it have been that deliberate, that much of a strain? Words like kick imply some resistance.

NÍ DHOMHNAILL: Yes. But a certain water level in Ireland will roll toward Irish, and if it doesn't—damn it all!—what can I do? But while I live, Irish doesn't die. That's as sure as God. When Seamus Deane[16] in the recent BBC series on English implied that now Irish was something that was behind us—it's in museums, it's mythological—that was tantamount to injecting me with formaldehyde. And I take very unkindly to such treatment. I walked around the house for three days like a madwoman. My husband said, "Oh, she's at it again."

McDIARMID & DURKAN: Do you think being born in England affected your attitude toward Ireland?

NÍ DHOMHNAILL: Yes. I have always been an outsider in the sense that when I was in England we were living in a little Irish community in Lancashire, and when I was in Ireland at the age of five, I was *an cailín Sasanach,* "the little Irish girl." We used to go out torching[17] in the night in winter and shine the torches on the birds' nests while the birds were asleep. It was wonderful to see the blackbirds sleeping, but I always had to come in early because I was cold. That was because I was "spoiled"; I was "brought up soft." So I've always had this thing of being brought up an outsider.

McDIARMID & DURKAN: Do you still feel that way?

NÍ DHOMHNAILL: I feel that what I represent is the aborigine Irish somehow. We've got English, and we can use it if we want to. What we've done with English is that we've made our own language out of it. Seamus Heaney has made valid and made public and made international a type of English which is really our own and types of interest and areas of deep concern and frames of reference that are really our own. Now we can go back to doing what we were doing when we were so rudely interrupted by the Norman invasion,[18] which is working out our psychodramas and "walking the land," living our lives, and dying. It's what the aborigines do in their homelands. They spend so much time with their wonderful rituals and their dance, and they live in peace with the air, with the land, around them. They don't have the urge to be conquering all they see. This is what we were interested in a long time ago, things like the sovereignty of Ireland and the Other World, and I am making valid and giving voice to these in literature.

McDIARMID & DURKAN: Were you saying that Heaney cleared the way for you?

NÍ DHOMHNAILL: I don't want to be jumping on any bandwagon and coupling myself with Seamus Heaney. But I do feel that what Heaney's doing in Irish-English is clearing home fields.

McDIARMID & DURKAN: Do you mean that by writing in English in a way that is distinctively Irish and that is international, he is therefore showing that it can be done, so there doesn't need to be any sense that English is not your language?

Ní DHOMHNAILL: It's quite complicated. For instance, English isn't *my* language, but *his* English is *his* language in a way that I understand perfectly and recognize immediately as being the way I would write in English if I had it. But I don't have it. I'm still too close to the native tradition. And so, Irish is my language. Aren't I damned lucky that I actually found it?

McDIARMID & DURKAN: What is the connection between what he's doing and what you do?

Ní DHOMHNAILL: What he's doing in English I'm doing the equivalent of in Irish. What I feel is "emerging" in our generation in Ireland, in Irish and in English, is your aborigine. We're both talking to ourselves about the things that concern us, without having to be looking over our shoulders and telling others out there what they want to hear.

McDIARMID & DURKAN: You mean if Lady Gregory came round—[19]

Ní DHOMHNAILL: If Lady Gregory came round to me, I'd give her all the *seanchas*[20] she wanted, but in my heart of hearts I'd be thinking something else entirely. I'd be thinking, how come she's up there with her silk skirt, and I in my *báinín*,[21] I would, and how's she better than me?

Now here you have a white aborigine who rejoices in being a white aborigine, who loves the sense I get of undermining all of us. The willful, unholy glee should never be underestimated. And I know—it's in my roots—I'm something they don't want to be reminded of, that I am well-fleshed and red-haired and high-cheekboned. In the establishment in the south of Ireland they hate me because I remind them of their tinker ancestry. And I play it up no end.

McDIARMID & DURKAN: But they are trying so hard to be respectable. It's only the poets and the writers who are honest.

Ní DHOMHNAILL: We poets in Ireland are like poets in Russia: we have psychic muscle, but it's not legalized. So it gives me great pleasure to get fatter and to let my hair get longer and redder and to get drunk in public, which no woman is allowed to do. I get this unholy glee from setting them up.

McDIARMID & DURKAN: You've been making sense of Yeats's line that providence has filled the artists with recklessness.[22] There seem to be two very different strands in you, and I'm not sure how to relate them to each other. On the one hand, you made yourself an expatriate at an early age; you're a woman who lives deeply in yourself and says to hell with the world. And then there's this strand that is so intensely concerned with Irish culture and carries the whole burden of the future of Ireland on your shoulders.

NÍ DHOMHNAILL: That's megalomania! Yes, there is this huge contradiction. I am just a mass of contradictions.

McDIARMID & DURKAN: You speak often as if communal voices were speaking through you, and you can't help it.

NÍ DHOMHNAILL: Even my name, Nuala Ní Dhomnhaill, is a princess name. She was Red Hugh's sister and married to her cousin Niall Dubh, and when he went over to the English side, she promptly left him.[23] She was a patron of the arts.

McDIARMID & DURKAN: Are there poets in your ancestral line?

NÍ DHOMHNAILL: On both sides. My grandfather, Pádraig Ó Dhomhnaill, was an Old Irish scholar and translated Old Irish poetry into modern Irish. That's on my father's side. On my mother's side, we get the poetry from the Seán Ó Duinnsléibhe, one of the last of the good local poets, mentioned by Tomás Ó Criomthan in *The Islandman*.[24] He and my great-great-grandmother came out of the one house in Baile an tSleibhe, in the parish of Ventry. We don't know what the exact relationship was because it was during the Famine and people were dying like flies and the survivors marrying again, but my great-grandmother told my mother; she was what's called in Irish a "noted" speaker. Her name was Léan Ní Chearna, bean Uí Fhiannachta.[25] I'm the dead spit of her.

When I was eighteen, I was acting in Seán Ó Tuama's *Maloney*,[26] and I was the whore. We decided that having been a success in Cork, we'd do a tour of west Kerry. We went to one of the halls there, and so there I was, acting my great female role, and there was an old woman in the front row. When I came out, she fell in a faint, and I thought, I know I'm bad, but I can't be that bad. Afterward, she came up to me and said, "You know, when I saw you I fainted." And I said, "I know," and she said, "You don't know why I fainted. Well, why I fainted was because I thought I'd seen a ghost when you came on because your great-grandmother was a near neighbor of mine, and she was very good to me when I was a young girl, and I remember her well. But now that I see you close up, you're too small." She was a big woman, 5'10", and I'm 5'2", so we have obviously gone into a decline during the last three generations.

McDIARMID & DURKAN: You seem to identify mostly with the female line in your family.

Ní DHOMHNAILL: When people say to me, "Are you a 'postfeminist'?" I think, who the hell cares? I don't want to be used and taken for a feminist.

McDIARMID & DURKAN: You're prefeminist, not postfeminist.

Ní DHOMHNAILL: I don't know what I am, but I know my grandmother was a feminist and my mother was a feminist and sometimes I am a feminist, but what feminism has to do changes from generation to generation. Now there was a generation where political equality was involved. It seems to me in my generation that an inner change is taking place. I have precious little time for the political and everything else; I think that was all done a long time ago. It is the inward implications of that which is the job of my generation.

I never get over my fascination with the Annunciation, the virgin birth, and parthenogenesis. When I write a poem, I have experienced inspiration, and that is being impregnated by the divine. There is no other explanation. The thing about being a poet with a muse is that the muse is always unavailable. That is a particular constellation that creates poetry. If I were meant to be a happy person, it would be requited love all the way.

McDIARMID & DURKAN: And it would be boring poetry, too.

NÍ DHOMHNAILL: Why would I write a word of poetry? Why would you even bother writing the damn thing?

McDIARMID & DURKAN: What connection do you feel with ancient Irish women?

NÍ DHOMHNAILL: A great one. There was Líadan, of the Corca Dhuibhne, my tribe of the Dingle Peninsula. She refused to marry her one great love, the poet Cuirithir, in case he stole her poetry, and[27] Then there was Eibhlín Dhubh Ní Chonaill, and her great keen of love and lust and hate.[28] And then in the *Táin* there was Fedelm Banfhile.[29] Patricia Lysaght in her great study of the banshee myth[30] traces one strand of it back to Fedelm Banfhile: she has just returned from a poetic tourney in Scotland, and Maeve asks her, What do you see? and she gets more than she bargained for. Fedelm's poem is prophetic; it has a Cassandra quality,[31] and I think that is what is emerging in our generation of women poets.

As we aborigines are just now getting back to what we were going on about before the Norman invasion, likewise we female aborigines are beginning to get back to what we were going on about before we were interrupted by the male side of the psyche that caused Christianity and witch burning. We are going back to where the Sybil was interrupted in midsentence by the invasions. Writing was as yet uninvented, except for inscriptions. That was true in west Kerry into this century. Léan Cearney[32] didn't have a word of English. She used to tie pieces of twine to her fingers when she went to Dingle to remind her of all the things she had to do. She couldn't write or read, so as she did each job she used to undo the piece of twine.

McDIARMID & DURKAN: Do you feel that paper gets in the way? or are you just as happy to have your poems on paper?

NÍ DHOMHNAILL: My inspiration is the spoken word, no doubt about it. But I read a lot, ever since I was eight or nine—the Bobbsey Twins, "What Katy Did." Recently, I bought a book of street songs, and my daughter Melissa loved it. She had her own hopscotch rhythms but found more in the book, so she was one-up on her friends. She'd say,

"Well, do you know this one?" It doesn't have to be all oral on one side and book on the other; there's this wonderful interaction.

McDIARMID & DURKAN: How do you see all the Irish women writing fiction? Is this part of the "interruption"?

NÍ DHOMHNAILL: The aborigine women were never writing fiction.

McDIARMID & DURKAN: Do you see that as genteel and Big House-y?

NÍ DHOMHNAILL: Yes, I do feel that's the Anglo-Irish. And they are them, and we are us. It is true that sometimes there are these bits of black angers in me. The wrath of being so poor so long when we were intelligent and we were kings. There is a relic of that in me, and I am inclined to be a little bit biased against the Anglo-Irish. Not against them personally—just a feeling that somehow they "done us wrong." It's quite unreasonable and definitely atavistic. It probably dates back to the trauma of the Famine. It took me years to read Nancy Mitford[33] because of this inbuilt prejudice, but then when I did, the books were so bloody funny. They keep taking the mickey out of their own things. I had to love them. Like Somerville and Ross: I'm afraid I don't appreciate them as I probably should. Molly Keane's[34] black humor I love; I'd forgive her anything.

McDIARMID & DURKAN: How do you react to Jennifer Johnston?[35]

NÍ DHOMHNAILL: Again, I find it's us and them, and she's them. I'm just not interested in the Big House theme; I'm mourning for a lost *tuath*.[36]

McDIARMID & DURKAN: Do you like Adrienne Rich?[37]

NÍ DHOMHNAILL: I do, yes. For instance, I read the poem "The Fact of a Doorframe," and it was good. She is using the door and doorframe as a metaphor for women's experience. But then she ruins it all by saying, "poetry, I gasp for you." But still there is the sheer extraordinary variety of female voices that haven't even begun to be heard yet. We are all women writers, but we all have personal gifts. I love that.

McDIARMID & DURKAN: With all this talk about the Other World and the drawing up of intense feelings I'm wondering if conduit is the right word for what you think you are.

NÍ DHOMHNAILL: Yes, I'm a vessel. I am a wind tunnel through which these cosmic storms break and explode, and it's my job to endure. But it's very hard. Yet it's all grist to the mill: use it; make it articulate; make speakable the unspeakable. My deepest sense is of being the vessel in which these great cosmic storms rage—at great cost to my nails. They're bitten down to the quick. What I hate is that because I write poems people expect me to turn around and be extraintelligent. When my poetic function is not working, and that's most of the time, I am very ordinary. I'm thinking: What are we going to eat tonight? Should I cook up a pound of mince? or should I go down to the store and get six chops? That is actually what's going on.

Tom Paulin

Interviewed by Eamonn Hughes

I'd like to be the kind of writer who simply writes poems and
doesn't engage in debate or polemics—I'm not made that
way. One has to engage with the status quo and stir up
debate and argument—that's the way I live.

—Tom Paulin

TOM PAULIN IS ONE OF IRELAND'S finest contemporary poets. His poetry
deals with both personal matters and public events, and it is always
marked by a sharp intellect that refuses to take anything for granted. This
same quality also distinguishes his critical writings and has placed him at
the center of literary and cultural arguments in both Britain and Ireland
over the past decade.

He was born in Leeds, England, in 1949 and grew up in Belfast. Since
taking his degree from Hull University, he has published on Thomas
Hardy (*Thomas Hardy: The Poetry of Perception* [London: Macmillan, 1975])
and has lectured at Nottingham University since 1972. In 1983–84 he
was visiting associate professor of English and Fulbright scholar at the
University of Virginia. This experience influenced several poems in his
most recent collection, *Fivemiletown* (London: Faber and Faber, 1987; reviewed in this issue), notably, "I Am Nature" and "Jefferson's Virginia."
Jefferson's words also inform the title of *Liberty Tree* (London: Faber and

From *ILS* 7 (fall 1988).

Faber, 1983). Apart from his collections *A State of Justice* (London: Faber and Faber, 1977) and *The Strange Museum* (London: Faber and Faber, 1980), Paulin has also published a collection of critical essays, *Ireland and the English Crisis* (Newcastle-upon-Tyne, Eng.: Bloodaxe Books 1984), two playscripts, *The Riot Act* (London: Faber and Faber, 1985; produced by Field Day, of which he is a founding member) and *The Hillsborough Script: A Dramatic Satire* (London: Faber and Faber, 1987), and has edited a controversial anthology of political poetry, *The Faber Book of Political Verse* (London: Faber and Faber, 1986). He is also a contributor to the forthcoming Field Day anthology of Irish writing.[1]

This interview took place at Tom Paulin's home in Oxford in the early winter of 1987, just after the publication of *Fivemiletown*. [Eamonn Hughes]

EAMONN HUGHES: Given your background, I'd like to ask you about your sense of kinship and culture. Did you, for example, have to make a conscious choice to be an Irish writer?

TOM PAULIN: Not at all. It must be great to be really Irish—or really English. I don't feel either identity. My father was stationed in the North of Ireland during the Second World War and met my mother there. He liked the North very much, and after a few years in England, they moved back to Belfast. I grew up there from the age of four, but most of my relatives were either in Scotland, the North of England, or in the Isle of Man, where one part of my family comes from. Looking back now after years of writing, I realize that at some level I'd always felt that I didn't belong anywhere and that, indeed, I didn't come from anywhere. There's tremendous pressure both in English culture and Irish culture to proclaim roots, ancestry, tradition, the past. I have no concept of ancestry. People often ask me where my surname comes from. I haven't a clue. It may be that I have some remote ancestor who was a French Huguenot; I just don't know—I've never investigated it. But I think that ancestor worship can be dangerous. All I know, all I feel, is some sort of Scottish Calvinism beating at the back of my mind, which is, I suppose, a cultural inheritance from my mother's side of the family.

HUGHES: You were educated in Hull University, which has connections with both Philip Larkin and Douglas Dunn.[2] Was there any prompting there to start writing?

PAULIN: I was friendly with Douglas Dunn; he was a great help to me when I was first trying to write. Douglas was a year ahead of me at Hull, reading English, and then he got a job in the library. I only met Larkin once while I was a student; Douglas introduced me to him, and I met him subsequently. Hull is a very remote city at the end of a railway line in Yorkshire. It's right on the North Sea and has an extraordinary poetic atmosphere. Many poets have been identified with Hull or have lived there. Back in the 1960s, there were poetry magazines produced there which had a very wide circulation. It's a city which was badly bombed during the Second World War. It feels to me like a dilapidated central European city, sort of Habsburg. But I'm romanticizing it. It's got a strange and very wonderful atmosphere to it if you like bleak, out-of-the-way places.

HUGHES: Your early poems are often about desolate middle-European areas. Is that the influence of Hull or Belfast?

PAULIN: In the end all the experience of growing up in a crazy society, an ahistorical, one-party state with a skewed and uncertain culture, must have something to do with it. In the community I grew up in—the Protestant community—we looked all the time to Britain; we listened to the BBC; all the children's books I read were British. Of course, something else was going into you all the time. There was a language that was speaking to you, though you wouldn't know how it was speaking to you or what you were for or what you were about. At the school I went to was a group of us who became interested in Irish writers. We read Joyce, Synge, O'Casey, and we were fascinated by the notion of writing. Joyce was the great god-figure for us, the writer who had flown through all the nets that, though we didn't understand it, trapped us. We probably thought we were free spirits, but we weren't. So the major figure, certainly for me as an adolescent, was Joyce.

HUGHES: And continued to be so?

PAULIN: For some years I stopped reading him, and I immersed myself in English writing. I spent two years researching the poetry of Thomas Hardy, and I think I became very empirical—the cult of experience, of the past, of memory that is so dominant in English writing. But at the back of your mind, there's some sort of original theology, something that's able to cut through all of that when you're under real pressure, when you're really thinking. So you would find yourself blown about between the essentially theological cast of mind people growing up in Ireland are given by whatever culture or community they're thrown into and that more empirical way of thinking where you're looking at bits and pieces of experience and reflecting on them.

HUGHES: Why choose Hardy? His reputation in the mid-1970s was as a novelist, not as a poet.

PAULIN: I got interested in the poetry because of Hardy's use of speech and speech rhythms. There were very few books on his poems; there still aren't many books on the poems. He's difficult to write about, and there are so many poems, and they are—as he said himself—scattered, random responses to experience. I tried to find a way of looking at them as a whole, but it was the speech rhythms that fascinated me. That came out of an experience in Belfast of reading Robert Frost's poems. His concept of writing was that it should come out of vernacular rhythms and trust in the speech around you. Rather than looking to an elite speech or to a language which exists in printed texts, writing should look to that primitive, original orality which any child is given from the moment they try to talk.

HUGHES: Do you aim for orality in your own poetry?

PAULIN: Some reviewers feel that the early poems were deliberately rough in texture, and I suppose over the years I've gone for even rougher textures, but, certainly, when I look back I can see that I was struggling for a language which I didn't have.

HUGHES: What do you regard as the function of the poet?

PAULIN: I'm uneasy with the title *poet*. It's very easy for writers to allow the forces of literary production which surround them to create this honorific title of *poet* and then believe in that title. I think there's been a damaging distinction made between so-called *creative writing* and so-called *academic writing*, and I look back to, say, a figure like Dryden who would write anything that came to hand: a piece of literary criticism, a play, a poem, a translation. One should think of oneself as simply a writer and yet that, too, has the charismatic glow of public attention around it. Barthes[3] has come up with an alternative term—*scriptor*—but that's no use either. The word being used in Britain now in the Murdoch press[4] is *journo*, which is a totally derogatory, contemptuous term. But that's how press barons think of journalists—indeed, I suppose of all writers.

HUGHES: Do you see yourself as having a public role?

PAULIN: From my own point of view all cultures depend on arguments. I don't think there is a place outside history where the sound of battles can't be heard, and while I'd like to be the kind of writer who simply writes poems and doesn't engage in debate or polemics—I'm not made that way. One has to engage with the status quo and stir up debate and argument; that's the way I live. I suppose it's the kind of feistiness that one gets naturally from the city of Belfast where everybody seems engaged in a polemic, a continuous dialogue with the world around them.

HUGHES: When you begin a review or a piece of critical writing, is it in the back of your mind to stir up trouble?

PAULIN: No, that would be reducing it to the level of simple mischief. My aim is to say whatever I want to say at the particular time of writing and, if possible, to praise.

HUGHES: A large part of the polemical effort you've been engaged in over the past few years has to do with changing critical and academic concepts of literature. Is it fair to say that you've moved away from the sense of the poet as a singular figure in the Hardy book to a much more historical consciousness?

PAULIN: In the Hardy book there's nothing about politics or society, at least not obviously so, but what I was concerned to do there was to investigate the literary influences on Hardy and to point out that he, like Eliot, had an imagination which depended on making an enormous number of allusions. Critics thought of Hardy as simply a sort of original writer with very little literary baggage. In fact, there's an immense weight of literary allusion in the poems of a a very complex kind. It's often disguised, but it's there. Certainly, I have shifted toward a much more historical form of criticism, but when I was working on Hardy, I was writing in a society which was much more consensual in which nobody bothered too much about historical argument. It was a rather placid time when one looks back. The Labour Government was in power, and there was a vaguely decent Conservative Party in opposition. Something happened then, and we are still trying to work out what it was that happened at the end of the 1970s.

HUGHES: How have your changing critical attitudes altered your own creative imaginative writing?

PAULIN: I wouldn't be able to answer that. You don't know what's happening deep down in your imagination. You aren't conscious of what's happening or why it's happening. My experience has been living through the breakup of an existing cultural idea both in Britain and in Ireland and trying to understand what's happening and why it's happening. It's the experience of living in a state which is not quite fully postimperial where many of the old-style imperial attitudes inform public life in all kinds of ways, where the pressure of a society in economic decline has forced people to identify themselves more tribally than they did in order ultimately to affirm the notion of a multicultural and multiracial society. You've got to remember that in Britain, unlike the United States, the concept of a multiracial enlightenment idea of citizenship has a very tenuous existence. Britain is a deeply racist society; anybody who lives in Britain as a member of an immigrant group knows that you're under daily pressure from the racism in the media, the racism in the attitudes of many people, and it will be a long time before those attitudes are fully exposed and demolished.

HUGHES: One response that you've made to those attitudes is to edit the *Faber Book of Political Verse*. What were you aiming for with the anthology?

PAULIN: It was an attempt to challenge the trivialization of poetry which arises from treating political poetry as simply a form of slogan mongering. It was also an attempt to say the obvious: the earth is round; John Milton is a great political poet who had a very definite ideology that succeeding generations of readers have ignored. This ignoring of Milton came out of the ahistorical vacuum in the study of English literature, a vacuum that was created very deliberately in the interests of creating an idea of cultural consensus. That consensus has now broken down though many critics have been slow to recognize it. I wanted to challenge the way in which critics had accepted Eliot's landscaping of English poetry in terms of the primary tradition being a monarchist one and say, "No, the primary tradition is a republican tradition, and the monarchist or royalist tradition is secondary." The anthology did stir up a good deal of argument, which pleased me.

HUGHES: Do you consider that an index of a healthy culture?

PAULIN: In Britain writers are under attack by government; you feel that all sorts of censorship are in operation, and at times you feel there's a mopping-up operation going on where writers who speak out against the orthodoxy are being singled out for attack by national newspapers. It does seem incredible to me that this supposedly democratic country is unable to value its own writers. The *Sunday Times* recently had an editorial naming certain writers and attacking them. This is an index of the grip which the present government has on the culture.

HUGHES: One of the criticisms at the time of the political anthology publication was that there were very few women poets in it. Was that because of its bias toward public politics?

PAULIN: I wouldn't accept the distinction between public and private. I based my anthology on the notion of national cultures and different traditions, for want of a better word, within those cultures. That's how I constructed it. I certainly didn't consciously exclude female poets. I have talked to a number of female writers who have expressed contempt for the notion that there is a special category called *female writer.* At the same time, I recognize that a feminist perspective needs to express itself polemically, and perhaps that's a fault in the anthology. I still can't make up my mind about it.

HUGHES: Let's turn to another public project you're involved in: Field

Day.[5] Why did you join it? What do you think its motives are? And what do you think its value is?

PAULIN: I don't think any of us in Field Day have any conscious program. There was no manifesto because we're not a political party, and you didn't know moment to moment where you would be going. It's only later that you look back with some form of historical hindsight and say, "that was the direction."

My own analysis is that something snapped in the political and cultural atmosphere at some point in the 1970s. Something snapped within Britain in regard to the North of Ireland. People switched off from this enduring and terrible problem, and the North of Ireland was adrift from Britain. This made me conclude that the Unionist ideology didn't have any life in it. Growing up in the North of Ireland, it was possible to take an anti-Unionist position, to support the Civil Rights movement, and to hope that you would get a democracy, which would be underwritten by Britain. The attempt to set up a power-sharing executive failed. Successive attempts to solve the situation have failed, and it's necessary to try and understand the reason for that. I see Unionism as a holding operation, essentially a throwback to a redundant form of British imperialism. That's not to say that I see Unionists as colonizers; I don't, but clearly, the Unionist people in the North of Ireland felt that their future was best served by remaining British in 1921, and they set up a state which was unjust and which has failed because of its internal contradictions.

HUGHES: Is Field Day an attempt to analyze that failure or even to remedy it?

PAULIN: No, Field Day is an attempt to allow the two major cultural traditions or communities to develop in relation to each other. It has been criticized as essentially nationalist; I don't think that is a fair criticism. I certainly am not a romantic Irish nationalist. I can't be, and I don't think Field Day affirms that type of romantic position.

HUGHES: I asked because Field Day has to do with community. Do you feel yourself part of a community of writers?

PAULIN: Yes, a community of writers isn't a physical thing. It's an invisible, even a spiritual thing. There is a strong element in Irish writing of the reply poem. Often allusions are buried, and they might not be visible, but, certainly, ideas are being bounced around among different poems.

HUGHES: Do you feel constrained by that community of Irish writers? or do you look to a very much wider community?

PAULIN: In *Fivemiletown*—when I analyze it with hindsight—I wanted to try and write a language that aspired toward the energy of American English. I had a year in the States, from 1983 to 1984, and I became fascinated by the way in which Americans speak and the extraordinary energy of the language. At the same time, I was trying to push my language into Northern Europe, Germany, and Russia to create a feeling of displacement—international displacement. That was the ambition.

For years I've invoked the spirit of Jackson Pollock[6] when I write—in other words, writing blindly and intuitively, not knowing what you're at but doing it. I kept thinking of Pollock while in the States. I went to see some of his paintings and read about him, and I discovered that he was Scots-Irish. I found in the Shenandoah Valley some sort of recognition of this displaced tribe that in some way I might belong to. I was trying to get a kind of redneck language in the book. I've always felt oppressed by that kind of kitsch poetic language that's so dominant in nineteenth-century English writing—for example, Tennyson—and I've always felt an identity with a much more fricative, consonantal kind of writing—hence the interest in Hardy and Frost. That's really what I was aiming at.

HUGHES: It seems to me that *Fivemiletown*, like some other recent volumes by Irish writers, is beginning to push at a sense of what it would be to be postcolonial, a situation in which having a history of oppression means that you have access to a range of cultures and possibilities which are allowable to you in a way that they're not to people from a dominant elitist colonial culture.

PAULIN: Perhaps, but I'd be uneasy at saying that I personally have a history of oppression behind me. It's not personally for me a concept at all. What I've felt in recent years is that the Unionist community feels itself within Britain and Ireland to be a sort of minority. There's a great deal of confusion, and for somebody nurtured in that community your historical recall is not of Irish history but of an international Protestant experience. Therefore, when the Anglo-Irish Agreement was signed,[7] the then-deputy leader of the Democratic Unionist Party, Peter Robinson, said that we'd been put out on the window ledge. Now, I interpreted that as being an example of historic recall—of the Defenestration of Prague in the seventeenth century[8]—because we, both Robinson and myself, went to the same school and we got the same history; we studied in great detail the history of Protestantism in Europe, and I found myself drawn to that experience in writing some of the poems in *Fivemiletown*.

HUGHES: Is *Fivemiletown*, then, more about the possibilities of identity than about its problems?

PAULIN: Perhaps. We've been given, until relatively recently, the notion of identity as a fixed concept, that identity is somehow like integrity: it's principled and it's unitary. In fact, identity is not like that. We are imaginatively bits and pieces and maybe they don't fit and maybe there are great gaps. Certainly, the Northern Irish experience has been one of fragmentation, and this may mean that imaginatively you have access to different cultures that you can raid for what you want. It means that things are fluid; they are unstable; and there can be a very astringent feeling of living moment-by-moment and not knowing what's happening or where you're going.

I'm concerned with the Unionist experience. I hope I understand the feelings of agony and displacement and not belonging that are part of that imagination, and I think that the historical experience of the culture needs to be treated sympathetically. There is, for example, a fascinating oratorical tradition within Northern Protestantism that, unfortunately, many members of that community have derided. It's a way of testifying to one's experience and one's belief, and it's there on its own.

HUGHES: What do you mean "on its own"?

PAULIN: It stands for certain values which cannot be diminished although in political practice they have not been successful because the North of Ireland was an inflexible state, and that was its tragedy. There isn't a Northern Irish state any longer: there is an administrative annex of the United Kingdom.

HUGHES: Are you agreeing with Robinson about Unionist culture being on the window ledge?

PAULIN: I think that's what it feels like.

HUGHES: In *Fivemiletown*, "The Defenestration of Hillsborough" contains the challenge of either jumping or being pushed, and it's followed by "The Caravans at Luneburg Heath." Is that poem your own leap into the possibilities of the history of Protestant identity?

PAULIN: Yes, but that's very abstract. If I could put it like this: I would not wish to be identified with a sectarian outlook, and I think I've probably spent enough time investigating the negative aspects of Protestant culture in "The Caravans at Luneburg Heath." I was trying to face what I take to be the experience of growing up in that postwar society. For example, I went to a high school that had four houses in it named for the four leading field marshals in the British army during the Second World War: Dill, Alanbrooke, Alexander, and Montgomery.[9] As it happens, they were all of Anglo-Irish background; all the families were from Ulster, I believe from the Clogher Valley, or roughly that area where the town of Fivemiletown is.[10] That obviously was a very powerful conditioning force on all the kids who went through that school. It was making a statement, just as if you went to a school that was named for Patrick Pearse, you would obviously have a quite different culture and community shaped in different ways. I wanted to face that.

HUGHES: Are you trying to put an end to arguments about identity which have figured in Irish writing?

PAULIN: I wouldn't know about that. Indeed, it would be taking yourself too seriously to agree with that. I just wanted to displace the concept of national identity, the concept of belonging to your tribe, the idea of tradition, and so on. I wanted to wreck that and replace it with something that's plural and infinite, something that's moving all the time.

HUGHES: One of the things which seems to be very important in your work is the idea of memory: this runs through both your poetry and your critical writing. You write about both Solzhenitsyn and Joyce performing acts of "mnemonic rescue." How does that sense of memory square with the sense of something that's free-floating and plural?

PAULIN: Memory is perhaps a form of fiction which is a kind of tyranny, but at the same time you can be terrified by living in a sort of ahistorical condition where history has been forgotten. I suppose it's a contradictory attitude to have, but for Unionists, what is there?— 1690, 1912[11]—that's it; it's a few dozen dates. In recent years history has become a growth industry in the North of Ireland: all sorts of history societies have been set up, lots of books published investigating arcane historical details. That's clearly a response to a crisis.

HUGHES: Do you think that's an invention, that people are trying to invent memories for themselves?

PAULIN: They're trying to discover things that have been buried or forgotten. The classic example of this was the moment when the Unionist leader Sir James Craig met Eamon de Valera.[12] De Valera spoke to him about the seven hundred years of oppression and injustice, and Craig was totally uninterested in that; he saw himself as a modernizer, as somebody who was looking to the future and believed in engineering and industry and wealth creation. Over the years that has changed, and certain writers and historians from that community have obviously started to look back.

HUGHES: The only two love poems in *Fivemiletown* are "Fivemiletown" and "Mountstewart," which are about the same place. What they share is a sense that love is something that happens outside identity. Do you regard love poems as being somehow separated from the political and historical?

PAULIN: No, I don't. Love is a cultural concept. There are many parts of the world where marriages are arranged. In the West we tend to think that the norm for marriage is the love-marriage. Love is personal, but it's cultural in many ways. I married outside my tribe. Anybody who does that understands something which I don't think is given to people who marry within their own race or tribe. It's difficult to define the experience, but you go into a territory where there are no comfortable institutions to support you.

HUGHES: Many reviewers, particularly English ones, have reacted to *Fivemiletwon* and *Liberty Tree*, to the Northern Irish dialect words. Do they resent being confronted with a language which is in certain ways private and secret from them?

PAULIN: I don't know. Clearly, there is a problem when you're using words which have a local existence and you're not glossing them. That is a difficult thing, but you just have to let it all hang out and see what happens. I'm fascinated by the riskiness, by the spontaneity of the spoken language, by its creative eruptions—that's what interests me. Maybe at some level, print is trying to melt into speech. You never know whether you're succeeding and clearly you carry all sorts of baggage and influences with you and they are very difficult to shake off. But the idea of linguistic purity is a form of racism, and I believe in radical linguistic impurity because I don't believe in the concept of race. I want to write in a way which breaks down notions like that. If you look at the way in which the English language has been historically described, the central concept is of the well of English undefiled. I hope to defile that well as much as possible.

Brendan Kennelly

Interviewed by Richard Pine

> I don't think any Irishman is complete as an Irishman until he
> becomes an Englishman, imaginatively speaking. . . . We can't
> solve our problems until Catholics become Protestants, and
> Protestants become Catholics, country people become
> Dubliners."
>
> —Brendan Kennelly

IT HAS BEEN SAID that after meeting Brendan Kennelly, "you know that he
has made little glosses in the margin of your psyche, that the direction
and the quality of your day have been altered." That's true. I've known
Brendan for over twenty years, and the following conversation, which
took place on 12 October 1989 in Kennelly's office at Trinity College,
Dublin, is set against the background of Kennelly as teacher and friend in
which those quoted words are constantly confirmed.

Brendan Kennelly, born in Ballylongford, County Kerry, in 1936, has
been publishing poetry since 1959. He began lecturing at Trinity College, Dublin, in 1963; became a fellow in 1967; and was appointed professor of modern literature in 1973. His chief publications (poetry) are
Dream of a Black Fox (Dublin: Allen Figgis, 1968), *Love-Cry* (Dublin: Allen
Figgis, 1972), *A Kind of Trust* (Dublin: Gallery Press, 1975), *Islandman*
(Dublin: Profile Press, 1977), *Cromwell* (Dublin: Beaver Row Press, 1983),

From *ILS* 9 (spring 1990).

and *Moloney Up and At It* (Dublin: Mercier Press, 1984). His *Selected Poems* appeared in 1985 (Dublin: Kerrymount). More recently, he has produced his first works for the stage: *Antigone* (1986; pub. Newcastle-upon-Tyne, Eng.: Bloodaxe Books, 1996), *Medea* (1988; pub. Newcastle-upon-Tyne, Eng.: Bloodaxe Books, 1991), and *The Trojan Women* (1989–90; pub. Newcastle-upon-Tyne, Eng.: Bloodaxe Books, 1993). In 1970 he edited *The Penguin Book of Irish Verse* (Harmondsworth, Eng.: Penguin).[1]

In this conversation Kennelly spoke about the dominant images in his life, which spring from his childhood experience of village life, the key words (and preoccupations) of which are: civilization, the meaning of love, of hope, of self, and the connection between violence and betrayal. These are discussed in the context not only of his poetry and academic career but also of his experience of marriage breakdown and his subsequent treatment for alcoholism.

We began by mentioning his early novels, *The Crooked Cross* (Dublin: Allen Figgis; Boston: Little, Brown, 1963) and *The Florentines* (Dublin: Allen Figgis, 1967), written while he was a graduate student at Leeds and in which there is a current renewal of interest. [Richard Pine]

Village

RICHARD PINE: You're a poet—you were always a poet. Why did you try to write fiction at all?

BRENDAN KENNELLY: In the 1950s I grew up in a village that was a very lively little place, but then I saw around me, when I was doing leaving certificate,[2] boys and girls going to England and America, and at that stage you begin to see things in a new way. I saw the place becoming emaciated, and I felt angry. This was in me for a few years, this anger, and finally I wrote a novel about emigration, and it was about the village, *The Crooked Cross*, because it was shaped like a cross.

I was trying to say that when life in the little places dies, the nation suffers, and the same is true today. Rural Ireland, the village, is really in danger of extermination. This may be a good thing, but I don't think so because the essence, the quintessence of civilization to me is the English village. I love it: in Blake's phrase, "the echoing green,"[3] the sense that houses are built around a green patch, children playing. I know it's idealistic, but you have to have these images for civilized living. Irish villages, on the other hand, are frequently furtive; they were built by people who seem to have been on the run. My own little village—there's nothing much to it, but there was terrific life in it. There was a drama group; there were a couple of football teams; a *feis*[4] where you learned how to recite poetry; an old priest who used to translate Dante into Irish; and it was ideal and totally acritical! To this day, I have to strain to think critically.

But my nature's more spontaneous, and the flaws in my writing, which are considerable, have to do with spontaneity. I suppose that now that I would consider myself reasonably trained as a critic, I would cite my native flaw as someone who transfers from an oral tradition into a written tradition, and this is why people frequently say to me, "Oh, but when you say your poems, they're so much more alive than when I read them to myself." That may be a comment also on the experience of actually writing a poem to be read.

But my tradition is oral: it's the ballad tradition. Whereas with *Medea*, which is an attempt at full expression, the danger is obviousness and explicitness, the value, if it's good, being that you involve people in a whole imaginative world—you bring them in.

PINE: When you talk about Ballylongford, I get a very strong sense of your village being the rival of all the other villages. Is that a healthy thing, the sort of rivalry that can begin in poetry and end in violence?

KENNELLY: The faction fights of North Kerry, which became the GAA,[5] were the explosive expression in violence of people who had no other way of expressing themselves. One forgets, for example, that the GAA has its roots in violence. There were and are still in many ways terribly narrow attitudes in rural Ireland which are connected with wonderful intensities, passions, and violence is very strange in that it does animate you, and there's no point adopting a bourgeois attitude that "it doesn't exist" or that you have to educate it out of yourself. It's part of your imagination; it's part of what fuels your dreams, your nightmares;

it's connected with your excitement in the presence of language. And, yes, I would say that the parochial, the parish atmosphere I grew up in, established immediately a number of tensions. There used to be battles—it's the only description I can give them—with the next parish, Tarbert. Then there was Listowel, Ballybunion—all these places had teams which were battlers, little armies, and fights were expected. I shifted from that Ireland into middle-class Trinity, middle-class Dublin, but I see violence here, too, but it's usually of the smiling, sophisticated kind.

PINE: Would you call it sublimated?

KENNELLY: I wouldn't; it's verbal, and it has to do with manners, *la politesse*, and money, and it has to do with taste. One forgets, for example, the amount of violence there is in establishing canons of taste. I've heard people at dinner tables expressing barbaric sentiments in sophisticated language about pictures and about poems and about people: It's violence—I know what it is. It is a tension in an individual that comes out, if he has the education, in a sophisticated idiom, and if he doesn't have it, it comes out in "fuckin'" and "blindin'."

PINE: I find that that kind of tension, the unease that causes that kind of expression, comes from a deep-seated fear of the unknown, the aesthetic challenge, let's say, of a picture or a theater experience that a person can't assimilate.

KENNELLY: Yes, and the fear of the unknown in people's lives, like the fear of sleep, the fear of dreams, the fear of sex, the fear of a woman or of any kind of sexual love, which is very strong still in Ireland, is a dynamizing factor. I realize that there are things one is afraid of and that they're everywhere. What interests me is what comes out of it: how you turn things to good. I'm not using *good* in a Victorian sense; I'm using *good* in the sense that you can make a poem out of your horror, that art is frequently transfigured horror and can be beautiful. The reason why much Victorian art is a lie to me is that it doesn't examine the roots of its own concept of beauty.

The roots of beauty, I think, can be horrible, frightening, and this is why I'm attracted to an amoral situation like what I tried to ask in *Medea*: "Is Medea's crime Medea's glory?" In our society that concept is rampant. Violence runs through education, ambition, the dream of middle-class parents for their children, the molding of personality. Violence is basically something in us that cannot leave other people alone: the violence of the missioner, the violence of the educator, the violence of the parent. The hardest thing for any human being is not to tamper with other people, and yet the deepest longing in most of us is a longing for solitude. We want not to be tampered with, yet we tamper with each other all the time. And that is the area where I would go to find the images and the resentments and the language of resistance and dominance that seems to be at work in all situations. Even within yourself, you're fighting yourself all the time. I fight myself. I have a genuine tendency, a desire to get beyond this sluggish, indifferent, nagging world into a world of genuine ecstasy. I say to myself, "You live for so many years; why shouldn't those bloody years be ecstatic?"

Images

PINE: Nothing you've said is irreconcilable with the man who wrote these poems, but I find, particularly while reading your poetry—we'll come to your plays in a moment—that you're a person who can keep an equilibrium, that they're very much happy poems, even when you're exploring the dangerous avenues you're describing, because you seem to go down those avenues with a considerable knowledge of your own inner strengths, and when you're confronting doubt, you seem to confront your own doubts and weaknesses out of a very strong knowledge of them. You seem to be a very secure person in that sense, even though you've gone through considerable crises in your own life. It seems to me that you're doing that because you keep going back to Ballylongford as a resource; everything that you know of life seems to come from Ballylongford. Nothing that you seem to have learned in

Trinity or Leeds or this little island around Trinity seems to challenge what you already knew before you left Ballylongford. Is that a reasonable view?

KENNELLY: I think what you're saying is that there are dominant images in any person's life and that you can spend the rest of your life unraveling the fears, terrors, hopes, and loves that dominated your childhood up to the age of probably ten. There's an awful lot to be said for that, and to that extent I would return to the village, my parents, my sisters, my brothers, the sight of men getting drunk in a pub, tinkers beating the daylights out of each other, a son whipping his father—images of unbelievable violence. In football, for example, in the late forties, early fifties, I saw a man get a kick in the balls. I never heard a man roar in agony until then; that roar is still in my mind. Then the repression in the church—the suicides of girls, the schools, the brutal teacher, the notion that a boy could get fifty slaps on the hand for stammering or for writing with his left hand, the total lack of any sexual education— these are all in retrospect comic in a way, but at the time you're going though it as an intelligent child, it was very puzzling.

On the other hand, you're quite right to point out about this other quality—I don't know what to call it—*hope* or *grit, survival,* coming from the brutality of life, in which people are battered and shoved about. Hope is an achieved thing, an earned thing. You have to fight for it; it's not a facile optimism. There's none of that in me as far as I can see, and yet I like getting up in the morning. I like to be alive. I like to put one leg in front of the other when I feel despair in my heart.

PINE: I remember—it must be twenty years ago—you giving a wonderful image of your father's pub, when you were a small boy, as a leggy world because at that height you were finding your way around the pub, and all you could see were legs like tree trunks, the huge, thick legs of the men, and that you had to thread your way among them to find the light. It seems that in a way you've carried on that quest for light, finding your way among the things that were stronger than you.

KENNELLY: Like a hand coming down on your head, a big hand. I was only a child and think that's a great image. Certainly I feel that poetry is written by blind men, groping for some kind of light. I've tried to educate myself, and the purpose of that education seems almost self-defeating at times because you realize that the more you read, the more you try to understand; the more ignorant you are, the less you know about things; and the older you get, the more pains you get in your mind and in your body. Nonetheless, there's always that questing of finding your way among people, among problems, among anything from a genuine urge to celebrate life to a genuine urge to abnegate, to opt out, to self-destruct. I love trying to get into close contact with my own language and with my own feelings and with people outside me, with the kids here in the college, with Dubliners, with women and with men who are willing to talk and reveal themselves a little. But also there is a part of me that just wants to give up, and I think a lot of us are like that. When you talk about hope or happiness, I think that what I understand by that is recognition. I feel like a battleground in which there is this fight between intelligent, enlightened surviving and loving, and a kind of black desire to fuck it up. [*Laughs.*]

Empathy

PINE: To come back again to your early writing, it seems that even when you're writing something like Cromwell, you're translating what you've just been talking about onto the public stage, onto the history of your country, but it's always—to come back to one of your most famous poems, "My Dark Fathers"—it's always your dark fathers and that image of the woman related to the man's breast bone. You are projecting strengths and weaknesses that you know about that house onto the great house of history.

KENNELLY: I think you're right, and I think that that's a perception which is probably *you* as well, Richard—that we do not ever escape from a certain house. One of the things I've noticed is that when you have a little self-knowledge and you realize that you're not important and that you are a creature of polarities but, above all, that you're not indispensable, then you find room in your heart for otherness, for others, genuine room, and I don't mean gesturing. I mean using your imagination for altruism.

An awful lot of my stuff is a genuine violation of inherited prejudices, egotistical, because prejudice to me is not unlike snobbery: it is basically a desire not to let others into your heart, a determination not to relate. So what I try to do in my poetry is to increasingly be the person, another person, or to give a voice to the other person that's in myself, and to that extent it's connected with my culture.

I don't think any Irishman is complete as an Irishman until he becomes an Englishman, imaginatively speaking. I was reared to hate and fear Cromwell, the legends, the folklore of my own parish, the unquestioning hatred of him, which was then transferred to England. That appalled me when I began to try to think. I'm doing the same now with Judas. I've spent six years trying to go beyond history into the religious roots, to see how you were got at, to find the place in your heart for the ultimate traitor, and to let him speak your capacity for treachery. I wrote a book called *The Voices* which was the beginning of it, far back [1973], which I wrote as a result of knowing that I don't matter that much to anybody. Part of this is giving a voice to the unthinkable, which to me is what our Irish problem is about.

I believe, imaginatively speaking, that we can't solve our problems until Catholics become Protestants, and Protestants become Catholics, country people become Dubliners. I'm talking about imagination and sympathy and empathy, and in Ireland, for all our talk about imagination, I think we are drastically deficient when it comes to profound sympathizing. I'm only talking about what we should be doing *ordinarily*. To me, *Cromwell* is an ordinary experiment in my own psyche: that I am giving a voice to a man who made trees wither. The worse thing you can say in the part of the country I grew up in is "the curse of Cromwell on you," and I wanted to turn that curse into a blessing; I wanted to let him speak. I got a punch in the jaw one night, crossing O'Connell Bridge, from a man who said, "Aren't you the bastard that had a good word for *him!* Aren't you the fellow that's making a hero out of him!" And I said, "No, he's a man; you're a man; I'm a man." And then he said, "Drogheda!"—he had all the clichés.

What I'm trying to say to you is that all of us are victims of clichés we don't even begin to suspect. One word is enough to engage you for years. I was in ten schools in England recently, and I asked the children what the line in Ted Hughes's poem about the pike, "deep as England,"[6] meant to them, and what they came out with was thrilling: history, fields, myth, family.

PINE: For you, that word is *village.*

KENNELLY: Yes, and it's *Cromwell* and *Judas* and *Christ* and *love* and *hate,* words around that, and the village mentality. Trinity is a village, for example, and Dublin's an extended village, and once you go outside a nodal community you're floundering. I've met lots of Americans, especially, who wouldn't have that attachment to the village, world wanderers who really intrigue me, the fascination of peripatetic rootlessness, but I like the pull of old antagonisms, old loyalties.

PINE: And is the village-ness being eroded?

KENNELLY: Yes. My brother told me on the phone, "They're thinking of closing the creamery." Of course the creamery is the morning, carts rattling, the milk coming in, the dallying in the pub, the chat, bringing news in from the countryside around, which is Homer to Kavanagh— this sense of personal bringing of news.

We're now confronting the age of the fax, the world being placed on your desk. I tend to recoil. I'm amazed at the genius of the technology, but there's nothing, *nothing* to equal a person telling you a story, face to face, and I think that's what we have in Ireland. I hope we keep that notion of you and me over a cup of coffee, telling a story or gossiping, and surprising each other.

PINE: In a sense, aren't you, in *Cromwell* or *Moloney,* taking on a persona in order to tell a story, a history—*"his story"*?

KENNELLY: They are that, and Moloney is the storyteller, the countryside, the tonal genius. It's hard to take it off the page, but if I say a poem, it'll be very different from the way you'd read it on the page [*recites a stanza from "Moloney"*]. It's tonal.

PINE: What you're doing to me is reversing the Joycean image. When you speak, my language becomes familiar and foreign to me![7] How do you find working in the English language, which is supposed to be familiar and foreign to you? [*Laughter.*]

KENNELLY: That is part of the pain, the alienation, the violence we were talking about, the notion of the *feis*, the notion that you have behind you all these pagan voices. When I was about eight years of age, I was able to recite the poems of Oisin.[8] Pagan Ireland was winning. The joy is with Oisin. I think, then, when you come on to language and develop your relationship with it, you're looking in English, or "the English," as it's called, for the joy. One of my favorite pastimes is reading the *Oxford English Dictionary*, and I'll take a word and trace its joyous history. It reminds me of my own life, the struggle of a work to survive its own stages, to stay alive, to serve a young boy or girl who's encountering that word for the first time, and behind it are centuries of experience, and it's in the mouth of that child, and that's joy to me, the word as survivor.

Rage

PINE: So, when you come to write plays, which so far in your case consists in adapting extant texts, it stops being Brendan Kennelly telling a story, adopting a persona. I don't yet feel comfortable with the idea that Brendan Kennelly *is* Antigone, *is* Medea:[9] you've moved into a completely different mode. Whether it has something to do with coming to terms with what woman means in your life, a gap in your experience that's only appeared relatively late in life, is for you to say, but for me it's quite different from what I've always known as a writer, poet, speaker.

KENNELLY: It is different, in the sense that it's a concentrated attempt to be, imaginatively, a woman, both Antigone and Medea, and now the Trojan Women.[10] To that extent, it's new. But to the extent that it's about letting your imagination be enhanced by a *difference*—woman, Cromwell, Judas, others—it is a logical . . . I don't know whether you'd call it a *development* . . . a logical *aspect* of a trend in my imagination, in my own attempt to know what this thing is in you, to know that your self is not important, and that what matters is your empathizing, and that paradoxically this is what creates the vitality in your nature: givenness, going-outness, the imagination as something that makes you more alive inside, that turns your despair, your depression, your desire not to be, into vital forces of being.

In *Antigone*, for example, I wanted to explore sisterhood, the loyalty that a sister will show to a brother, against law, against marriage, against everything. There's no relationship like it; it has all the passion of your whole nature, this side of incest. I don't know if it was brought out in the production, but it was a study of a girl all of whose impulses defied everything in order to bury the boy, to give him dignity.

I wrote the first version of *Medea* in St. Patrick's,[11] listening to Irish women from all over the country, who were depressed, who were in for nervous disorders, and who were talking about men, about society, family, brothers, but husbands mostly. After I wrote *Antigone*, a girl came up to me in O'Neill's[12] and said, "I don't know you, but you strike me as being one of the most enraged men I've ever observed, and I'd like you to have a look at *Medea*; it's always considered a play about jealousy, but it's a play about rage."

PINE: *Medea* represents a problem for me in the sense that what you have done has disturbed other people's view of you, which is a dangerous thing to do. Your poems are sometimes nothing more or less than massive chunks of sexual imagery; I'm thinking of "Love Cry," for example, which begins with this enormous lifting and shafting of the woman against the background of the Shannon, and the whole thing is sexual action. In *Medea* you're abandoning the sensitive, sensual way in which man has approached woman in the poems, and you're saying, "I've discovered another kind of woman, the mind of woman, which I've never encountered before, a mind that does not create the great congruences that I've celebrated in the love poems. I'm moving into another mode where I've got to encounter the other side, the antagonisms, the emasculating knives that are in the woman's mind. Woman's potential for that, the vagina dentata—I'm addressing that." The shock consists in the fact that it comes so late in a huge body of work you've produced up to that point.

KENNELLY: I take that point. I think it came as a result of violence, disruption in my own life, very profound disruptions of commitments, of expectations, of the actual sense of one's function in life, of my reasons for being me. The breakup of a family is a terrible thing, and in our society, without divorce,[13] a breakup in Ireland for the ordinary Irish person—and I see myself as that; I do not have recourse to clever strategems of getting a divorce in Honolulu or that kind of thing; I don't go in for it—is a special disruption. I think also the alcoholism had a deep influence; it was a logical strain in my character.

There is a side to me that revels in ecstatic self-destruction, *revels* in it, and loves to upset. *Cromwell* was the start of my upsettedness, but I was holding on to form because at the back of my mind is always the notion that until your chaos is formed, it has no meaning—it's only to be suffered, not shared. *Medea* is chaos of a kind; it's chaos in her mind, *my* mind sympathizing with *her* chaos, and it asks the question, "Is murder ever an instrument of justice?" I was surprised that nobody picked that up, in terms of politics, in terms of emotional murder, that people do kill—maim and kill—emotionally, around them. It's very strong in Dublin pubs, the way we emotionally assassinate each other. "Is Medea's crime Medea's glory?" That's the last line of the play, and it goes right back over it.

PINE: One of your best and most committed critics is your old friend John Moriarty,[14] with whom I've spent many hours talking about this. Moriarty says that it seems unforgivable to have written *Medea*, unforgivable in the first place but also unforgivable for you to have made a version of it.

KENNELLY: He feels I've betrayed myself, does he?

PINE: He feels that to portray someone who will destroy to the uttermost in order to exact revenge is unforgivable, that it is such an unthinkable thing he cannot encapsulate, accommodate that concept, a rage so vast that she has to do these things.

KENNELLY: Well, in a sense, there's a thrilling immoral tribute in that, to me, because Moriarty I love and respect. He has a fantastic imagination and a wonderful mind. He's a philosopher and a mystic, and I am neither. I have grains of both in me, but I know it when I come up against him. It saddens me that he would think of *Medea* like that, but he knows that I'm a for-better-or-worse man, and he knows also that my attraction is to the boundary-breakers, the limit-smashers, both in myself and in society. I wonder what he'd think of Judas; I wonder what he'd think of trying to find the Judas in the heart, in the voice. And beyond that, I would ask him, "What is love?" because at the back of it all, that's what I'm trying to find out. I want to define love.

PINE: I don't think any of us know that, do we?

KENNELLY: No, but we push toward it, and I think that murder has something to do with it, emotional maimings have something to do with it, or they're part of it, of the ultimate, final fluency we can achieve in our life. The woman who kills her children *is* unbelievable. The mind cannot grasp it: it's killing the future; it's killing the one thing on which my poetry rests—hope. I think that what appalls Moriarty is that Medea does kill hope, deliberately, in order to bring a man to the state of pained consciousness that she suffered and that she considers he caused her to suffer, until they're now equal.

PINE: He began as an arrogant, strutting, ignorant fool, and we were made to laugh at him. In the second part we are almost made to cry with him as he shrank until he was gone, invisible, a nothing, and we reveled in her triumph, but at the same time we felt for the utter destruction of his world. You bring it to the point of reducing them both: they are standing on either side of a grave that has been filled with everything that was once them and is gone. Is that what you were aiming at?

KENNELLY: Yes. But she doesn't do him the favor of killing him. There's more bleakness that way.

PINE: I think Moriarty is saying that no one should do that to any person for any reason whatsoever. Shouldn't you do them both the justice of writing a sequel, when they next meet?

KENNELLY: That is what our civilized sense of symmetry and, perhaps, even our love of justice would demand. I would say no. I would be an inferior writer if I tried to balance the scales. The justice in me says yes, but not the imagination.

Betrayal

KENNELLY: Judas is a fairly logical follow-on from Cromwell, from the scapegoat figure in the spiritual world, as Cromwell was in the political, historical world that I experienced. I started in December 1983 writing about him in prose and then in ballads and then in dialogue, and then one day I sat down and instead of "Judas did this," I said, "I did this," and that was the start because it's the Judas in myself, the Judas in my society, the Judas in Irish Christianity, and betrayal as a principle. In the poem there's Christianity and there's Judasinity and there is the implication that we follow the Judas in the heart, that we betray ourselves a lot, and that it may be necessary. The unasked questions are the ones I like to ask: "Is it necessary?" "Is Christ tolerable?" "If he came in today . . .?" It's easy to pay deference in retrospect, but if there's a mere disturber, an amateur Christ knocking around, he gets locked up; we get rid of him. What's the maddest thing you can walk up to a man or woman and say? "I love you." People think you're fucking nuts!

PINE: It's that compulsive interference in another person's life, isn't it?

KENNELLY: And after that, then, "I own you."

PINE: The worst thing is if that expression of love is a disinterested one. It's not, "Let's get in bed together and I'll show you how I much love you"; it's that disembodied love that we can't really accept.

KENNELLY: I don't fully understand that, but I know what you're saying, all right, in that it rings true to me.

PINE: I mean that we are only able in a sense to appreciate physical expressions of love, the only thing we know, and the disembodied love isn't possible, and that's what Christ was offering. Even when you're beating up someone, you're showing how much you love them; otherwise, it's war on the streets.

KENNELLY: It is. Anyone who experiences love knows the violence in it, in the tenderness. The unasked questions that prompted Moriarty to say what he did and which I'll think about are in everything, and especially as regards the violent element. Images that come into the mind as you've loved somebody. . . . I don't think that any active psyche, any stirred imagination, anyone who loves intensely can be freed from the terrors and the horrors of love.

PINE: Did Judas love Christ?

KENNELLY: Yes, loved him, admired him, studied him, and pestered him and wanted to know certain things about him and, therefore, of himself; wanted to know if he could do certain things with him, and put himself to the test of his consciousness and the limits of his consciousness; asked himself the questions: "Dare I do this?" "Can I do this?" My Judas, of course, would just like to be my God, my Christ, my capacity to imagine them, him. The Judas I have in mind is a comic, intelligent, sympathetic, detached, vigilant observer, reluctant to participate in life, irritated by triviality and folly; and with designs, with plans for people, and then not easily putting up with people who violated his plans; into sexuality and yet realizing its ultimate inadequacy and its fascination.

One of the things that has intrigued me always is the idea of the kiss. I've a long section of the poem about kissing—this kissing, this intermingling of germs, if you will, on the one hand, and this helpless display of something, on the other, mouth to mouth. The idea that a man will walk up to another and kiss him—we are told that Judas kissed him on the side of the face; that's okay; he well may have—on the butt of the ear or the forehead, Adam's apple, or right on the mouth, and that this was the stroke of treachery, the sign, the recognition, the moment given to the soldiers to move in, to the world to move in, fingering: Judas the *fingerer*, a beautiful word, in the context. Then I make that a criticism of various forms, whether you fuck life, kiss it, finger it, stroke it, caress it: What does poetry do? What does the novel do? What have I tried to do in my work? Have I messed up my own life up in some way? Have I betrayed myself?

PINE: It touches life somewhere, and what you're interested in is how, in what way, it touches? What you're saying about the ultimate need for betrayal of the beloved as an affirmation of the self accords closely with what Brian Friel and Tom Kilroy have recently been pursuing: the need for betrayal.

KENNELLY: These men understand politics and history. I have tried to understand it in *Cromwell*, but I have to admit that what interests me is the man and sex and friendship. Maybe we should go back to the village, to the idea of intimacy and closeness. I like intimate things, the intimate ways of connecting with people. I see betrayal of that in education: that you do educate certain vital impulses out of you and that our language becomes too careful; you betray your capacity for spontaneity.

What interests me, man to man, is this friendship thing. How many friends have I? I'm fifty-three. How many friends have I known? What is a friend? That's the kind of question at the back of it all. It's true that in pushing forward toward your death you're pushing forward toward some definition or oblivion or some ultimate, mocking laughter, and I'm trying to ask the question, What do I do as I push forward? The Judas thing of my treatment of friends, my experience of friendship, my experience of education—that intrigues me. What have I gained? What have I lost? How have I affected people? Have I loved enough? Have I betrayed enough? Have I betrayed so that somebody could become himself or herself? Morality says, "No, not that, ever." But who knows consequences? If Judas had not betrayed Christ, would you have loved anybody as you do? Would your consciousness be absolutely different? Would you be capable of the kind of interests or passions that you have or the guilt or the fear of the nightmare?

PINE: There's another side to morality, which also has its own morality?

KENNELLY: Absolutely. I think that it's possible, as you push toward your honesty, you can become honest enough not to bother with morality. You can become so honest that you have to create morality for your life, and I would like to write honestly. I don't think I've done it yet.

Hugh Leonard
Interviewed by S. F. Gallagher

I have no political leanings, but my plays do *not* want for
social commitment. . . . This accusation of "shallowness" is an
old and handy tag. It simply isn't true, but because my plays
have proved popular, then *something* must be wrong with
them.

—Hugh Leonard

HUGH LEONARD—the pen name of John Keyes Byrne—was born in Dublin in 1926 and, but for a sojourn of several years in England, has lived in
Dalkey, a small coastal town on the southern outskirts of Dublin and
habitat of a remarkable number of Irish writers and performers. Playwright, adapter, journalist, theater critic, and book reviewer, Leonard has
also served as a literary editor at the Abbey Theatre and as program
director for the Dublin Theatre Festival, to which he has contributed no
less than eighteen original plays or adaptations.

Leonard's adaptations include several screenplays for television, works by
Georges Simenon, Dickens, Emily Brontë, A. Conan Doyle, Doestoevsky,
Somerset Maugham, Flaubert, Wilkie Collins, H. E. Bates, Chesterton,
Sean O'Faolain, Jennifer Johnston, James Plunkett, Giovanni Guareski,
Molly Keane, Somerville and Ross and, for the stage, works by Ibsen,

From *ILS* 9 (spring 1990).

Joyce, Eugene Labiche, Flann O'Brien, John McGahern, and Keith Water-house and Willis Hall. His adaptation (1967) of Frank O'Connor's "Silent Song" received the Italia Prize.

Of his original plays the best known and most widely performed is the autobiographical *Da,* an outstanding success on Broadway and winner in 1978 of the Tony Award, the New York Drama Critics's Circle Award, the Outer Critics' Circle Award, and the Vernon Price Award. The film version (1987) of *Da,* starring Martin Sheen and Barnard Hughes, drew not only on the play but also on Leonard's *Home Before Night* (Bath: Chivers, 1979), an exquisite account of his early years, supplemented by *Out after Dark* (London: A. Deutsch, 1989).

Leonard's columns in *Hibernia* and, later, the *Sunday Independent* have been outspoken and controversial with public figures and celebrities as the prime target of his caustic wit: he once defined a "movement" in Irish literature as two contemporary playwrights on speaking terms. Three collections of the *Sunday Independent* columns—*Leonard's Year* (Dublin: Cana-vaun Books, 1985), *Leonard's Log* (Dublin: Brophy Books, 1987), and *Leonard's Log-Again* (Dublin: Brophy Books, 1988)—have been published by Brophy Books.[1]

The following interview was conducted in late August 1989. The allusion in Leonard's first response is to his description of his initial visit to the Abbey Theatre to see a production of Sean O'Casey's *The Plough and the Stars,* whose cast included F. J. McCormick and Cyril Cusack. It runs in part: "But it was more than the acting that made Jack [Leonard] stand outside the theatre afterwards, looking towards the roof tops for the red glow of Dublin burning that he had seen through the window of Betty Burgess' attic room. The life that roared through the play itself had spilled over from the stage, sweeping him with it so that he would never again be content just to sit and watch and applaud with the rest of them. The thought burned him like a fever" (*Home Before Night*). [S. F. Gallagher]

S. F. GALLAGHER: Can you pinpoint your initial impulse to write plays?

HUGH LEONARD: The second-last chapter of *Home Before Night* provides a kind of answer here: the experience of *The Plough and the Stars* at the Abbey.[2] I had always wanted to be a writer and made a few abortive beginnings; when I took part in amateur drama, my ambitions swung further toward play writing. It is hard to nail down an impulse; rather, one is looking back at an evolution.

GALLAGHER: In your early years as a playwright were there significantly encouraging or discouraging experiences?

LEONARD: I remember a most encouraging review from a critic named Coton in the *Daily Telegraph*—a comparison with O'Casey, actually!—which was my first "green light." A later *Telegraph* critic would say that I wasn't a playwright at all, but an adapter, so there was a canceling out. I wasn't encouraged, but didn't expect to be: Ireland isn't that sort of place. Besides, the "free-lunch" syndrome applies—what you get you pay for later. I just ploughed on. I had no knowledge or expectations of the future.

GALLAGHER: You spent most of the 1960s in England. Was that a useful or rewarding period?

LEONARD: In England I wrote for television for nine months of the year and a theater play in the remaining three, usually for the festival here. I liked writing for television; I found it challenging and could alternate adapting with original work.

GALLAGHER: During the 1970s several of your plays premiered at the Olney Theater in Maryland. How did your association with Olney come about?—end?

LEONARD: A sad question! Jim Waring directed the "Olney plays." He presented *Stephen D.* and did a play of mine yearly in summer stock. Then I wrote *Da* expressly for the theater there. We shared a New York agent, Gilbert Parker of William Morris Agency. When, at long last, *Da* was to receive not a Broadway production but, to our disappointment, an off-off-Broadway showing with the actors receiving only carfare, Gil asked Jim if he would direct it for one hundred dollars a week. Jim said he couldn't afford to, and so we looked elsewhere. Later, when the play was a success, others said that Jim *Year* said, "the theater, like children, is often ungrateful." I think Jim himself came to

believe this. In an interview he said that "Leonard made easy decisions," forgetting that it was he who made the decisions. Olney had
done *Stephen D., Madigan's Lock,* and *The Patrick Pearse Motel* before *Da*
and afterward did *Summer, Irishmen (A Suburb of Babylon),* and *A Life—*
they turned down *Time Was* as too far out!—but there has been a
definite cooling on Jim's part.

GALLAGHER: *Da* had a lengthy run—about seven hundred performances?—
in New York and swept almost every award for which it was eligible.
What other plays of yours were performed there, and how did they
fare?

LEONARD: *Stephen D.* was the subject of Clive Barnes's first-ever notice
for the *New York Times*[3]—a good review, but not an outright rave, so it
didn't transfer to Broadway. *The Au Pair Man* played the Lincoln Center and won a Tony nomination; but Charlie Durning was hopelessly
miscast, even if the play launched his career. I begged "them" to let
me cut the play, but dear Julie Harris was too fond of it. As New
York drew near, cuts *had* to be made, and there was a hacking job—
not done by me. *A Life* got respectable notices, but Roy Dotrice
wasn't right for it nor was the director, Peter Coe. They were all we
could get, but we needed a star and a warmer treatment. We won
another "posthumous" Tony nomination.

GALLAGHER: What were the swings and roundabouts of transposing *Da* to
film?

LEONARD: It took five years to get *Da* from Olney to Broadway, and the
film took another nine—1978 to 1987. The deal—sell the play and
for me to write a script—took eons; I think I was lost in the vastness
of the William Morris Agency. Then the Russell Murphy debacle happened.[4] I wanted to put back some of the money, so I parted company
with Gil Parker and the play was sold within three weeks. It took
another three years for the production money to be raised; meanwhile,
one forgot the whole thing and went on writing.

The film of *Da* gave me great scope to open the play out and catch the flavor of the town and its surrounds, particularly the Enderly garden where the filming was done among my father's roses. Significantly, though, the bit that worked best was the "drowning" of the dog because it was cinematic. Film depends on images, drama on words, and in that sense the film *Da* must always remain a non-film.

GALLAGHER: Why do you consider *Summer* your best, though not your favorite, play? What is your favorite play, and why?

LEONARD: *Da* is my favorite play. It has been good to me—as simple as that. *Summer* I no longer think to be my best. I considered it so because I brought off a very difficult feat: static, naturalistic but dramatic. On balance, though, I think *A Life* is a better play; it cuts deeper. Have you noticed that all my plays are coping with the advent of death—an anticipation?

GALLAGHER: Have there been productions of, or performances in, your plays that you would regard as definitive, or even as close to such?

LEONARD: The first Jim Waring production of *Summer* and the Broadway opening of *Da*—these were as good as one would expect. And there was a significant showing of *Some of My Best Friends Are Husbands* at Watford, north of London—quite perfect, but the critics didn't come out to see it.

GALLAGHER: Which of your adaptations for the stage do you regard as most successful? And of your numerous adaptations for television?

LEONARD: *Stephen D.* was greatly acclaimed, but I thought it a scissors-and-paste job; it left me cold. *The Passion of Peter Ginty* (*Peer Gynt*) was good, I thought. On television, I liked adapting O'Faolain's "Dividends," O'Connor's "Legal Aid" and "The Mad Lomasneys," and H. E. Bates's "The Four Beauties."[5]

GALLAGHER: Have you ever consciously modeled your own work on that of another dramatist?

LEONARD: Not really. I have always admired structure and enjoyed Lennox Robinson. I loved his *Church Street* but haven't seen or read it in years. And I revered Kaufman and Hart[6] as supreme architects.

GALLAGHER: What has been your most disappointing experience as a dramatist?

LEONARD: I don't dwell on disappointments. *Kill* should have been given a second chance, I feel, and the hostility of certain colleagues, Friel and Murphy,[7] is stupid, self-defeating, and depressing if one broods on it. One doesn't.

GALLAGHER: How would you respond to those who readily acknowledge your craftsmanship but find your plays lacking in social and political commitment?

LEONARD: How on earth *can* one respond? I am much quoted for saying that in Ireland there is much genius and absolutely no talent. *Genius* absolves one of the right to learn one's craft. I have no political leanings, but my plays do *not* want for social commitment. See *The Patrick Pearse Motel;* Da's inability to question and rebel against his exploiters; the moral issue in *A Life*—who are the most valuable? Lar, who is idle, shiftless, untrustworthy, boozy, and yet life-embracing? or Drumm, who is scrupulous, honest, industrious, and misanthropic? This accusation of "shallowness" is an old and handy tag. It simply isn't true, but because my plays have proved popular, then *something* must be wrong with them.

GALLAGHER: On balance, have you been helped or hampered by critics and reviewers?

LEONARD: I remember a bad review until bedtime and a good one as far as tomorrow, and that's the end of it. Answer: neither.

GALLAGHER: Like Shaw's, O'Casey's, and others', your formal education was limited, yet your writing bristles with literary allusions. When did you do most of your obviously extensive and intensive reading?

LEONARD: The Dun Laoghaire Carnegie Library was my university. I read omnivorously, preferring to read plays, seeing them in my head, than go to the theater, where actors and directors got between me and the playwright. I read on trams, buses, walking, over meals, on park benches—wherever. Still do.

GALLAGHER: At risk of my sounding a bit like Drumm in *Da*, who are your all-time favorite authors?

LEONARD: I liked L. A. G. Strong,[8] who wrote novels about the roads I walk everyday. He taught me the value and uniqueness of what we take for granted, the life we foolishly try to shed like a snake sloughs off its skin. I liked O'Faolain and O'Connor when I was growing up. Alan Coren[9] is a humorist I admire. Alan Ayckbourn[10] is a superb dramatist, but he is "darkening." I liked J. B. Priestly,[11] but he isn't wearing well. And I think Feydeau[12] is the daddy of us all.

GALLAGHER: Assuming that, apart from the books you review, you still find time for reading, what do you most like to read?

LEONARD: I read biography. As a film buff, I'll read almost anything about cinema, even trash. I have almost ceased to read fiction entirely; I have no idea why, especially since I have written the first chapter of a novel.

GALLAGHER: In a similar vein, what do you like or dislike in contemporary theater?

LEONARD: As said, I like Ayckbourn, Sondheim.[13] In Shakespeare, *Much Ado* and *Twelfth Night*. Beckett's *Happy Days*—unbearably moving. I dislike whatever reeks of the author's contempt for his audience, the disdain for entertainment, even at its highest level . . . the humorless self-indulgences of John Arden[14] . . . the emptiness, while admiring the skill, of Pinter.[15]

GALLAGHER: Given the popular and critical success of your first autobiographical novel, *Home Before Night*, have you revised your earlier (1972) opinion: "I don't think I'm very good at writing stories. I tie myself in knots with prose."?

LEONARD: Yes, I have revised my opinion. Writing *Home Before Night* wasn't half as hellish as writing a play, and much of *Out after Dark* was at times a pleasure cruise. The trick was in accepting that in writing "stories" you can afford to give yourself elbow room; you struggle, you drown, you float, you survive.

GALLAGHER: The publication of *Out after Dark,* your second volume of autobiography, is imminent.[16] How far does it take us? Are you planning a third volume?

LEONARD: *Out after Dark* is not a sequel but the other face of the coin. It ends as I become a professional writer, and its theme is how we spend the time waiting for "real" life to begin. There will be *no* third volume.

GALLAGHER: More than a few people thought it odd that you were not among those invited to the International Writers' Conference held in Dun Laoghaire last year as part of the Dublin Millenium celebrations. I've read that you were "publicly hurt" by—and "publicly resented a private suggestion by Seamus Heaney" apropos of—that exclusion. Perhaps your provocative address to the Monaco 1986 conference on "Irishness in a Changing Society"[17] had something to do with with it? Care to comment?

LEONARD: I wasn't at all upset by not being invited to the conference—I wouldn't have subjected myself to the boredom, if invited—but wanted to highlight the fact that I had been excluded, in short, that there was and is a clique. I don't know of any private suggestion by Heaney. At a meeting of the Irish Academy of Letters, I once made a passing and uncritical comment about Brian Friel, and Heaney said, quite amicably: "We can talk about him; *you* can't." I thought this strange and took it to be a Northern thing. I doubt if anyone paid any attention to the Monaco address. I wish they had!

GALLAGHER: How significant a setback was the "Russell Murphy affair"? and how well have you weathered it?

LEONARD: Russell Murphy took money that I would probably have not gotten around to spending, but it was earmarked as a bequest for my wife and daughter. It was an annoyance, but it's past. I was amazed to discover that I was not nearly as materialistic as I had thought!

GALLAGHER: May we look forward to more plays by Hugh Leonard?

LEONARD: America has *Our Town;* Wales has *Under Milkwood.*[18] No one has tried to do the same for Ireland. I'd like to have a stab at it—a play called *Moving*[19]—but won't try unless I can steer a course between Wilder and Thomas. It may not be possible. Otherwise, I really have no compulsion to write again for the theater. And, as far as my relations with the Irish critics are concerned, they may be likened to policemen watching a drunk weaving around his car, waiting to pounce if he dares get in. No, I'm not a masochist.

Medbh McGuckian

Interviewed by Kathleen McCracken

Poetry is not the servant of politics. The Troubles affect my
life and enter my poetry that way, but I avoid them as a
subject as I avoid taking arms against a sea. The crisis informs
my work, naturally, but I can't confront it there; it is too
complex. . . . I just suggest an attitude of compassion in what
is part of a universal tragedy.

—Medbh McGuckian

MEDBH McGUCKIAN WAS BORN in Belfast in 1950. She was educated at the
Dominican Convent and Queen's University, Belfast, where she com-
pleted an M.A. on Irish writers and Gothic fiction. After graduating, she
became a teacher at the Dominican Convent, then at St. Patrick's Col-
lege, Knock. She began publishing poetry in anthologies and literary
magazines in the 1970s and has published five collections to date.
Among the literary prizes she has been awarded are the British National
Poetry Society Competition (1979), the Eric Gregory Award (1980), the
Alice Hunt Bartlett Award (1983), the Cheltenham Award and the Bass
Ireland Award for Literature (1991). *Marconi's Cottage* (Oldcastle, Ireland:
Gallery Press: 1991; Newcastle-upon-Tyne: Bloodaxe Books, and Wins-
ton-Salem, N.C.: Wake Forest University Press, 1992) was a Poetry Ire-
land Choice (1991). Medbh's term as writer-in-residence at Queen's
University, Belfast, marked the initial appointment of a woman to that

From *ILS* 9 (fall 1990).

post. She has been visiting fellow at the University of California, Berkeley (1991), and is currently writer-in-residence at the University of Ulster. She lives in Belfast with her husband John McGuckian, their three sons, and one daughter.

Medbh's early poems were published in two pamphlets, *Single Ladies* (Budleigh Salterton, Eng.: Interim Press, 1980) and *Portrait of Joanna* (Belfast: Ulsterman Publications, 1980). Shaped by the outbreak of the Troubles in 1969 and by her involvement in the "second wave" of the Group at Queen's University, these poems introduced a voice at once lyrical and disturbing in its probing of intimate psychological dramas and its delineation of feminine perspectives. The sometimes threatening domestic interiors and the proliferation of flower, water, and lunar imagery of her subsequent collections *The Flower Master* (Oxford: Oxford University Press, 1982), *Venus and the Rain* (Oldcastle, Ireland: Gallery Press; Oxford: Oxford University Press, 1984), and *On Ballycastle Beach* (Oxford: Oxford University Press; Winston-Salem, N.C.: Wake Forest University Press, 1988), position marriage, pregnancy, and birth as definitive experiences in women's struggle for artistic autonomy. Medbh's persistent exploration of the territory between physical and emotional realities combined with her technical experimentation with speech patterns and traditional form continue to inform the poems in *Marconi's Cottage, Captain Lavender* (Oldcastle, Ireland: Gallery Press, 1994; Winston-Salem, N.C.: Wake Forest University Press, 1995) where increasingly sophisticated structural and thematic dynamics allow for acute examination of notions about masculinity and femininity, and political divisions in Northen Ireland.

This interview took place at Medbh's summer home near Ballycastle during the summer of 1987. At that time she had just completed her third major collection of poetry, *On Ballycastle Beach*, the "late summer house" and environs of whose title piece had framed our conversations. The original discussion was discursive, meandering, instructive, revelatory. What survived into print is a distillation, the kernel of those talks about early influences, feminism and female writing, motherhood, politics, the importance of place. [Kathleen McCracken]

KATHLEEN McCRACKEN: Could you say something about your literary background?

MEDBH McGUCKIAN: I was a fellow student of Paul Muldoon's[1] at university in the early 1970s, and Seamus Heaney taught me. On the other hand, the Bible, hymns, and missal of the Catholic Church are what I think imbued me earliest and deepest. I feel I exist somewhere on the Tree of Poetry on the same limb as Blake and Yeats but many phone calls below them.

McCRACKEN: One tends to look at other women writers, Eiléan Ní Chuilleanáin or Eavan Boland,[2] for instance, for points of contact, but the poet whose style and outlook seem closest to your own is Paul Muldoon. Would you agree?

McGUCKIAN: I find that Eiléan deals in philosophy and abstraction while Eavan's territory is domestic and middle class. Perhaps I'm nearer to Nuala Ní Dhomhnaill's[3] earthiness than to Paul's wit and irony. I feel his subtlety of rhyme and mastery of form is something I'll never reach. There is also a detachment and coolness that I don't share. He might be the one I would emulate most, though, or be most anxious not to disappoint.

McCRACKEN: How do you see your growth as a poet?

McGUCKIAN: Do I see it? I feel very much a child there, though a mature woman physically. I feel positively embryonic, and yet what I'm writing now does seem at once more innocent and more experienced than it was. I see my growth as intersecting my physical prime or decline. I do feel less alone than I did. I just write about the unbearable heaviness of being, at the minute at least.

McCRACKEN: Do you choose to write poetry as opposed to fiction?

McGUCKIAN: Yes, although my stories come in and out of my head when I feel poetically ill.

McCRACKEN: Do you have any ambitions to write literary criticism or drama?

McGUCKIAN: No, ambition lies elsewhere. If I were ambitious, it would be to love, but I am not. Literary criticism seems very loveless, but I like sometimes to review other poetry or women's books. I do not know enough people well enough to attempt a play. I do dream films, like everyone else.

MCCRACKEN: Much of what "happens" in your poetry seems personally very near to the bone. In what ways do you find the poems translate fact into something that is beyond private experience?

MCGUCKIAN: I would say near to the flesh or to the blood. They don't so much translate fact as build fantasy on fact. I'm not sure they don't remain private, at least until some scholar totally identifies with me. When I read one, I know who it was for, what I felt, what they felt, or what I felt they felt. Many are about deaths, which could not be other than a fantasy for me, although such a fact for the bereaved or the dead. I would have to look at each poem to describe the ways. Each one is different. But there's usually one special person the poem is a private message to. For instance, "The Time Before You" is a funeral rite for Paul leaving Belfast and highly personal, yet since his presence meant so much to so many, I think I speak for many of us. Emigration is a common tragedy here, so it is about that and could be my mother to my brother in New Zealand.

MCCRACKEN: There is in your poems what I feel is a collision—or is it collusion?—between an apparently innocent domestic surface and a sinister, menacing environment. Is this an effect you work for? Do you intend it to explore any specific thematic?

MCGUCKIAN: I have a poem called "Collusion" about a begonia that was staked up artificially, and used this as a symbol of my guilt feelings about using contraceptive oral tablets. I think the menace comes from within, and our nature is capable of such deception that it's sinister to me in itself. I am sinister to myself. The environment is an inner one; the sea and sky are mental attributes. I suppose it is the old microcosm thing. I do tend to explore the delicate balance of the human and female organism, which can suddenly soar or drop from productivity to sterility.

MCCRACKEN: One adjective that has been applied to your work is mysterious. Do you hope your poems will establish and retain an element of mystery?

McGUCKIAN: In O'Casey's[4] sense of the mystery of a woman being a mystery no longer, I would not hope for that quality of enticement and disillusion. I hope my poems will draw the reader into the particular mesh of thoughts and nexus of feelings, but I hope in the end to have spelled something out clearly. If the poem is swallowed whole, it won't be digested. I want it to become part of the person, as I might recite a line from Dylan Thomas without understanding, but for the music. A rose dissected loses its perfume but is still a miracle of creation or a work of art whatever its biology.

I don't mind if part of the poem remains elusive, but most of it, with attention to the actual meaning, should yield a definite meaning. Too many poems are all meaning and no reserve. They are no more mysterious than a woman can help being to herself. Sometimes a specialized knowledge throws up a volcano of meaning, but aestheticians would say the question of meaning and who gives or takes it is a vexed one. Those whose main pleasure is from ignorance had better not be informed. I think my poems travel on a spectrum, and what would mean one thing to a child of ten would mean another to a farmer of forty or an academic of sixty. I think I want to surprise rather than boggle. Language has been devitalized by advertising and news; poetry must almost dismantle the letters.

McCRACKEN: Each of your books concentrates on certain images and symbols—flowers and seeds, stitching and sketching, light and water—which give the volume unity and texture. Your entire oeuvre might be described as a seedbed where tulips, daffodils, gentians, and orchids complement a macrocosm of insects, crustaceans, leaves, and fossils. Do you work toward an interlinking design as you write the poems? or do patterns emerge when they are set together?

McGUCKIAN: Flowers and seeds preoccupied me when I was germinating myself, as a young mother, or when I was first married. Art always concerns me as a subject—hence the stitching and sketching. Light and water belong to a broader, more mature consideration of the elements and our place as 99 percent or whatever in them. The other kinds of life serve sometimes as mirrors. I invest certain things with my own associations, but generally what a word brings to mind is what I mean by it. Sand is nearly always suggestive of time ebbing and decay, the sea of the opposite. Patterns only emerge when the poems are grouped and I see what I've repeated subconsciously. For instance, the last word of part 1 of *On Ballycastle Beach* is *dark,* and the last word of part 2 is *light,* but I didn't do that intentionally though the significance is what I must have intended.

MCCRACKEN: The term *metaphysical* seems to give an apt indication of the way your poems operate. Do you feel you are working somewhere within the tradition established by Donne, Herbert, and others?

MCGUCKIAN: I've been called religious, and it is Blake who says God is the true subject of all art. I think it is fair to say I feel part of that heritage, closest to Hopkins and Eliot, with a sense and sensuousness clashing with sensibility. As a trained Catholic, Heaney also is imbued with rituals and observations and guilt. As an adolescent, I sublimated a desire to be a priest, as these poets actually were, and like Keats, had to be content with being "Nature's eremite."[5] (Chaucer had succeeded in putting me off nuns absolutely.[6]) I envied the priest's role and his sacred inviolability, his oratorical authority, the silence he could command and the spells he could bind, his special knowledge. Yet real priests were so much more frail than laymen, so proud and blind, so abusive of their power; I am terrified of becoming proud as a poet. It would cancel everything out.

I hope I don't preach or moralize, but if I'm erotic, maybe *agapé* has a lot to do with it. People say the first seven years of life are the source of all poetry, and my state then was centrally Christian. I was baptized and sinless; dreams go back to perfection, and that's what you aim for.

MCCRACKEN: Would you concede that your poetry is antirealist and anti-surrealist, that it resists both mimesis and the symbolic to interrogate formal and contextual conventions more thoroughly?

MCGUCKIAN: I'm not anti-anything, but I don't depict the real world or represent it. I think *interrogate* is the right word since these conventions are traditionally male and don't belong to me. But I do play around with some kinds of symbols—houses and gardens, for instance. I don't set these up as being perfect expressions. I suppose what I set up in one poem I knock down in the next.

McCRACKEN: From 1986 to 1988 you were writer-in-residence at the Queen's Univerity in Belfast. Did you find this a rewarding experience in terms of your own writing?

McGUCKIAN: In terms of my writing, yes. I was free partially, at least, from a full-time teaching post to write creatively and get paid for it. My job as wife and mother still took priority, but my poems lengthened, dallied, wavered in a way they had not done. Psychologically, it was a disaster because I was made so aware of my age and loneliness; but I met some good young poets and will, I hope, continue to be friends with them.

McCRACKEN: Do you intend your poems to speak mostly about yourself and your world? or do you also want them to express communal points of view?

McGUCKIAN: Sometimes, I think I am very odd; sometimes, that everyone is like me. So when I feel out of line, I want to express that, and when I feel the same, I want to express that universality. I feel as a woman I am sharing most things; as a poet I share only with a few.

McCRACKEN: Would you agree with the statement that your poetry is "a mimesis of a distinctly feminine experience of the world"?

McGUCKIAN: I would like to agree. It certainly is not a masculine experience. It's mostly moody and menstrual in a way a man's poetry never is. Its subject matter is the sea and its flux, the world of water and matter that females dominate or that dominates them. I would say it is the experience of a mammal. Men don't like to think of themselves as mammals; we have to. I've tried to write poems about the special feminine experience, but not very successfully. You're cutting through forest and rock, like menarche, the first penetration, the first orgasm, the first birth, the recovery from that, the acceptance of the beginning of the end of fertility.

McCRACKEN: In your view is the dreamlike, surreal quality of your work generated by a conscious dislocation of syntax and semantics, part of what one critic has called a "feminine or feminist antilogic"?

McGUCKIAN: I don't dislocate things deliberately. I don't think my language is irrational: it has its own logic which may be the opposite of men's since we are of the opposite sex. I feel utterly opposite and utterly the reverse, not a mirror image: but where they end or leave off, I start; where they have a fullness, I have an emptiness; where they have an emptiness, I have a fullness. I am not against sense; I am just following my own sense. The dislocation is unconscious or guided by it. I feel everything from within, and most women's reflexes are deeply hidden. It's like the center of the earth that has its own mountains and rainfall, parallel to the surfaces but all internally controlled. It depends whether Blake was right or wrong to say of Wordsworth, "there is no such thing as natural piety" because to him nature was evil, and Satan was the self.[7]

McCRACKEN: Many of your poems are either spoken by or are about women. Whether they give voice to an isolated consciousness or focus on male/female relations, the perspective is almost always that of the woman. Do you consider yourself a feminist writer?

McGUCKIAN: I'm beginning, at this point, to identify more closely with women. Before, I think I was trying to compete with men or be androgynous and to appeal as much to one sex as to the other, to old people and children who fade into sexlessness. But my being a woman at this stage seems all-embracing of my life and dominates it. My poems are taken more seriously by women; men often dismiss them or like them for the wrong reasons. So sometimes I think the majority of my audience is female. I find young girls especially responsive to them. Young men are generally bewildered. I'm not feminist in an angry way. I've not been ungenerously treated, and men don't make me feel inferior, on the whole.

McCRACKEN: Is the muse masculine or feminine?

McGUCKIAN: To me a muse is the driving force of the poem. The person concerned may be male or female. If the emotion is passion or desire, it's likely to be a male love-object. If it's sympathy or empathy or an equal feeling, it's probably a female friend. I might pretend to be a man in love with a woman to intensify the course of things. I can make use of a muse for a single poem and then abandon it or be abandoned. Recently I've not written a sequence to the same person, which does not mean flightiness, just a reservation of involvement.

McCRACKEN: Mothers and children are important figures in your poetry. The cover illustration of *Venus and the Rain*, a detail from Jan Toorop's "The Younger Generation,"[8] shows a mother watching over her daughter. A recent poem is entitled "Girl-Mother and Child." Are these references present for purely autobiographical reasons? or do they have a larger significance within your mythology?

McGUCKIAN: I have an obsession with the mother/daughter relationship due to my own complex, one-way experience of it. Having no daughter makes me constantly search for one. I don't find Persephone very useful as a theme, and it's worn out anyway. The *Venus* book was a postnatal darkness and dealt with how birth is the suggestion of death, even its symbol, or how life is stolen. I have Catholic tattoo marks about the Madonna and Christmas cards: the mother/son relationship is sacred rather than Oedipal in my race memory. I personally am convinced if I had not had children my poetry would have been very different, like skimmed milk. I am going against the traditional childless woman-artist grain, but most Irish women poets have a highly developed maternal dimension, and many write even while their babies are young. I find de Beauvoir's[9] sterility a killing of a vital part, lessening one knowledge while increasing others.

McCRACKEN: Does your role as wife and mother complement or disturb the poetry?

McGUCKIAN: When I'm balanced, the roles can be juggled evenly. I switch smoothly enough from the backseat of domestic responsibilities to the exciting driver's wheel of poetry. But I can't carry both things at once. The children have to be unconscious, asleep, before I can write,

and my husband and I must be at peace with each other. Any disturbance and I can't fulfill either function. It's very delicate, very fine; I
fall off the wire about twice a week. Most difficult is to go away and
do readings; most easy is to sit at my desk and juggle the words.

McCRACKEN: A 1983 survey showed only 11 percent of the books published in Ireland were by women. Of these, 9 percent were published
by Arlen House, the only women's press in Ireland at that time. The
Attic Press hopes to remedy the situation. How do you view the status
of women writers in Ireland? Where do they stand in an international
context?

McGUCKIAN: I noted at the recent International Poetry Conference in
Dublin that only two Irish women were included, neither of them
poets. Women writers here are still very much out on a limb and
considered eccentric. I find my work is taken more seriously in America than in Europe although I've been assured I am "very big in Es-
tonia." I think countries that understand oppression understand women
and, therefore, Irish women, with their dual form of it. Status is not
the same as achievement: whatever respect we command we must earn
with great difficulty. To be considered equal to men you have to outdo
them, which is not very acceptable.

McCRACKEN: Several of the younger poets—Nuala Ní Dhomnaill, Michael Davitt, Caitlín Maude—have returned to writing their verse in
Irish. Have you considered making this move?

McGUCKIAN: No, because it is not even my subconscious language, although I've attempted to translate Nuala because she's so brilliant and
dynamic. But Irish was imposed on me in such a parochial way I still
have a horror of it, like the chill I feel in the Gaeltacht areas.

McCRACKEN: Do you feel any connection with ancient Irish women
poets?

McGUCKIAN: I guess I must feel a deep tribal kinship. I called my son Oisín
after the male poet and might have called a daughter Líadan.[10] I don't
know enough about them. I am more imaginatively stirred by the warrior-
queens, Grainuale and my namesake.[11] I feel even less continuity with Eva

Gore-Booth and Katherine Tynan,[12] since, again, I have no knowledge of them historically. But Maire O'Neill[13] had a legendary, magical influence as a native mystic and folklorist from my own landscape. Her monotony and impersonality hurt me into art, like mad Ireland.

McCRACKEN: *Venus and the Rain* is dedicated to your mother and your mother-in-law. There is a poem to your grandmother. In what ways have familial connections contributed to your writing?

McGUCKIAN: My first book is dedicated to my husband and son, my third to my father and second son. My fourth book, if it happens, will be for my three sisters. I have poems in it for all my sisters and brothers, for my aunts. Blood and blood-links of all kinds are so basic that they are inevitable material. The maternal instinct is one even motherless and orphaned women poets find fascinating. I feel as a person very similar to my mother's mother, who was at once gregarious and superstitious. My strongest female impressions are of her. Also, I think women can be mothers and daughters to each other, perhaps even more tenderly than through the blood-tie—in the tie of marriage, the bond of friendship, the academic or literary world. The family is an institution that in Ireland is both a curse and a blessing: one constantly spurns it and returns to it. It's so closely connected to Joyce's nets[14] that most of us need to keep redefining what it means. I don't think I do that any more than others, divorced or not, divorce being the ultimate gesture of family defiance.

McCRACKEN: Place—geographically and historically—seems to shape your perception of people and events. To what extent do you feel your places enter into the poetry?

McGUCKIAN: Place is a metaphysical as well as a geographical and histori-cal concept for me. When you say *"your* places," I immediately think of places on the map of the body. I don't really perceive people and events through place, but, certainly, the people here are colored by the events that make the place so important. I began to name places in order to exorcise them; perhaps I should name the people instead. Belfast as "my" city interacts symbolically with rural childhood memories of County Antrim and County Down. I guess I am an urban poet trying to be a nature worshipper.

McCRACKEN: Your poetry suggests that, like many Northern Irish writers, your preferred position is that of an outsider, an observer of, rather than a participant in, political and religious disputes. Do you have any fixed political allegiance, and if you do, is that bias consciously eliminated from your poetry?

McGUCKIAN: I don't have a fixed allegiance. I have inherited grievances, but while these *are* consciously eliminated, they subconsciously obtrude. No one here can be an observer. Everyone has lost someone or been scarred over twenty years. More than half of my life—all my adult life—has taken place in this war. It's impossible not to see the poetry as a flower or defense mechanism, so the relationship is a complex one. I'm not, however, a political animal.

McCRACKEN: Several of your contemporaries, the so-called younger generation of Ulster poets, have, like many of their literary forebears, gone to live in the Republic, England, or North America. What makes you stay in Belfast?

McGUCKIAN: I lived outside Belfast when first married and couldn't stand it. On a cold night, Belfast is warm. It could be that it's home. My family is here; there is a hardness; people are sharp and humorous and share ironies and a knowledge that make elsewhere naive. One side of me recoils from the place; another can live or write nowhere else. Maybe I need the tension. I can't see myself moving, except farther north. Other poets have been males, free to follow their careers, whereas my husband works here, and his job is not a flexible one, nor he a flexible person.

McCRACKEN: Seamus Heaney once referred to those writers at work in the North as "a very necessary and self-sustaining group." You are one of a number of Ulster poets, including Michael Longley, Derek Mahon, Paul Muldoon,[15] and Frank Ormsby, who have gained international recognition in the past two decades. There is talk of an Ulster Revival, a Northern School. Do you have a sense of being a member of a definite movement? and if so, how would you define it?

McGUCKIAN: I have a certain sense of membership because of groupings and anthologies. Heaney's being a Catholic and speaking for Catholics made success seem not impossible. That there were women writing in the South also made me feel a kinship with *that* subculture. Paul and Frank were contemporaries I could talk to as friends and with mutual respect. I've never had the same intimacy with the older poets; their generation has problems with women that extend to women poets. Reading these poets was part of my education, but we've no common aims other than to uphold our traditions and to ply our trade when we've learned it. I feel attempts to draw *me* into a scheme are difficult since my subject-matter and style are so different.

McCRACKEN: While you refrain from addressing the "Troubles" directly, the pervasive social and psychological disturbance implied by the euphemism can, I believe, be detected in the imagery and rhythms of many of your poems. Is this a subject you avoid? Do you feel that Northern Irish writers must necessarily confront the ongoing crisis in their work?

McGUCKIAN: Poetry is not a servant of politics. The "Troubles" affect my life and enter my poetry that way, but I avoid them as a subject as I avoid taking arms against a sea. The crisis informs my work, naturally, but I can't confront it there; it is too complex. What other writers do is not for me to lay down. If they live in England and America, outspokenness is easier because safer. I have touched on the subject implicitly in poems like "The Dovecote," written at the time of the hunger strikes, or "The Blue She Brings with Her," for a mother whose son was destroyed. But one could argue that I don't deal with or solve anything; I just suggest an attitude of compassion in what is part of a universal tragedy.

McCRACKEN: Do women writers have any particular responsibility to come to terms with this issue?

McGUCKIAN: The responsibility of a woman writer is to fulfill her art. If it means making political commitments or public statements, then she must decide. I can't generalize. I just don't feel any onus on *me* in particular to limit my mind or distance my vision by supping on horrors. It's not an issue that one can come to terms with, at least directly, in poetry. All a poet can do now is warn, said Wilfred Owen over seventy years ago. I think he would say that now they cannot do even that. Yeats set an absurdly rhetorical example which I don't feel able to follow. Also, it got him too involved with reality: being a senator marred his vocation.[16]

McCRACKEN: Is it possible to talk about a Catholic as opposed to a Protestant writer? Are differences in sensibility evident in the language, subject-matter, and cadences of the poetry?

McGUCKIAN: If it were not possible, there would be no "Troubles." The English hierarchy went to extremes here to make it so. But it's not fruitful to engage in debate about exactly where Frank Ormsby ceases to be a Catholic and becomes a Protestant writer, or the motives of Derek Mahon and Tom Paulin in attempting to do the reverse. There are broad similarities among Louis MacNeice, John Hewitt, and James Simmons as there are among Patrick Kavanagh, Heaney, and Muldoon—the poetry of the settler as opposed to the poetry of the outsider. It would take a full-length thesis that would become so controversially hurtful that it would militate against the power of poetry to heal wounds, to bridge divisions. All of them are only too capable of biting satire and savagery, and where the venom remains unresolved there is no poetry, however many cadences.

McCRACKEN: There are obvious linguistic differences between Irish, Irish-English, and English, most notably in melody, intonation, and diction. But are there also qualities which distinguish an Irish from an English poet, a Northern Irish poet from one writing in the South?

McGUCKIAN: The Irish poet will differ from the English in his sense of security though it depends whether the English poet is a WASP or a woman. The Northern Irish poet will also differ from the Southerner in a *different* sense of security. The Northern Protestant will have the sense that what precious little security he has or had is disappearing, the Northern Catholic the sense that he has never had any security anyway and is not likely to find any. So the position and equality of the last is the most existential of all, and being a woman to boot removes the last drop of wind from your sails, so you might as well be a love poet or a prophet and forget all capitals.

Eavan Boland

Interviewed by Nancy Means Wright and
Dennis J. Hannan

I'm not a separatist. I would be much more subversive by
inclination. Ireland is a country with a strong history of
subversion. I think the subversions in this literature have an
interesting past. . . . I want to subvert the old forms. Where
those elements of the Irish experience are repressive, I would
rather subvert them than throw the baby out with the
bathwater.

—Eavan Boland

EAVAN BOLAND is one of the most important poets in Ireland and indeed
in any country today. Born in Dublin in 1944, the daughter of diplomat
Frederick Boland and artist Frances Kelley, Boland was schooled in London and New York as the family moved with the father's career as ambas-
sador to England and later Ireland's representative to the United Nations.
Back in Dublin, Boland attended Trinity and has lived in the Dublin area
ever since.

Boland's first book, *New Territory* (Dublin: Allen Figgis) came in 1967
when she was twenty-two and newly graduated from Trinity. Stereotypical of the Irish literary tradition and reflecting a Yeatsian model, the
poetry of that first book provides a baseline revealing how far Boland's
individual talent was to develop over the years. In the almost three de-

From *ILS* 10 (spring 1991).

cades that brought her to her present preeminence she has published eight books of poetry, innumerable articles, and in 1995, *Object Lessons: The Life of the Woman and the Poet in Our Time* (New York: W. W. Norton).[1] In the *American Poetry Review*'s special supplement on Boland,[2] the poet looks back over the road she has traveled since leaving her *New Territory* for more productive fields, bringing women out of silence: "out of myth into history I move to be / part of that ordeal / whose darkness is / only now reaching me from those fields."

The increasing critical acclaim of those years, however, has not eliminated the vestiges of Irish patriarchal gender prejudice from attacking Boland as a "separatist" and/or "angry" woman.[3] Nonetheless, since the time of the interview, the critical atmosphere has undergone some change for the better. Recently commenting on this improvement to us, Boland has written the following:

> I think there has been a subtle but definite shift in attitudes to Irish women over the last few years. . . . Certain public events—among them the election to the presidency of Mary Robinson—showed a new ability in Irish people to think of women and their achievements differently. And I think Mary Robinson's presidency has had a real imaginative, as well as cultural, effect in Ireland. Then again, the debates over the *Field Day Anthology of Irish Writing* made articulate the debate about the voice and vision of Irish women—and the importance of their inclusion—in anything we want to claim as a representative Irish literature. . . . Finally, however, . . . there have been more poems by Irish women poets over the last six years. . . . Paula Meehan and Rita Ann Higgins and Mary O'Malley and Phil McCarthy and Joan McBreen and Katie Donovan all have books in print now, when most of them didn't six years ago. Their poems have been the main agents of change.

Eavan Boland and her husband, novelist Kevin Casey, and their two daughters now reside in Dundrum, a Dublin suburb. Reading Rosemary Mahoney's *Whoredom in Kimmage: Irish Women Coming of Age* (Boston: Houghton Mifflin, 1993), we remembered our own visit to the comfortable Boland home: "The furniture in the small living room was arranged in a haphazard fashion. A low coffee table in the middle of the room was so overloaded with trinkets and figurines, tiny carvings, painted eggs, a pocket watch, and other small, highly detailed artifacts that the table surface was barely visible." Our visit was an afternoon of good talk, pleasantly interrupted once or twice by one of the daughters and some concern as to where the cat had disappeared. [Nancy Means Wright and Dennis J. Hannan]

NANCY MEANS WRIGHT & DENNIS J. HANNAN: A first-rate Irish woman poet would appear to receive less recognition in Ireland than even a third-rate male poet. Do you find this to be true?

EAVAN BOLAND: I was on a panel in Boston recently at a festival of Irish poetry, and exactly that point was with me. In the audience, there were a number of male poets, but I knew of five or six wonderful Irish women poets that nobody in that audience would have heard of. And the breaking-through point for them is more at risk, I think, than for the male poet. My problem is, and certainly my ethical worry is, that the woman poet doesn't even get considered: she's under so much pressure in this particular country.

WRIGHT & HANNAN: Can you describe these pressures?

BOLAND: We like to think that in a country like Ireland that is historically pressured and has been defeated and has had minorities within it, that people get the permission equally to be poets. We like to think that, but they don't. There is not an equal societal commission here for people to explore their individuality in an expressive way—for a woman to cross the distance in writing poetry to becoming a poet. "If I called myself a poet," a young woman in one of my workshops told me, "people would think I didn't wash my windows." This was a piercingly acute remark on the fracture between the perception of womanhood in a small town in the southeast of Ireland and the perception of the poet.

So the second part of the equation of not getting an equal societal permission is that I couldn't say that the people who have had permission—in other words, the bardic poets, who are male—that they have in every case generously held out their hand to these women, that they have equally encouraged them, given them a hearing. The proposals that happen under the surface to make a canon—that are subterranean and invisible—have been radically exclusive. The male writers in Ireland traditionally, in both prose and poetry, do have a kind of bardic stance; they do see themselves as inheriting a kind of bardic role. They have been disdainful of women writers with women's themes; they use language I don't think you'd see in Canada or the United States. Only recently, for example, someone well involved with literary things in Ireland got up in a conference on "Women and Writing" to complain of the "pornography of childbirth and of menstruation in Irish women's writing."

WRIGHT & HANNAN: This kind of discrimination has certainly existed in the United States.

BOLAND: Yes, but you have the huge diversity, that wonderful diversity of pressure and voices and liberalism. Ireland is a very small country, and its literary community is, over the past forty years, very staid in its perceptions. There isn't a lot of oxygen for the young woman poet, who is tremendously vulnerable to how she's perceived.

WRIGHT & HANNAN: Rita Ann Higgins, for example, the young working-class poet in Galway or Moya Cannan or Eva Bourke, who can't find their books in the Dublin bookstores?

BOLAND: Yes. There's a huge amount of literary activity going on in Galway. Jessie Lendennie was in my national workshop in 1984—a wonderful presence in it. I've known of those tentacles of energy for years, but it hasn't been easy to get any visibility for them. It's easier for me because I'm older, because I've always lived in a metropolitan area.

WRIGHT & HANNAN: Is it easier for a woman poet in academe, like yourself, to attain recognition?

BOLAND: I'm not in academe. I was a writer-in-residence last year at Trinity and this year at University College, Dublin, but I would think of myself as academically far from grace.

Interestingly, the contemporary poetry course in Trinity this year carried not one woman poet! It's extraordinary to be taught outside in other countries and not anywhere in your own. This is the reason why when I'm in Boston I'm not inclined to be quiet or conciliatory about it: because these things have happened again and again and because they have been passively sanctioned. The male Irish poets have treated exclusion as invention, but there is absolutely no doubt that that exists. There is no give on this issue. It is a matter of fact.

WRIGHT & HANNAN: Are there academics in Ireland who would promote the work of women?—women academics? The theme for the American Conference for Irish Studies conference this fall is "Women and Children First."

BOLAND: Yes, that's very interesting. If you look back at *Éire-Ireland*, for example, there are almost no references to women's writing. The ACIS—yes, there are wonderful women there, but I think that ACIS itself has been conservative, the institution itself. The academic in Ireland has had remarkably little to do with the writing of poetry, but it has a great deal to do with the dissemination of it. The problem, I think, is a compound psycho-perception in this country that women are in many ways the caryatids of community. They hold on their shoulders the lives and the shelters—and it's not to say a great regard is not had for them—but as the unindividualized generic feminine presence.

WRIGHT & HANNAN: In your *American Poetry Review* essay, "Outside History,"[4] you rue the fact that male poets have made "the image of the woman the pretext of a romantic nationalism."

BOLAND: Certainly, and the nation is an old woman and needs to be liberated. But she's passive, and if she stops being passive and old, she becomes young and ornamental. Therefore, within our perception of women as being in the house, as being in the kitchen, holding things together, there's the perception of the male very often as the active and anarchic principle, and, therefore, nominated as male is the individual, the bardic, the dangerous, the expressive, partly because those were male, but partly because the transaction between the male and the female in literature is an active-passive one. But basically this community nominates women as the receptors of other people's creativity and not as the initiators of their own.

Then we have the church to support and give a sacro-quality to these perceptions. If you take a woman in a town which no doubt is strongly influenced by its Catholic past and its rural customs where women were counseled patience and its silent virtues—a woman who suddenly says, "Now I'm going to express myself"—that society is not going to give her the same permission as to a twenty-three-year-old male with black, curly hair. So she's already under a lesser set of permissions to explore her own gift and a greater sense of inferences that that gift is dangerous to her tradition of womanhood. These are huge pressures!

WRIGHT & HANNAN: Enough to make feminists out of women poets?

BOLAND: I think it's important that women don't have to be feminists, don't have to be anything. They just have to have enough oxygen to write. I don't care what their political persuasions are.

WRIGHT & HANNAN: You're not a separatist?

BOLAND: No, I'm not a separatist. I think that separatism in a small country like Ireland would be another form of censorship. In a funny way, being a separatist might have been advantageous to me. It would probably have made me a less suspect figure on the left of the women's movement here—who, I think, have had difficulties with me. They wouldn't see me as feminist enough, you see. It's the old story of the hare and the tortoise: they always see me as the tortoise. They don't understand that often you're just trying to get discriminatory funding out of the Arts Council so there are not six traveling fellowships for women under thirty, or artists under thirty, so that women with children can't take them up. But I think the maximum pressure should be kept up to bring these male resistances into the open.

About five years ago, you would have found male writers saying, "Yes, there are women writers." But the inference would be: "These are women writers and not Irish writers; they don't belong to the great main discourse." One very eminent Irish poet said to me in New York: "I do accept that the energies of women writing are unctioned." Big deal! It's a very-late-in-the-day recognition! You can't be congratulating people on the recognition of human rights and the expression of it. So I think male writers might consider that I have an unconciliatory pose, and I think some of the left of the movement, as I said, too moderate. So it's an awkward position.

WRIGHT & HANNAN: Your themes come out of women's experience. Won't the male poets and critics continue to object to that?

BOLAND: But it's the male poets who are separatist, you see; this is their separatism. They want to say: "There's a niche for this, a category for this. There's a cupboard for this—we can get rid of her; this is women's poetry." I certainly call myself a woman poet, and I don't allow them to contaminate that particular category. But there is no way that they are not saying that ours are poems of human resonance and human import. I could certainly recommend to all women poets in this country that they argue on their own terms whether a poem is good or bad. We are not going to have an Irish poem to be a poem about a city or a bull or a heifer, but all the poems we write about—houses or children or suffering in the past—are women's poems. And that is where the argument is at the moment.

WRIGHT & HANNAN: You won't get into a Virginia Woolfian dialogue on the aesthetics of the female sentence?

BOLAND: No. It's wonderful to talk about, but this argument may be in a cruder stage here. I think it may be at a more pressurized stage, and the ugly part is the intimidation for a woman to write a poem, get a book together, wonder where it's going to be published, how it will be received. In other words, the ugly part in every single minority in a writing culture is, "Where does the power lie? Who has the power?"

I remember a woman poet who said to me: "I can't publish with a woman's press; I have to publish with another one so that I have credibility." To me that was a heartbreaking sentence because it represented all the oppressions women are under in this country. A well-disposed male poet said to me: "If Salmon publishes just women, which it doesn't, it will do them harm." I said, "Why will it do them harm? You have been publishing just men for years!" Tears come into these chaps' eyes because they think, here's Eavan on a social occasion, saying these hard things to me. Here is one window that is shut off. I think you must be very careful and try to open the window and not break it. You come to a point, you know, where you feel like breaking all the windows. And I have really been getting near that point.

WRIGHT & HANNAN: Can you talk about the critique in Ireland: where does it come from?

BOLAND: Everything I've been talking about is owed to the fact or emanates from the fact that the critique in this country remains obdurately male and patriarchal. It's a complex matter where a critique in a country comes from. It comes in a very simple way from the contracting out to reviewers by the literary editors, and that's a complicated system. I no longer review any Irish writers. Five years ago, I decided not to do that anymore; I wasn't going to waste time. Therefore, you have a critique partly made by the reviews contracted by the literary editors. Then there are the critiques undoubtedly made in the universities, and there's a minimum interaction between the newspapers and the universities. Then there's the sort of hum in a literary writing community which is made up of short-hands and off-the-cuffs—that sort of hand-to-mouth critique, which I have a great respect for. Although a great deal of vital work by women has been done, the critique is really sitting on top of it. It's made up of the defense mechanism of an older writing culture that is predominantly male, and it's made up of everything, I'm afraid, from sneers to pious statements of what makes excellence. The great cry is that all this terrible sewage that people like myself have released into the literary waters is diluting the excellence of our great literature—though how you can get an excellent literature if it is exclusive, I don't know.

WRIGHT & HANNAN: And the language used in this critique?—words like *miniature* and *painterly* and she's not representative of her sex as a kind of backhand approbation?

BOLAND: Yes. There are all these code words like *domestic*, which imply a restrictive practice within the poem itself. A woman said to me of a male editor: "He said the best poems I wrote were the least female"—instead of looking at the thing—the right way around, which is to look at the work of young women, and asking, "How are they putting together the Irish poem differently?" That is the real question. They are putting it together differently, and that means in itself to cast a light around what is being done in other ways and at other times. We need to look at all this as part of the legitimate energies that affect one another and country. But if you look at it that way, the critique is actually obstructing the perspective on that. So we are not able at the moment to consider in this country: How do young women put together that poem? What do they put into it, and what do they leave out of it? We can't see that because the whole jargon surrounding it is very emotive. The most significant review to me was one in the *Irish Times* on my pamphlet "A Kind of Scar"—the same essay that appeared later in the *APR* as "Outside History."[5] The work was utterly dismissed. My editor said, "Should I do something about it?" I said, "Leave it." It's always to me a good thing when the murky undertows come to the surface.

WRIGHT & HANNAN: Is it difficult for these young women poets to be reviewed?

BOLAND: Yes, and, therefore, they get truly demoralized. The working conditions for young women poets are infinitely poorer than the conviviality and congratulations that surround their male counterparts.

One of the important hidden agendas in this country is that poets emerge differently. The young male poets tend to emerge in their early twenties. They tend to be economically independent; even if they're restricted, they don't have dependence. They're mobile; they can move to the centers of activity; they can move from the rural areas to the metropolitan areas. Although very often pressured, they have some flex on how they can move around.

The traditional young Irish woman poet is in her thirties, at best in her late twenties. She may well at that point be economically dependent, be married, have small children, and above all be fixed in one place. She can't get to the local library easily, let alone get to Dublin. She doesn't have many of the available sustenance and none of the amenities. Yet I don't think either the critique or funding or the perception or the community support has followed her the way it has the young male writer.

WRIGHT & HANNAN: The poet Rita Ann Higgins advises that women poets refuse inclusion in an anthology unless there is equal representation. Would you concur?

BOLAND: It's an interesting idea—one I'd be emotionally in sympathy with. But I would probably be cerebrally not in sympathy with token representation of any kind. I don't favor a woman being in an anthology just because she's a woman. I favor her being there because I know that many of the younger writers who are best in poetry are women. I think the right way is that women be the anthologists and editors. I think it would be very interesting if Rita Ann would edit *Poetry Ireland*—and include men. And we could see what she saw of what is around her.

WRIGHT & HANNAN: The periodical *Krino* has just brought out an edition dedicated to women and writing. Is this a sign that the situation is changing?

BOLAND: I think it's changing, but it's changing slowly. It's changing in ways that have to be closely looked at. I think that token representations in periodicals or conferences are not all the same as looking with a discriminatory eye at the body of literature in a country and saying, "If A is A, then B must be B. If there is a wonderful poem written in Galway in which the bus is put in and a woman on it, and she looks out the window—that has got to affect a poem written in Dublin five years before it or four years after it." I don't think we have recognition here, really. The names are known, but there is still tremendous controversy. There were no women in the communities in the fifties and sixties calling themselves *poets*.

WRIGHT & HANNAN: Your first book came out in 1967.[6]

BOLAND: Yes, but you would find it hard to believe how persona non grata I was. I was regarded as a straight-up lyric poet with the first two books. There was no support of any kind from any male poet, and that was very difficult. I was growing uneasy about the way the thing was handled, from the minus of congratulations for women to the kind of bardic posturing of men at readings. The assumption was that all Irish poets drink, that they behave to women in a certain way. I am a poet who grew up in my generation hearing Sylvia Plath routinely slandered by male poets; I have to except from that some of the male English poets, whom I think were surprisingly graceful and attuned to her work. But the Irish poets have continued to slander her.

WRIGHT & HANNAN: Because they consider her too "confessional"?

BOLAND: Absolutely. And then, as I said, I became persona non grata. They were fairly happy to sit back and let me disappear. When I didn't completely disappear, I don't know that they knew I didn't disappear for a very long time. I do think you can pick up a number of books by Irish writers that make no reference to any woman writer in those years. *Irish Poetry after Joyce,* written by Dillon Johnston, came out in the middle of that decade.[7] I think there are five hundred pages in that book and two are on Irish women poets. The funny thing is that in my case it made the working conditions more definite; I found it liberating. It liberated me from the slightest interest in their views on these matters. It didn't stop me from liking some of the work they did, but it stopped me from having a huge regard for their views because I thought they were thoroughly retrograde in many cases.

WRIGHT & HANNAN: Adrienne Rich suggests the need for a woman poet to break with the male tradition and create her own personal myth, as she does in a poem like "Diving into the Wreck." Do you find this too separatist a view?

BOLAND: Well, of course, I love her work, and the last line in that poem is just prophetic: "a book of myths / in which / our names do not appear." But no, I'm not a separatist. I would be much more subversive by inclination. Ireland is a country with a strong history of subversion. I think the subversions in this literature have an interesting past. Joyce's *Portrait of the Artist* is simply a subversion of the Jesuitical program—that's what Joyce was out to do. He wanted to take the original repressive stance and subvert it to show that in another life, when you turned it backward, it could be liberating. Yeats was more subversive of the British poet at the time than he appears. But by instinct, I wouldn't wish to throw out capital labor or any of those things, and if I wished to I wouldn't find it possible because we are daily rooted in the past. People who say you can live in Ireland and not have an interest in the nation—they haven't lived in Ireland. They don't know how powerful these things are! The separatists want us to see the poetic past as patriarchal betrayal. I see that ideology as dangerous to the woman poet; I want to subvert the old forms. Where those elements of the Irish experience are repressive, I would rather subvert them than throw the baby out with the bathwater.

Derek Mahon

Interviewed by James J. Murphy, Lucy McDiarmid,
and Michael J. Durkan

I would like to take this further opportunity to correct a few
misconceptions. First of all, I am not sophisticated; I am not
cosmopolitan. . . . People say, you have to do do this
reading, and you have to invite everybody who's important,
and it's not in my nature to go out and do that. I believe in
the lonely impulse of delight. I hate the "business."

—Derek Mahon

ON THE HOTTEST DAY in Philadelphia since the beginning of time, James
J. Murphy, Lucy McDiarmid, and Michael J. Durkan had the privilege of
speaking with Derek Mahon and with one another. Mahon had recently
finished a semester as artist-in-residence at Villanova University and was
soon to return to Dublin for the summer before taking up a new position
in the English Department of Queens College, City University of New
York, in September 1991.

Mahon, who was born in Belfast in 1941, is the author of many volumes
of poetry, including *The Hunt by Night* (Oxford: Oxford University Press;
Winston-Salem, N.C.: Wake Forest University Press, 1982) and *Antarctica*
(Dublin: Gallery Books, 1985), and is widely considered to be one of the
most distinguished contemporary poets. His new *Selected Poems* (Har-

From *ILS* 10 (fall 1991).

mondsworth, Eng.: Penguin, 1991) has just been published and was praised by John Banville in the *New York Review of Books* (30 May 1991) for its "great richness, elegance, and technical brilliance." He is the editor, with Peter Fallon, of *The Penguin Book of Contemporary Irish Verse* (London: Penguin, 1990). A selection of his prose pieces will be appearing later this year [1991].[1] [Lucy McDiarmid]

JAMES MURPHY, LUCY McDIARMID, AND MICHAEL DURKAN: How many syllables are there in your last name?

DEREK MAHON: Two: I pronounce it Ma-hon. Spenser[2] cites us as a bunch who were originally Norman and were called *Fitz-Urse,* like the man in *Murder in the Cathedral.* According to Spenser—and he deplores this, of course—the Fitz-Urses became Hibernicized and changed their name to *MacMathuna.* They were "Olde Englishe," *Hibernicis ipsis hiberniores.*

MURPHY, McDIARMID, & DURKAN: What part of Ireland were the McMahons from?

MAHON: There was a big McMahon clan in County Fermanagh, and Hugh O'Neill picked up Cuchonnacht McMahon on his way to Kinsale in 1601.[3] The story goes that the night before the battle took place—the well-organized Brit striking down Paddy as usual, in icy fog—there had been a possibility of the Irish winning. But McMahon had been fostered in one of those Big Houses in England; Taafe was the name of the people. McMahon also had a drink problem, and he sent his little son over to the English camp to talk to Captain Taafe the night before the battle of Kinsale: "You go over and talk to Taafe and bring back a jug of whiskey." And so, of course, Taafe asked the wee lad, "When's your Daddy going to attack?" And the wee lad said, "Well, I think we're going to have a go tomorrow morning, if Daddy's up to it." So he came back with the jug of whiskey from Taafe, and the English were all prepared the following morning when the Irish attacked. And the usual thing happened.

MURPHY, McDIARMID, & DURKAN: What did your parents do?

MAHON: My father was an inspector of engines in the Harland & Wolff shipyard in Belfast. He was apprenticed as a fitter initially, like his father before him, and later became an inspector of engines. My mother worked in the York Street Flax Spinning Company. So my parents embodied the two principal industries in Northern Ireland, ship building and linen. She didn't work there long. After she got married, in the fashion of the time, she simply became a housewife and mother. This is a great pity because I think she should have done other things. Belfast is the only part of Ireland that the industrial revolution impinged on, and it contains an industrial folklore. There used to be a lot of talk about the *Titanic*.

MURPHY, McDIARMID, & DURKAN: The *Titanic* was built in Belfast, wasn't it?

MAHON: Yes. My grandfather was responsible for the loss of the *Titanic*. He was a boiler-maker in Harland & Wolff, where they built the *Titanic*, and I've long been convinced that he did something wrong over there. Both my grandfathers, my father, and all my uncles worked in Harland & Wolff or went to sea in the Merchant Navy or did both. All the men in the family were concentrated on ships and the sea, except for those of us who were half-blind. I wanted to go to sea myself, so I was taken down to the Custom House in Belfast when I was about sixteen and given a preliminary examination, which involved looking at the chart on the wall. You know: O, X, Z, Q. The doctor said, "Read off the chart on the wall." So I said, "What chart?" And that was the end of my seafaring career.

MURPHY, McDIARMID, & DURKAN: You talk in *Autobiographies* about being hidden under a stairway during the bombing raids.

MAHON: I think that's actually incorrect because I was born in November of '41, and the bombing raids on Belfast took place in March. I was born after the raids, but they were very much a childhood memory in the sense that everyone spoke of them. I remember people talking about "poor Mr. This" or "poor Mrs. That" who were killed in the next street. The Germans went for Belfast, all right, the way they went for

Coventry and any industrial city, but they missed the shipyard and the aircraft factory. And consistent with their usual practice, when they missed a target, they just dropped their bombs indiscriminately all over residential districts, including the area where we lived.

MURPHY, McDIARMID, & DURKAN: Was your neighborhood mixed, Protestant and Catholic, when you were growing up?

MAHON: Yes, it was. But I didn't really understand this stuff about Protestant and Catholic. We'd a family round the corner called Matthews who were Catholic. And we—the Protestant kids—used to play with the Matthews kids and probably other Catholic kids as well. And there was absolutely no problem. I was particularly interested in Deirdre Matthews, but she was strangely coy—not sexually coy; we're talking about youngsters—and she wouldn't let me into her house. She was going off somewhere one day with her brother Jim, and they had to stop their play. I said, "Where are you going?" They said, "To confession." I said, "Can I come too?" And they said, "No, it's only for Catholics." I said, "What are Catholics? What do you mean?" And they wouldn't tell me. It was a long time before I understood. I understood the difference between Christians and Jews because there were Jewish kids in my primary school who stepped out when morning prayers were said, but the Protestant-Catholic thing I didn't understand at all.

MURPHY, McDIARMID, & DURKAN: What kind of Protestant are you?

MAHON: Lapsed. I was brought up in the Church of Ireland.

MURPHY, McDIARMID, & DURKAN: In a very churchy family?

MAHON: No, though my mother used to say, "Don't criticize the clergy; you never know when you'll need them." Church was very important because I was a chorister at St. Peter's on the Antrim Road, and that involved singing a lot of hymns. We used to stand with our ruffs, holding the hymnals like wee angels. But if you looked in the back of the hymn book, there were the most extraordinary drawings.

MURPHY, McDIARMID, & DURKAN: "Abide with me"?

MAHON: We were a little bit more up-market, in fact. I still remember a lot of those hymns. Sometimes I find myself humming them—for example, "Praise, my soul, the King of Heaven."

MURPHY, McDIARMID, & DURKAN: "To His feet thy tribute bring."

MAHON: And my favorite line: "Ransomed, healed, restored, forgiven." Wouldn't that be nice? Heaney has this thing in *Preoccupations* about the Litany of the Virgin Mary and the BBC shipping forecast. After the ordinary weather forecast, you know, it wouldn't be raining in London, but it would be raining in Leeds. They'd do the shipping forecast, at which point most people turned off. But Heaney listened, and curiously enough I did, too. I was engrossed in this litany of *Malin, Faroes, Dogger, Irish Sea, Finisterre*, which I suppose related to him, as it did to me, local interests. I would list also the church hymns and the BBC late Saturday afternoon sports results with all these second- and third-division teams, some of them, especially the Scottish ones, with exotic-sounding names: *Hamilton Academicals, Arbroath, Heart of Midlothian.*

MURPHY, McDIARMID, & DURKAN: Did you take the sermons seriously?

MAHON: The sermons were very boring. We had a very boring rector although he did liven us all up one day before an election by expressing the hope, in his sermon, that we would all support the government—in other words, vote Unionist.

MURPHY, McDIARMID, & DURKAN: How did your parents feel about that?

MAHON: I don't remember how my parents felt, but one uncle was very annoyed. The men in my family were all very left wing. In a curious Ulster way they were Belfast, working-class socialists. That doesn't mean they weren't sectarian; they were. Everybody's sectarian in Northern Ireland. But they were anti-Unionist inasmuch as Unionism was Conservatism, Toryism. The men—all those uncles! God, hundreds of uncles!—were all Labour voters. Perhaps a little bit unusual in Northern Ireland, where everybody on the Protestant side of the fence has always really voted Unionist. The women all voted Unionist.

MURPHY, McDIARMID, & DURKAN: *Why?*

MAHON: This was just the way things were. Strong feelings were involved. It was taken for granted that the women were conservative and the men mildly radical—one or two of them more than mildly. My uncle Roy, who's still alive, was a member of the Belfast Communist Party in the 1930s.

MURPHY, McDIARMID, & DURKAN: What school did you go to?

MAHON: A place that had a long eighteenth-century title to itself [the Royal Belfast Academical Institution], but everybody called it Inst. It was founded in 1791, and a lot of its early schoolmasters were United Irishmen, and the Linen Hall Library[4] was just round the corner. Tom Stoppard called Edinburgh the "Reykjavik of the South," but there was a time when Belfast was called the "Athens of the North," in the 1790s and early 1800s, because of men like Thomas Russell and Henry Joy McCracken.[5] Wolfe Tone[6] drew upon that; he had tremendous support in Belfast among radical Protestants. And Inst was still staffed by people like that when I went there.

MURPHY, McDIARMID, & DURKAN: Are you thinking of anyone in particular?

MAHON: There was a brilliant teacher there, a Dublin man named John Boyle. He was a Trinity graduate, a tremendously impressive man. He taught three subjects, English, French, and history; and he taught us *Irish* history, too, which was not in those days taught in Northern Irish Protestant schools. We read J. C. Beckett's *A Short History of Ireland;* it's Unionistic, very conventional. It wasn't going to ruffle any feathers in a Protestant school. But John Boyle really did give us a new perspective on things. He wasn't long in Belfast before he joined the Irish Republican Labour Party. He was involved in left-wing, anti-Unionist politics. He'd been there for about a year—this was wartime, of course—when the RUC[7] called on him one night: "Excuse me, Mr. Boyle, I'm afraid we have instructions to search your flat." "Oh, do come in. Search away." So they searched away and found nothing incriminating except one book: *The Republic.*

A further refinement: I told this story to Marie Heaney, and she said: "That doesn't make sense. I know the story. It's not John Boyle;

it's *Sean O'Boyle* of St. Patrick's College, Armagh, the collector of folk-lore and traditional music. A different man. The RUC turned up in 1940 in his flat in Armagh and searched the place and found only one incriminating book, *The Republic*. And moreover," said Marie, "the sergeant was standing with his arse to the fire and the constable came out from the study, holding a copy of *The Republic*, and the sergeant said, 'What's that you got there?' And the constable said, 'Well, this is all I can find. It's called *The Republic*, and it's in thon ould Free State writ-ing'." That was Marie's version of the story I was quite convinced had been told me by John Boyle.

MURPHY, McDIARMID, & DURKAN: In "Courtyards in Delft," you call your-self "a strange child with a taste for verse." When did that come over you?

MAHON: There was a wonderful school anthology called *A Pageant of English Verse*. It started with "Summer is icumen in," and it finished up with "Fern Hill." I think it was that book that did it for me. The first poem that really turned me on—aside from the hymns—was "The Stolen Child."

MURPHY, McDIARMID, & DURKAN: And then what?

MAHON: My next enthusiasm was Dylan Thomas, especially the early lyrics, like "Where Once the Waters of Your Face." That particular poem had a tremendous effect on me at one time. At Inst, there was a thing called the Forrest Reid Prize. He was an old boy of Inst, a not-very-much-read Belfast novelist, and he endowed this prize for poems and short stories in alternate years.

When I was in the fifth form. I wrote a poem which was un-abashed Dylan Thomas, and I put it in for the prize. Several smarty-boots in the sixth form had put in their poems, but mine won be-cause Joe Cowan, the head of the English Department, liked it. I think that's the moment at which I decided this was the thing for me. So a year later, when I was about eighteen, I saw this thing adver-tised in a newspaper, the May Morton Prize, a hundred pounds. Dylan Thomas had died in 1953, and as far as I knew, no one was writing poetry anymore. I thought, I'm the only one does it, so, of course, I'm going to get the prize. I sent them another Dylan Thomas pastiche, and to my astonishment and indignation I didn't win! It was won by John Montague with a poem called "Like Dolmens Round My Childhood, the Old People." So then I realized that people did write poetry still.

MURPHY, McDIARMID, & DURKAN: When did you realize there was a poetry-writing community you could be part of?

MAHON: When I got to Dublin, I realized it wasn't just Montague and me; there were a hundred others.

MURPHY, McDIARMID, & DURKAN: Had you given any thought at all to Queen's University, Belfast?

MAHON: There was a kind of hierarchical system at Inst whereby the very brightest boys went to Oxford and Cambridge, the next brightest boys went to Trinity, and so on. . . . Somehow it was assumed that I would go to Trinity. The Northern students who went there picked up an all-Ireland view instead of the provincial view. There are still cross-border things that assume Ireland to be one country—AA, for example, and golf. There are two different soccer teams, but there's only one rugby team. The presence of Northerners at Trinity was an aspect of that. Politically, Northern Ireland shouldn't exist, of course. I've been a United Irishman since I was about fourteen.

MURPHY, McDIARMID, & DURKAN: What happened at fourteen?

MAHON: I looked around me. I knew there was something very wrong with the environment in which I had grown up. It may have had to do with relations, or lack of, with the Matthews family. I didn't formulate it to myself: "I can't stand this political system. I hate Lord Brookeborough, Stormont, and the Unionists."[8] But I thought, this place is sick.

MURPHY, McDIARMID, & DURKAN: Is that why you speak of your childhood as muddy?

MAHON: I was thinking of my shoes. But if you want to impose another meaning on it, I'm perfectly happy.

MURPHY, McDIARMID, & DURKAN: Do you still think of Belfast as home?

MAHON: No. This is very close to the bone: where is home now? Where do you want to be buried? They've widened the bridge; they've destroyed the beach; but I suppose home for me would be a little place in County Antrim called Cushendun, where both my children were baptized. It sounds sentimental, but the Glens of Antrim are a little bit of "real Ireland."

MURPHY, McDIARMID, & DURKAN: So you're not altogether an "urban" person?

MAHON: I would like to take this further opportunity to correct a few misconceptions. First of all, I am not sophisticated; I am not cosmopolitan. I was not a member of Philip Hobsbaum's fucking Belfast group.[9] I was in a different city. I was a member of my own group in Dublin. I went *once* to Philip's group, and never again. Mind you, Philip was good fun, sure enough, but in a pub. He was no fun in his group, which was dogmatic and Leavisite[10] to a nauseating degree. I liked Philip a lot. He threw a lot of light around in Belfast where people were frightened of their own shadows. He used to say, "Things happen wherever I go! Fights break out!" So, let's get that clear once and for all: Philip's group didn't do anybody any good, except perhaps Philip and Seamus, who carried it on after Hobsbaum left to go to Glasgow.

MURPHY, McDIARMID, & DURKAN: Who went to Trinity in your time who was writing poetry?

MAHON: Michael Longley.[11] He was at Inst with me, but he was two years ahead. We were aware of each other, but we couldn't talk. He maintained a dignified aloofness until we met at Trinity. Brendan Kennelly and Eavan Boland[12] were also there, but Dublin being Dublin, it wasn't just Trinity: there was a whole kind of pub culture, so I had frequent sightings of people like Kavanagh and Myles.[13] I went to Trinity in September 1960.

MURPHY, McDIARMID, & DURKAN: How difficult was it to publish then?

MAHON: There were three places you could publish. There was *Threshold,* put out by Mary O'Malley in Belfast. It described itself as a quarterly, but it was an Irish quarterly, if you know what I mean—once every two years. There was the *Kilkenny Magazine*, which loomed very large. But the immediate place was the student magazine *Icarus*, which was started by a delightful man called Alec Reid.

The faculty at Trinity in those days were lousy; the Dowden[14] ethnic of dull Anglocentric mediocrity survived into my time there. This was in the days of Archbishop McQuaid,[15] who made it a mortal sin for any Catholic to enter Trinity, even to enter the gates.

MURPHY, McDIARMID, & DURKAN: All the faculty were "lousy"?

MAHON: Alec was an exception; also Con Leventhal, Beckett's best friend, and Owen Sheehy-Skeffington. At a time when it was neither profitable nor popular, he would adopt a radical stance, which was uniquely his own; so that made it possible for people to write him off with, "That's only Skeff being Skeff again." He taught French, and his particular interests were Gide and Camus. He taught what you might call the "French Protestant tradition." Camus wasn't Protestant, of course, but the way in which Skeff presented these two figures was to equate Protestantism with Existentialism. He was a little bit self-righteous, a little bit too much "my-father-was-shot-by-by-the-Brits,"[16] but he was a very fine teacher.

There's a story about Paddy Kavanagh in 1956. He receives a letter from London saying, the judges have decided that you have won the Guinness poetry prize, one hundred pounds. So Paddy goes to his bank and waves the letter at the assistant manager, who's called Colthurst, and he says, "On the strength of this letter, perhaps you could advance me fifty pounds." And Colthurst says, "I think we'll have to wait for the check to put in its appearance." "Well, fuck you." So Kavanagh goes off to the Bailey in high dudgeon and falls in with his cronies: "I've just been talking to that bastard Colthurst, the assistant manager; he wouldn't advance me a penny on the strength of the letter. 'Course, it was his father that shot Skeffington." "Actually, Paddy, you've got that wrong: they're different Colthursts." "I know," says Kavanagh, "but I'm putting it about all the same."

MURPHY, McDIARMID, & DURKAN: In your new *Selected Poems*, you made a notable change in "Afterlives," your poem dedicated to Jimmy Simmons, which is always anthologized.

MAHON: Yes, I had this line, "What middle-class cunts we are," and being a reconstructed kind of fellow and looking at it again, I thought, this is deeply wrong and has to be changed, so I changed it to "twits." I remember reading "Afterlives" to a ladies' book-reading society at Trinity, and I saw they all had copies on their knees, and after three stanzas I—whew!—turned the page.

MURPHY, McDIARMID, & DURKAN: Was it a deeply philosophical decision or was it a marketing decision? Was it really a matter of being "reconstructed," or did you think reviewers and feminists would be upset?—I'm[17] asking a crude question.

MAHON: It's a question worth asking. I discussed it with friends, and it became apparent that it was an unacceptable use of the word, and to perpetuate that use of the word was invidious. It wasn't a marketing decision, God forbid, merely good manners, if good manners have any place in poetry.

MURPHY, McDIARMID, & DURKAN: The big question is, what does Jimmy Simmons think of it?

MAHON: I know what he thinks. I don't even have to ask him.

MURPHY, McDIARMID, & DURKAN: In the new poem in your *Selected Poems*, "Dawn at St. Patrick's," you say you don't want your children to know where you are, but isn't it implicitly addressed to them anyway?—for when they're adult enough to understand?

MAHON: Yes. The principal weakness there is, it's too Lowellish, too Life-Studies-y. The stanza-form is a bit like "Skunk Hour." I think I've come to the end of tight, structured forms. One of my latest, "The Yaddo Letter," is very chatty and loose.

MURPHY, McDIARMID, & DURKAN: You refused to read the "Disused Shed" at your book-launching last week.

MAHON: Well, sometimes I can and sometimes I can't. "A Garage in Co. Cork"—I always like to read that.

MURPHY, McDIARMID, & DURKAN: You're fond of poems that begin with a painting.

MAHON: I've done too much of that. There's something frantic about it; it's a search for subject matter—the circus animals' desertion.

MURPHY, McDIARMID, & DURKAN: In putting the new book together were you looking for a thematic sequence?

MAHON: I write individual poems and then put them together in what seems, for the moment at least, to be some kind of sensible order, which may be simply pictorial. If you've two poems written in three-line stanzas, you put them together. I'm very conscious of the page, very conscious of poetry as a visual experience, and so it may not be for narrative or sequential reasons at all that I put two things together. I may want to put a poem so it starts on the left-hand page. And the texture of the letter on the page makes the thing a tactile experience. The typewriter is important to me: I want to see how things might look on the page, printed. I like a typewriter that goes "plunk," a good solid sound and kind of hairy letters.

MURPHY, McDIARMID, & DURKAN: When do you feel you have enough poems for a book?

MAHON: This is a sore point, because some poets—Montague, Heaney, for example—write books of poems, books like *The Great Cloak*, or *North*, and the books are almost novels. I don't write books of poems; I write individual poems. I'm slightly terrified of something I noticed in London, the kind of every-three-years-you-bring-out-a-book syndrome. I think there's something a little exceptional and distinguished about being silent for ten years and then bringing out a thin pamphlet which is hard to come by. The next best thing to being a bestseller like Seamus is being a much-sought-after rarity.

MURPHY, McDIARMID, & DURKAN: Do you see translation as something to do to keep active in a lull, to keep the pen moving?

MAHON: When the real thing isn't happening, it's a way to keep the pen moving. But, of course, translation takes on its own life. I've done two Molière plays, *The School for Husbands* and *The School for Wives*, and Fintan O'Toole, the new literary advisor at the Abbey, says they want to do the two together to make up an evening's theater. They want the whole thing updated to contemporary Dublin and set in somewhere like Fitzwilliam Square, among the haute bourgeosie. I've also done a version of *The Bacchae.*

MURPHY, McDIARMID, & DURKAN: Do you think the literature from the North should be considered separately from the literature of the Republic? Or is it all one thing?

MAHON: As far as I'm concerned, it's all one.

MURPHY, McDIARMID, & DURKAN: Then there isn't a "Northern Irish Renascence"?

MAHON: No. You can't *renasce* something that was never *nasce.* There is, however, as always, an Irish renascence.

MURPHY, McDIARMID, & DURKAN: Renascing from the Revival?

MAHON: No. It happens all the time. In Ireland people are always writing poetry, and everything else—fiction, plays. It's always going on. There's a continuing nascence with every generation. What about MacNeice, Rodgers, Hewitt?[18] What about them?

MURPHY, McDIARMID, & DURKAN: Did you ever meet MacNeice?

MAHON: Maybe two or three times, and he was never quite sober. What I remember is the length of his teeth. He was very long in the tooth, and that gave him a sneering look on his face. Somehow, Ulster Protestants are expected to be ironical. This is a way of explaining the liberal Ulster Protestant and apologizing for him, be it Louis MacNeice or Terry Brown or myself or whoever. By being ironical we somehow escape culpability.

MURPHY, McDIARMID, & DURKAN: Do different kinds of people read poetry in both Irelands from over here?

MAHON: There might be people living in trailers in North Dakota who read poetry, but my impression is that in America poetry is read in academe and very little elsewhere.

MURPHY, McDIARMID, & DURKAN: And by some few poets.

MAHON: Who are mostly in the universities anyway. In Ireland, however,

I think all kinds of people walk into bookstores and buy books of poetry. I see people walk into Fred Hanna's[19] saying, "Where's the new Paul Durcan?"

MURPHY, McDIARMID, & DURKAN: Ireland sells more volumes of poetry per capita than any other nation. That's always quoted.

MAHON: In Dublin, what they do is, they stand in Fred Hanna's thinking, Jesus, I'd love to have this book, but am I going to spend ten pounds to buy it?

MURPHY, McDIARMID, & DURKAN: But he's reading tomorrow night, and I'll get to hear him for five pounds, and I'll have five pounds for a drink afterward.

Is there any point in all this literary business besides the "business"?

MAHON: My answer is a quotation from Yeats, which is quite simply, "A lonely impulse of delight." To tell the honest truth, I try to fend off thoughts of those things, and I think most of us do. From time to time you have to make an effort. People say, you have to do this reading, and you have to invite everybody who's important, and it's not in my nature to go out and do that. I believe in the lonely impulse of delight. I hate the "business."

MURPHY, McDIARMID, & DURKAN: If the lonely impulse weren't there, the rewards aren't enough to keep going.

MAHON: You know those terrible sessions after readings, when they have questions too? People say, "Why do you write poetry?" I think it was Mike Longley replied, "I'm only in it for the money."

MURPHY, McDIARMID, & DURKAN: Does it do any good?

MAHON: I think it does good. I wouldn't be doing it if it didn't do good. "The great instrument of moral good is the imagination; and poetry administers to the effect by acting upon the cause"—Shelley: *A Defence of Poetry.*

MURPHY, McDIARMID, & DURKAN: You're a Shelleyan?

MAHON: I suppose so. Somehow my comments always seem to take the form of quotation. So this from *The High Consistory,* by Francis Stuart:[20] "The artist at his most ambitious does not seek to change maps but, minutely and over generations, the expression on some of the faces of men and women." That and the Shelley quote.

MURPHY, McDIARMID, & DURKAN: What do you do when you're not being literary? Do you play ping-pong? snooker? things you can't mention?

MAHON: Things I can't mention.

Eiléan Ní Chuilleanáin
Interviewed by Deborah Hunter McWilliams

I suppose I see the issue of national identity largely in terms
of accepting responsibility and also of confronting the fact
that many things are not different here. . . . I think we have
to . . . recognize that there are universal problems to resolve
because, you know, we can't always take refuge behind the
idea that we Irish are all so different and, therefore, do things
differently.

—Eiléan Ní Chuilleanáin

FOR EILÉAN NÍ CHUILLEANÁIN the idea of a literary coherence lies at the
level of expression, not expectation, that is, the connection between the
literary audience and the Irish national ideal as negotiated by the poet's
language. Ní Chuilleanáin intends for her poetry to articulate the native
Irish voice, not in the native Irish language but rather through native
images and motifs. She focuses on the influence and significance of exter-
nal objects, social patterns, political forces, and on using her poetry as a
way of relocating the Irish voice. This voice, according to Ní Chuilleanáin, is not to be found wholly within the sovereignty of the national
canon, principally because that collection of voices has historically
elected to exclude the voice of the Irish woman writer. Place and position—each reference constructs of the writers identity, but locality con-
textualizes what the writer seeks to reveal—the textual message. Ní

From *ILS* 12 (spring 1993).

Chuilleanáin explores existing demarcations between historical events and human experiences, employing as primary literary devices the constructs of myth and history. These two structural elements act as a type of containment; that is, they provide an enriching analytical framework inside which Ní Chuilleanáin's poetic voice peacefully resides.

Added to the issues of place and position, then, is the issue of perception. The poet writes about, and critiques, the comparisons and contrasts between social constructions and individual perceptions; between singularity and multiplicity; between relativity and universality; between cultural conditions and human contextures; and between isolation and integration. Through her poetry Ní Chuilleanáin articulates the question of the political force of the literary imagination. She contends that women, in particular, are powerless if they do not revisit their self-perception and creative imagination to reform and relocate our current sense of self.

Eiléan Ní Chuilleanáin began publishing book-length collections of her poetry in the 1970s: *Acts and Monuments* (Dublin: Gallery Press, 1972), *Site of Ambush* (Dublin: Gallery Press, 1975), and *The Second Voyage* (Dublin: Gallery Press; Winston-Salem, N.C.: Wake Forest University Press, 1977). In 1981 she published *The Rose-Geranium* (Dublin: Gallery Press). A decade later, she borrowed, critically recollected, and published some more recent poems under the title *The Magdalene Sermon and Earlier Poems* (Dublin: Gallery Press, 1990; Winston-Salem, N.C.: Wake Forest University Press, 1991). Since this interview, she has brought out another collection, *The Brazen Serpent* (Oldcastle, Ireland: Gallery Press, 1994; Winston-Salem, N.C.: Wake Forest University Press, 1995).

Deborah McWilliams interviewed the poet on 16 July 1992 in her office at Trinity College, Dublin, where Ní Chuilleanáin teaches. During their dialogue the two explored, among other themes, issues involving the concept of the Irish woman writer in contrast to that of a woman writing in Ireland; the poets interest in continental Europe, Italy, in particular; the medieval and renaissance periods; and religious iconography.[1]
[Deborah H. McWilliams]

DEBORAH McWILLIAMS: What is your view on the role significance of technical merit among the contemporary scene in Ireland?

EILÉAN NÍ CHUILLEANÁIN: I think that people, that contemporaries, respond to a poet in terms of how interested they are in what the poet has to say *and* how a poet is able to write about things that are interesting, and that is what gets a response. I'm inclined to think that maybe, many years later, people are more inclined to look at the language and the technical skill, but that's my feeling about it in this country.

McWILLIAMS: So, in your view, what texts survive of poet over time are those measured against their technical merit as well as the message, and what may be heard in the short term is principally the thematics of poetry and of the poet's voice?

NÍ CHUILLEANÁIN: Yes, . . . I think the wider audience is less aware of what you're doing with language than with what you are actually saying.

McWILLIAMS: As I mentioned in a letter once to you, I don't find that your poetry is very well-known in America. My sense is that your own poetry is largely not well-known outside of Ireland because of the images and imagery you choose to use in your poetic work. And also, for the most part, you choose not to promote your poetry through participating as a lecturer. In this accurate?

NÍ CHUILLEANÁIN: Well, I was in California last October, for example. But I don't give lectures because I don't want to become involved in the academic study of Anglo-Irish literature. I find that that would give me a kind of psychological bind. I much prefer to teach an earlier period.

McWILLIAMS: Medieval or Renaissance?

NÍ CHUILLEANÁIN: That's right. And this kind of thing is so relative because obviously a lot of American poets, a lot of American readers, have only heard one Irish poet, and that's Seamus Heaney. Within that, there are people who have begun to study women poets. And I can see that Eavan Boland and Nuala Ní Dhomhnaill have had more exposure. But I can say that this isn't a subject you can talk to me about because it is not a subject that interests me greatly. I mean, I'm writing for an Irish audience in Ireland. And if other people want to read it, I find that actually quite interesting, quite liberating, quite surprising in a way, but it's not what I'm interested in. It's not what I'm writing for. What I feel is that poetry is something that demands a lot of concentration. . . . I'm interested in who's going to read it here because, I suppose, I share something of the language with them, but as far as I'm concerned, you're talking a different language. You're talking a foreign language to me because your idiom is different.

I've a lot of good American friends, and I've a lot of good friends who speak other languages, but I feel that I'm writing both in an idiom and, to some extent, using references that are available to an Irish audience, and, it seems to me, it's not that likely that those beyond that audience would understand it very well. I've read various critics about my work, and I've been told about others. And I haven't systematically gone after them because, really, with perhaps two exceptions, I haven't come across any really good criticism about my work. I haven't read anybody who seemed to have anything to say that wasn't to some extent misreading it. And that's probably because, first of all, people are starting to read my work, some of it maybe twenty years after it was written, and their sense of some of the things that have happened—that were happening, say, in the later sixties and early seventies—has changed since then. But also, I suppose, people are, for example, reading my poetry in the light of a dichotomy between masculine and feminine, which to me is not a very real dichotomy, except that I think imaginative literature is constantly transforming and transgressing boundaries and always being interested in ways in which one can get a perspective which isn't entirely masculine and isn't entirely feminine. So, when I come across these reviews, I don't feel that they understand what they are doing.

McWILLIAMS: Writing to an Irish audience, I find it interesting that your references, your images, the idiom in your poetry reflect a theme of migration, of shifts and movements within the native landscape, of rethinking what a rural Irish past means within an urban Irish landscape today. With this in mind, your poetry raises three points of interest which I'd like for you to discuss with me: the notion of movement and of migration; the notion of the sacred in history; and the idea of national identity within a transforming, postmodern Ireland.

Ní CHUILLEANÁIN: I have traveled a lot, especially in Europe, and I think I don't like much writing about a foreign landscape because I think I can't know it as thoroughly. But something which has certainly affected me a lot has been the experience of traveling, of being on a train or in an airport, the sense of being on the move. And I think, in a way, that's the place that I'm in. If you want to talk about it in terms of place, my place is on the move. I certainly am drawn back to Ireland, but, I suppose, my experience has been fairly untypical of most Irish women—in that sense, someone like Eavan Boland, who has been a freelance writer, but she's also lived in the suburbs with her family and written about that. I've got family, but since I've always been a breadwinner, I've never been a domestic woman. It's a subject I occasionally contemplate from a distance, but I don't feel it really suits me.

McWILLIAMS: But neither do you get actually involved in the current academic debates about the contemporary Irish landscape.

Ní CHUILLEANÁIN: I'm an academic woman who is much more interested in reading sixteenth-century Latin because I think—in fact, I know— that what attracts me is that which I do not know, but also, I suppose, the linguistic differences between now and the past, and the kind of scholarship which enables us to recuperate the past. I'm not an academic in the sense of someone who wants to talk about the here and now. I'm the kind of academic who, like many others, if you were to knock on the doors in this building . . . not many of them are interested, actually, in talking about the debate in Anglo-Irish literature. [Academia] is something that one gets drawn to because it is strange, and it's also very much a family tradition in my case. Both my father and grandfather were academics . . . [my father] was professor of Irish in Cork, and my grandfather was a professor of chemistry at Galway, actually. So that to me, in one sense, I have been following the male side of my family, but this is what women do when they go out and get jobs.

McWILLIAMS: What other jobs are open?

NÍ CHUILLEANÁIN: I could have been and, actually, I wanted to be a chemist. But . . . schools couldn't provide me, and were very unwilling to provide me, to even try to provide me, with the kind of background I needed to start off in chemistry.

McWILLIAMS: As one of the more prominent female voices in Ireland today, you're more well-accepted than many.

NÍ CHUILLEANÁIN: That's right. But I've been around for longer. I have been here . . . I've been writing and being published since 1966. . . . I got into it because I was also getting into the academic world, and there's no doubt that there is a connection between the academic world and the world of publications. I happened to win, anonymously, a poetry competition sponsored by the *Irish Times* in 1966. So they got to know what I was made of though I suspect they thought the writer was not female. I suspect they thought I was male.

McWILLIAMS: Do you think, had they known otherwise, it would have affected the judges' decision?

NÍ CHUILLEANÁIN: Yes, I believe that for at least one of the people it would have meant that they wouldn't have approved if they had known who I was. But . . . if you're interested in the question of whether I'm a popular poet or not, then you'll want to go talk to the readers, not to me. I suppose I have been a bit uncompromising in the sense that quite often I write difficult poetry.

McWILLIAMS: Difficult in terms of its complexity and layering? or difficult in terms of technique?

NÍ CHUILLEANÁIN: I think difficult in the sense of complicating to the reader. . . . I suppose there's much which might or might not be accessible to anyone.

McWILLIAMS: You are not writing to the common reader?

NÍ CHUILLEANÁIN: You see, it's very difficult to tell how *common* the common reader of poetry is. I think that poetry may, very well, put something unfamiliar in front of the reader. Any particular reader might not know about it right away and would have to look it up in a dictionary. I think that there's a type of historical moment here. I think in the sixties, when I was just starting up, I was becoming rather self-conscious of people's expectations. There was still some kind of respect for difficult poetry, and I think that's gone. I think there's a much more impatient attitude with what you might call originality, unusual expression, in poetry. I like to find English poets who are obscure. Though some find the poetry of Seamus Heaney obscure, I really think that they're laboring too hard at it.

McWILLIAMS: What about the notion of the sacred in history? You've mentioned this in your writing.

NÍ CHUILLEANÁIN: I grew up in a very traditional society, quite a traditional society, of a small Irish city in which there was a religious context for most things: one in which going to church could be very aesthetically exciting in terms of the liturgy and the visual experience. But it also brought the whole community together. You could see people at church. You got a sense of the whole community. And, obviously, in terms of Irish history, I'm very interested in the sacred in history. It's something I'm very conscious of here and also in other societies—again, to discover what it is that is gone, what has changed, why communities don't relate to each other in a religious way any more. I think Italian communities in the United States very often do, and not just Catholic communities either, but Protestant groups do it as well. And so it's just something that interests me. It interests me as an academic, and it keeps on sort of teasing me as a poet; I keep on coming across examples of it.

McWILLIAMS: But, in a sense, it's not really definable. You can see it depicted. As a Catholic myself, and as an Italian-Irish Catholic . . . I'm very familiar with what you are referring to, but it would be hard for me actually to define it. I could describe it in Italian or Catholic terms, but I couldn't define it in universal terms.

NÍ CHUILLEANÁIN: Yes, I think that's one thing about it. It's designed to be particular and attached to particular places and groups. I don't know, say, the difference between the Italian-in-Italy and the Italian-in-America identity, and, of course, the Italians throughout the European community. One obvious example is the notion of death. The Irish deal with death on the level of a party. The Italian response seems to be—well, it's rather different: the cult of the grave, the cult of visiting the grave and of bringing flowers, of having anniversary masses and things like that. As soon as I start thinking about this, I find it so interesting that I want to write about it. I just am drawn to various ways of ritual with people.

McWILLIAMS: As I recall in "Acts and Monuments," you suggest, through the use of particular images, what constructs our sense of identity. Is it possible that the sacred in history is really an aspect of our own identity?

Ní CHUILLEANÁIN: I think that's a fair description. We are inclined, or at least I am inclined, to read history with a sense of how relevant experience is, especially the history of injustice, deprivation, victimization. So that I feel that this is all somewhat filtered out of it, that it is not what [people] want to hear. They—we all—know it's full of injustices and deprivation, and I think that is what I do want to talk about.

McWILLIAMS: Why?

Ní CHUILLEANÁIN: Because it's real, because if it really happened, it's real. On the other hand, I'm interested in the sense of the sacred as something that people . . . think of as folklore and folk beliefs, and historical beliefs and sacred observations—as belonging to the past. And I think people think this even when these beliefs are, in fact, alive and vital. For example, you can see that in the eighteenth-century writings about the Irish belief in the banshee; she is a very supernatural spirit who comes crying at night when someone is about to die. In fact, they write about the banshee in the eighteenth century, and they talk about this as a dying superstition, but the banshee is alive and well in Ireland at this day. There are still people who claim to have heard [her]; often they are older people. But, obviously, when we are writing about the eighteenth century, it just wasn't so: it just wasn't a dying belief; it wasn't something that would be gone in a couple of generations. Again, how we feel about the past, the way in which we are inclined to associate certain things with the past as something vanishing, where in fact, one is constantly made aware of the fact that the past does not go away, that it is walking around the place and causing trouble at every moment—I mean, this may be particularly true in Ireland, but it's true in an awful lot of places.

MCWILLIAMS: What about the notion of national identity?

NÍ CHUILLEANÁIN: Well, that's interesting because it is created by, in Ireland, so many overlapping criteria, like living in the country or the Irish language. There are people who would consider, and certainly when I was growing up, there were people who said, that if you didn't belong to the majority religion, you weren't really Irish—you were kind of there on sufferance or [you were] becoming Irish or nearly Irish. To me, to some extent, national identity is something shifting and constituted for me by the presence, especially, of two languages, but also of two different religious traditions, but as groups of people who understand what the argument is about.

MCWILLIAMS: And not as a particular political environment wherein we can place some sort of ideological debate?

NÍ CHUILLEANÁIN: I think that the ideological debate is going on all the time. And in Ireland it has that national pride in one sense. It can be involved in a sense of the assuming of responsibility for problems; it is something we've only been able to do rather gradually. I mean, we weren't able to do, say, on a certain day in 1922 and to say, right, from now on we run the show. All kinds of things, because of the presence of England in so many different ways, were—and are—very slow to change. I think, for example, . . . the Irish are very much going to have to confront the [abortion] issue as an Irish problem to be solved here and not somewhere else. So I suppose I see the issue of national identity largely in terms of accepting responsibility and also of confronting the fact that many things are not different here. I mean, there are a lot of differences between Ireland and other countries. On the other hand, I think we have to . . . recognize that there are universal problems to resolve because, you know, we can't always take refuge behind the idea that we Irish are all so different and, therefore, do things differently.

Notes
Suggested Readings
Index

Notes

Introduction

1. Mary Dalton's interview with Paul Durcan appeared in volume 10 (fall 1991) of the *Irish Literary Supplement*, hereinafter cited as *ILS*.

John McGahern

1. McGahern's recent publications include these titles: *Amongst Women* (London: Faber and Faber, 1990); *The Power of Darkness* (a play; London: Faber and Faber, 1991), and *The Collected Stories* (London: Faber and Faber; New York: Knopf, 1992).

2. Eamon de Valera was *taoiseach* or prime minister of Ireland from 1937 to 1948 during the time to which McGahern refers. The Trade or Economic War began in 1932 when the Irish government withheld its promised annuities from the British Exchequer and the British retaliated with tariffs on Irish cattle and agricultural products; it ended in 1938 with the Anglo-Irish Agreements.

3. University College, Dublin—Kennedy.

4. Flann O'Brien, the fiction pseudonym of Brian O'Nolan (1911–1966).

5. *The End of Beginning of Love*—Kennedy.

6. John Charles McQuaid (1895–1973), Roman Catholic archbishop of Dublin and primate of all Ireland (1940–72).

7. The Dáil Éireann, or Irish Parliament.

8. The Irish Constitution of 1937, Article 44.1, emphasized the special position in the Republic enjoyed by the religion of Ireland's majority, the Roman Catholic Church. Although this article also recognized equal rights for other religions, it was deleted in 1972 by referendum. The constitution's recognition of the Catholic Church's importance, McGahern maintains, contradicted in part the Irish Provisional Government's proclamation first read publicly by Padraig Pearse on the steps of Dublin's General Post Office on Monday, 24 April 1916: "The Republic guarantees religious and civil liberty, equal rights

and equal opportunities to all its citizens, and declares its resolve to pursue the happiness and prosperity of the whole nation and of all its parts."

Jennifer Johnston

1. Johnston's more recent novels include *The Invisible Worm* ([London]: Sinclair-Stevenson, 1991) and *The Illusionist* (London: Sinclair-Stevenson, 1995).

2. Edith Somerville (1858–1949), Violet Florence Martin, or "Martin Ross" (1862–1915), and Maria Edgeworth (1767–1849) were Anglo-Irish writers of fiction.

3. That is, before the Easter Rising of 1916, which initiated Ireland's war of independence.

4. The Irish Free State was established in 1922.

5. See the interview with John McGahern.

6. Bernard MacLaverty (b. 1942), Northern Irish writer of fiction, published his novel *Lamb* (Belfast: Blackstaff Press) in 1980.

7. Published in London and New York, 1980, and Dublin, 1988.

8. During World War II, or the Emergency as the Irish refer to it, Taoiseach Eamon de Valera and his government maintained a policy of neutrality toward the Allied and Axis powers.

9. The battle of the Somme, which began 1 July 1916 and which resulted in 419,654 British casualties (see John Keegan, *The Face of Battle* [New York: Barnes and Noble, 1993], 233), decimated several Irish units, particularly the Ulster Volunteer Force or Division.

10. From 1 March to 20 August 1981 IRA prisoners in the H-Block of the Maze prison went on hunger strikes to force world attention on Great Britain's refusal to treat them as political prisoners of war rather than as common criminals. Eleven prisoners starved to death before the hunger strikes ended.

11. Published in 1977. For Kiely's perception of his novel see his interview.

12. Brian Friel's (b. 1929) play *Translations* was first presented in 1980 and published the following year.

13. The Northern Irish Civil Rights movement began in 1968.

14. John Paul II became pope in 1978.

15. See the interviews with Derek Mahon and Michael Longley.

16. See Timothy Kearney, "An Interview with John Hewitt and John Montague on Northern Poetry and the Troubles," *The Crane Bag of Irish Studies*, 1977–81 (Dublin: Crane Bag, 1983, 722–29 (a reprint of the 1980 interview).

17. *Ticking over*, "marking or wasting time."

18. The production in 1980 of Friel's *Translations* inaugurated the Field Day Theatre Group.

19. That is, Ireland. (Cathleen Ní Houlihan, as in Lady Gregory and William Butler Yeats's play of the same name, is one of several traditional personifications of Ireland as a beautiful young woman.)

20. *The Railway-Station Man* (London: Hamish Hamilton, 1984).

21. Johnston published several plays, among them *The Porch, The Invisible Man,* and *The Nightingale and Not the Lark.*

John Montague

1. Published in 1984 in Winston-Salem, N.C., and Mountrath, Ireland. Since the interview, Montague has published several important collections, including the following: *Mount Eagle* (Oldcastle, Ireland: Gallery Books, 1988; Newcastle-upon-Tyne, Eng.: Bloodaxe Books; Winston-Salem, N.C.: Wake Forest Univ. Press, 1989); *The Figure in the Cave and Other Essays* (Dublin: Lilliput Press, 1989); and *Collected Poems* (Liverpool: Gallery Books; Winston-Salem, N.C.: Wake Forest Univ. Press, 1995).

2. Teilhard de Chardin (1881–1955), French Jesuit, paleontologist, and philosopher, whose best-known work is *The Phenomenon of Man* (1953; English trans., London: Collins; New York: Harper and Row, 1959).

3. William Butler Yeats in *A Vision* and throughout his poetry employed the geometric figure of the cone or gyre, or two such interpenetrating gyres, to illustrate and describe phases of change.

4. The Fenian cycle, or *Fianaigheacht,* is one of the great medieval Irish compilations of heroic tales. It centers on the deeds of Finn mac Cumaill (Finn McCool) and the Fiana, sometimes also known as the Red Branch Knights.

5. The Irish writer and critic Austin Clarke (1896–1974).

6. John O'Hara (1905–1970), American fiction writer and journalist.

7. Constantine Cavafy (1863–1933), Greek-Egyptian writer.

8. The Venetian composer Antonio Vivaldi (1678–1741) wrote his *L'estro harmonica* about 1711. Anton Bruckner (1824–1896), Austrian composer.

9. *Duende,* fiery spirit (Spanish).

10. That is, "that it's shit."

11. The German philosopher Immanuel Kant (1724–1804) published his *Critique of Pure Reason* in 1786. Blaise Pascal (1623–1662), French philosopher and mathematician important for his distrust of reason's ability to resolve metaphysical problems.

12. Johann Sebastian Bach (1685–1750), composer whose intellectual explorations of the fugue form climaxed in his *Art of the Fugue.*

13. In Greek mythology Oedipus killed his father and married his mother; Electra avenged her father's murder by killing her mother; and Psyche eventually destroyed herself in pursuing the boy-god with whom she had fallen in love.

14. Apollo and Lugh ("the Shining One") are, respectively, the classical and Celtic gods of the sun. (More often, however, Lugh corresponds to the classical Mercury/Hermes.)

15. Ezra Pound (1885–1972), American poet. T. E. Hulme (1883–1917), British poet;

D. H. Lawrence (1885–1930), British writer. William Carlos Williams (1883–1963), American writer.

16. French writers Francis Ponge and Charles Baudelaire (1821–1867).

17. William Carlos Williams began publishing his long poem *Paterson* in 1946.

18. Possible references to American poets John Berryman's *Homage to Mistress Bradstreet* and James Merrill's "The Summer People."

19. William Langland (c. 1330–c. 1400), author of the long poem *The Vision of Piers the Plowman*.

20. Dante Alligheri began his *Divine Comedy* about 1300.

21. Each writer successfully authored at least one long poem: William Allingham (1824–1889), *Laurence Bloomfield in Ireland*; Ludovico Ariosto (1474–1533; Italian), *Orlando Furioso*; John Ashbery (b. 1927), *Self-Portait in a Convex Mirror* (or, possibly, *Fragment*).

22. Gillaume de Salluste Du Bartas (1544–1590), French writer remembered chiefly for his *Divine Weeks and Works*.

23. Charles Olson (1910–1970), *American Maximus*. Edward Dorn, *Gunslinger* (1968).

24. For Bruckner see n. 8. Gustav Mahler (1860–1911), Austrian composer.

25. Olivier Eugéne Prosper Messiaen (1908–1992), French composer.

26. Hugh MacDiarmuid (1892–1978), sometimes considered the greatest Scottish poet since Burns, and David Jones (1895–1874), a strongly religious Welsh poet.

27. Pablo Neruda (1904–1973), Nobel prize–winning Chilean poet.

28. Galway Kinnell (b. 1927), American author of the *Book of Nightmares*. "The Bridge" is an allusion to Hart Crane's poem.

29. See interview with Irish poet Paul Muldoon.

30. Miles Davis (b. 1926), American jazz trumpeter.

31. Sean Dunne died in 1995.

32. Desiderius Erasmus (1466?–1536), Dutch humanist.

33. That is, the *New England Review and Bread Loaf Quarterly*.

34. See Timothy Kearney's interview with Montague and John Hewitt (1907–1987), in *The Crane Bag of Irish Studies, 1977–81* (Dublin: Crane Bag, 1983), 722–29 (this is the reprint of the original Crane Bag interview, 4 [1980]).

35. Marshall McLuhan (1911–1980), Canadian cultural historian and theorist on mass communications.

William Trevor

1. William Trevor's fiction explores both long and short forms. Beginning with the London publication of *The Old Boys* (London: Bodley Head) in 1964, his principal novels include the following: *The Boarding House* (London: Bodley Head, 1965), *The Love Department* (London: Bodley Head, 1966), *Mrs. Eckdorf in O'Neill's Hotel* (London: Bodley Head, 1969), *Elizabeth Alone* (London: Bodley Head, 1973), *The Children of Dynmouth* (London: Bodley

Head, 1976), *Other People's Worlds* (London: Bodley Head, 1980), *Fools of Fortune* (London: Bodley Head, 1983), *The Silence in the Garden* (London: Bodley Head, 1988), *Juliet's Story* (Dublin: O'Brien Press, 1991), *Two Lives* (two novellas; New York: Penguin, 1992), and *Felicia's Journey* (New York: Viking, 1994).

His first collection of shorter fiction, *The Day We Got Drunk on Cake* (London: Bodley Head), appeared in 1967 (London), and he has published numerous subsequent collections since then. His *Collected Stories* came out in 1992 (New York: Viking Penguin). Trevor has also written a memoir, *Excursions in the Real World* (London: Hutchinson, 1993).

2. The collection *The Ballroom of Romance and Other Stories* was published in 1972 (London: Bodley Head).

3. Later reprinted in *The Collected Stories* (New York: Viking Penguin, 1992).

4. Published in 1975.

5. Published as *The Collected Stories* (New York: Viking Penguin, 1992).

6. That is, the Irish Civil War, 1922–23.

7. In his novel *Howards End* (1910), E. M. Forster (1879–1970) uses *connecting* to denote the importance of community and social relationships.

8. James Thurber (1894–1961), American writer and humorist.

9. Film director Silvio Narizzano established his reputation with *Georgy Girl* (1966), featuring James Mason, Lynn Redgrave, and Alan Bates. As Trevor goes on to indicate, the poorly scripted *Blue* (1968) proved a failure.

Michael Longley

1. Now the American Conference for Irish Studies.

2. "Salamander and Gallery Presses; reviewed in the last issue [spring 1986] of *ILS*"—Dillon Johnston.

3. During the late 1960s Englishman and lecturer at Queen's University, Belfast, Philip Hobsbaum held weekly seminars often credited with helping crystalize a consciousness of a Northern Ireland tradition of poetry.

4. *Poetry in the Wars* (Newcastle-upon-Tyne, Eng.: Bloodaxe Books; Newark, N.J.: Univ. of Delaware Press, 1986)

5. In recent years, Longley has published several works: *Tuppeny Stung: Autobiographical Chapters* (Belfast: Lagan Press, 1994) and *The Ghost Orchid* (London: Cape Poetry, 1995).

6. During World War I, in 1916, the Thirty-sixth, or Ulster Division, was effectively destroyed during the Somme offensive that began in July.

7. Clement Attlee (1883–1967) and Harold Macmillan (1894–1986) were prime ministers of Great Britain 1945–51 and 1957–63, respectively.

8. Located near Queen's University, the Eglantine Inn was a meeting place throughout the 1980s for Belfast writers.

9. Eamon de Valera (1882–1975) was prime minister, or *taoiseach*, of Ireland, 1932–48, 1951–54, and 1957–59.

10. Wellington Park Bar, or Hotel, near Queen's University, also served as a meeting place for a number of Belfast writers.

11. See the interview with Paul Muldoon, for another disussion of Muldoon leaving Belfast.

12. British poet Robert Graves (1895–1985) advocated a "return" to recognizing the creative power of the female principle, the muse, the anima.

13. Mark Rothko (1903–1970), Russian-born American painter.

14. An allusion to the ending of William Butler Yeats's poem "The Circus Animals' Desertion."

15. See the interview with Montague.

16. British poets Wilfred Owen (1893–1918), Edward Thomas (1878–1917?), John Clare (1793–1864), and George Herbert (1593–1633).

17. Gaius Valerius Catullus (c. 84–c. 54 B.C.), Sextus Propertius (c. 50–c. 16 B.C.), and Albius Tibullus (c. 60–19 B.C.).

John Banville

1. Since the interview, Banville's publications have included the following: *The Book of Evidence* (London: Secker and Warburg; New York: Scribner's, 1989), *Ghosts* (London: Secker and Warburg, 1993), and *Athena: A Novel* (London: Secker and Warburg; New York: Knopf, 1995).

2. Imhof alludes to Banville's "those high cold heroes who renounced the world and human happiness to pursue the big game of the intellect" (cf. Banville, *The Newton Letter* [London: Secker and Warburg, 1982], 50).

3. *[Die] ewige Wiederkunft*, that is, "return," "eternal recurrence" (see Imhof's study, *John Banville: A Critical Introduction* [Dublin: Wolfhound Press, 1989], 157–59, for a discussion of this point).

4. That is, "season in hell."

5. In Greek mythology the aged and poor couple Philemon and Baucis entertained Zeus and Hermes, disguised as humans. Because they received the two gods hospitably after the rich had turned them away, Philemon and Baucis were rewarded, their lives saved during a flood, their house transformed into a temple, themselves metamorphosed into intertwined trees after they were allowed to die together.

6. For a discussion of how Banville's Philomena and Uncle Ambrose invert these antecedents see Imhof, *John Banville*, 163–64.

7. Heinrich von Kleist (1777–1811), the German Romantic author.

8. Wilhelm Friedrich Nietzsche (1844–1900), the German philosopher and writer.

9. The Greek philosopher Democritus (c. 460–370 B.C.) elaborated an atomic theory of the universe.

10. Thomas Mann (1875–1955) published *Doktor Faustus* in 1947.

11. Prof. Heinz Kosok is a professor of English literature at Wuppertal University in Germany.

12. *Kosok*, spelled backward, remains *Kosok*.

13. German physicist Werner Karl Heisenberg (1901–1976) elaborated the "uncertainty principle," a hypothesis that measuring one observable quality (e.g., position and momentum, energy and time) will produce uncertainty in the measurement of the other.

14. Published in 1989 as *The Book of Evidence*.

Benedict Kiely

1. Kiely's publications since the interview suggest the diversity of his efforts: two collections of short stories, *A Letter to Peachtree and Nine Other Stories* (London: Gollancz, 1987) and *God's Own Country* (London: Minerva, 1993); a memoir, *Drink to the Bird* (London: Methuen, 1991); and children's fiction, *The Trout in the Turnhole* (Dublin: Wolfhound Press, 1995).

2. Until 1972 the parliament of Northern Ireland met in Stormont, outside Belfast.

3. "For god order is the supreme rule, and all things are ordered by god."

4. (London, 1949).

5. Robert M. Smyllie (1894–1954), Irish journalist known for his advocacy of both maintaining ties with Great Britain and preserving Irish independence.

6. Michael Joseph MacManus (1891–1951), literary editor of *Irish Press*, 1931–51.

7. Edward Gibbon (1737–1794), author of *Decline and Fall of the Roman Empire* (1776–1788).

8. A distance of some 30–40 miles.

9. See the interview with John Banville.

10. Richard Ellmann (1918–1987), American literary critic respected for his work on modern Irish writers.

11. Flann O'Brien is the fiction pseudonymn of Brian O'Nolan (1911–1966).

12. William Saroyan (1908–1981), American fiction writer.

13. Allan Tate (1899–1979) was an American poet and critic.

14. Published in 1991 (London: Methuen) as *Drink to the Bird*.

15. Included in the collection *A Letter to Peachtree and Nine Other Stories* (London: Gollancz, 1987).

Paul Muldoon

1. An Allusion to Muldoon's poem "Why Brownlee Left" in the 1980 collection of the same title.

2. Published in Newcastle-upon-Tyne and Cranbury, N.J., 1986.

3. James F. Fenton (b. 1949).

4. From "Immran."

5. The poem to which Barry refers and which Muldoon discusses is "7, Middagh Street." The note in *Meeting the British* (Winston-Salem, N.C.: Wake Forest Univ. Press, 1987) reads as follows: "'7, Middagh Street' takes its name from the Brooklyn-Heights residence of George Davis, fiction editor for *Harper's Bazaar*. In the autumn of 1940, W. H. Auden, Chester Kallman, Gypsy Rose Lee, Benjamin Britten, Peter Pears, Salvador Dali, Carson McCullers, Louis MacNeice, Paul and Jane Bowles, and a trained chimpanzee were among the residents and visitors there" (64).

6. *The Sphere Book of Modern Irish Poetry* (London: Sphere, 1972).

Nuala Ní Dhomhnaill

1. Nuala Ní Dhomhnaill's *Selected Poems/Rogha Dánta*, trans. Michael Hartnett, was published in 1986 (Dublin: Raven Arts). Since the year of the interview, she has published several shorter volumes of verse: *Pharaoh's Daughter* (Oldcastle, Ireland: Gallery Press, 1990; Winston-Salem, N.C.: Wake Forest Univ. Press, 1993), *Feis* (Maynooth, Ireland: An Sagart, 1991), and *The Astrakhan Cloak* (Oldcastle, Ireland: Gallery Press, 1992; Winston-Salem, N.C.: Wake Forest Univ. Press, 1993).

2. The poem entitled "Parthenogenesis."

3. Aodhagán Ó Rathaille, or Egan O'Rahilly (c. 1670–c. 1728), and Eoghan Rua (or Ruadh) Ó Súilleabháin, or Owen Roe O'Sullivan (1748–1784), Irish poets.

4. "Do you know [or can you speak] Irish?"

5. Ventry is located in the western section of the Dingle Peninsula.

6. Irish for "small gate."

7. That is, songs performed in the traditional style or traditional Irish songs.

8. Throughout the interviewers' part *I* refers to Michael Durkan.

9. Thomas Moore (1779–1852), the Irish poet and song writer.

10. Phrase used to criticize someone of Irish nationality with a distinguishing British sensibility, or Anglophilia.

11. Máire Mhac an tSaoi, or MacEntee (b. 1922), Irish writer, and Conor Cruise O'Brien (b. 1917), Irish essayist, critic, and political commentator, are wife and husband.

12. Frank McGuinness, born in County Donegal in 1953, is a writer and teacher.

13. Hiberno-Irish for "rustic, unsophisticated person."

14. "Grant" or "monetary award."

15. Myles Na Gopaleen is the Irish pen name of Brian Ó Nualláin (1911–1966), also known under another pseudonym, Flann O'Brien. His book of modern Irish humor *An Béal*

Bocht (1941) was translated by Patrick C. Power in 1973 as *The Poor Mouth* (London: Hart-David, McGibbon).

16. Seamus Deane (b. 1940), Irish writer and literary critic.

17. That is, "spotting," using a flashlight to locate animals at night.

18. The Norman invasion commenced in 1169.

19. Lady Augusta Gregory (1852–1932), one of the leaders in the Irish literary revival. Referred to here is her practice of visiting the cottages of native Irish speakers, often her own tenants, to transcribe their tales of Irish folklore.

20. Irish for "traditional lore," stories and tales inhering in the oral tradition.

21. Irish term denoting a garment made from coarse white wool or flannel; "homespun."

22. Yeats's ideal of heroic recklessness recurs throughout his writings. The poems "September 1913" and "Pardon, Old Fathers" are often cited as celebrating this ideal.

23. Near the end of the Nine Years' War, on 3 October 1600, Niall Dubh, better known as Niall Garbh, O'Donnell changed sides and allied himself to the English who were commanded by Henry Dowcra. For this defection his wife, Nuala, sister to the Irish leader Red Hugh O'Donnell, left him.

24. Tomás Ó Criomthan, or Criomthain (1856–1937), published his memoirs, *An tOileánach*, in 1929 (translated by Robin Flower in 1934 as *The Islandman* [London: Chatto and Windus; Dublin: Talbot Press]).

25. Irish for "Mrs. Ó Fiannachta" or "Mrs. O'Finaghty."

26. Seán Ó Tuama (b. 1926) published *Maloney* in 1967.

27. In the episode alluded to, Líadan refused to marry Cuirithir for fear that he might steal her poetry.

28. Eibhlín Dhubh Ní Chonaill (fl. 1770), an aunt of Daniel O'Connell, was married to Art Ó Laoghaire. Ó Laoghaire was killed in 1773 by the bodyguard of the Protestant high sheriff of County Cork, Abraham Morris, the ultimate result of a quarrel. Nuala Ní Dhomhnaill refers here to the famous Irish keen (*caoineadh*), "The Lament for Art Ó Laoghaire," Eibhlín Dhubh wrote after her husband's murder.

29. Early in the *Táin* the prophetess-poet Fedelm foresees defeat for the army of Maeve, queen of Connaught.

30. In Irish folklore the banshee's unearthly wailing forewarned of death. See Patricia Lysaght, *The Banshee: The Irish Supernatural Death-Messenger* (Dublin: Glendale Press, 1986).

31. In Greek myth Cassandra, the daughter of Priam, king of Troy, possessed prophetic powers, which everyone disregarded or dismissed as mere madness.

32. Leán Ní Chearna is Nuala Ní Dhomhnaill's great-grandmother mentioned earlier.

33. Nancy Mitford (1904–1973), an English novelist.

34. Molly Keane, or "M. J. Farrell" (b. 1905), an Anglo-Irish writer.

35. See the interview with fiction writer Jennifer Johnston.

36. That is, "country" or "countryside."

37. Adrienne Rich (b. 1929), an American poet.

Tom Paulin

1. Published in three volumes (Derry, 1991). Paulin's recent works include the following: poetry, *Selected Poems, 1972–1990* (London and Boston: Faber and Faber, 1993), and *Walking a Line* (London: Faber and Faber, 1994); criticism, *Minotaur: Poetry and the Nation State* (London: Faber and Faber, 1992) and *Writing to the Moment* (London: Faber and Faber, 1996).

2. Philip Larkin (1922–1985) and Douglas Eaglesham Dunn (b. 1942), noted English poets.

3. Roland Barthes, French linguist and structuralist, 1915–1980.

4. Named for Keith Rupert Murdoch, Australian journalist (b. 1931), who relied upon a combination of sensationalism, sex, scandal, and outspoken conservatism to found a successful newspaper empire.

5. Formed in 1980 by playwright Brian Friel and actor Stephen Rae, the Field Day Theatre Group has grown to include a number of prominent Northern Irish writers dedicated to demythologizing the myths and images that have divided Northern Ireland in hope someday of achieving a united Ireland.

6. Jackson Pollock (1912–1956) was an American artist.

7. Designed to break the cycle of violence in the six counties of Northern Ireland, the Anglo-Irish Agreement was signed in 1985.

8. The Second Defenestration of Prague took place during the Thirty Years' War, in 1618. (The euphemism *defenestration* in this context denotes "resolving" a political crisis by throwing opposition leaders out of high windows.)

9. Sir John Greer Dill (1881–1944) was born in Lurgan, Northern Ireland. Alan Francis Brooke (1883–1963), first Viscount Alanbrooke, was born into families (Brooke and Bellingham) with deep roots in the counties Fermanagh and Louth. Harold Alexander, Viscount Alexander of Tunis (1891–1969), began his career in 1911 with a commission in the Irish Guards. Bernard Law Montgomery, Viscount Montgomery of Alamein (1887–1976) was of Ulster stock.

10. Fivemiletown is located in County Tyrone near the border with County Fermanagh about ten miles east of Enniskillen.

11. Protestant forces led by King William of Orange defeated the Catholic and basically Irish army commanded by the deposed James II at the Boyne River on 1 July 1690. In 1912 Ulster Unionist and British Conservatives mounted a successful campaign against the Home Rule Bill introduced into Parliament by the Liberal Party.

12. Unionist leader, and later prime minister of Northern Ireland, Sir James Craig met

Irish nationalist and later prime minister, or taoiseach, Eamon de Valera in Dublin, April 1922. The two discovered they had no common ground for discussing Ireland's future.

Brendan Kennelly

1. Since the year of the interview, Kennelly's published works have included the following: *A Time for Voices: Selected Poems, 1960–1990* (Newcastle-upon-Tyne, Eng.: Bloodaxe Books, 1990); *The Book of Judas: A Poem* (Newcastle-upon-Tyne, Eng.: Bloodaxe Books, 1991); *Breathing Spaces: Early Poems* (Newcastle-upon-Tyne, Eng.: Bloodaxe Books, 1992); *Journey into Joy: Selected Prose* (Newcastle-upon-Tyne, Eng.: Bloodaxe Books; Chester Springs, Pa.: Dufour Editions, 1994); and *Poetry My Arse* (Newcastle-upon-Tyne, Eng.: Bloodaxe Books; Chester Springs, Pa.: Dufour Editions, 1995).

2. That is, studying for the final examinations resulting in a secondary-school diploma.

3. See William Blake's poem "The Echoing Green" from *Songs of Innocence*, in *The Poetical Works of William Blake*, ed. John Sampson (Williamstown, Mass.: Corner House Publishers, 1978), 87–88.

4. That is, a "celebration," "festival."

5. The Gaelic Athletic Association, founded in 1884.

6. See British poet Ted Hughes's poem "Pike": "A pond I fished, . . . It was as deep as England."

7. In chapter 5 of James Joyce's *Portrait of the Artist as a Young Man* Stephen Dedalus confronts the disturbing fact that the English-born dean possesses a profound appreciation of English that he, Irishman Stephen, can never achieve: "His language, so familiar and so foreign, will always be for me an acquired speech."

8. Oisin, third-century Gaelic bard and supposed author of poems actually forged by the eighteenth-century Scottish writer James McPherson (1736–1796).

9. In Greek mythology Antigone was executed because she refused to allow her brother's body to lie unburied, the punishment decreed by the king of Thebes, Creon. Medea enjoyed a reputation as a murderess. In one instance, rejected by Jason, the man she loved, she murdered their children in revenge, depriving him of heirs. The two women thus polarize female attitudes toward self and justice.

10. "A public reading of Kennelly's *The Trojan Women* took place in the Project Arts Centre a week after this conversation," Pine. In Greek mythology, and in Euripides's play based upon the story, the women who survived the sacking of Troy epitomized the tragic plight of all women who must endure living after the slaughter of their menfolk.

11. "The psychiatric hospital where Kennelly was treated for alcoholism," Pine.

12. A pub in the vicinity of Trinity College, Dublin.

13. At the time of the interview, of course, divorce in Ireland was not a legal option.

14. "Kerryman, formerly professor of literature at the University of Manitoba, now living and writing in Connemara," Pine.

Hugh Leonard

1. Leonard's more recent works include the biographical novel *Parnell and the Englishwoman* (London: A. Deutsch, 1991) and the play *Moving* (London: Samuel French, 1994). His *Selected Plays*, ed. S. F. Gallagher (Gerrards Cross, Eng.: Colin Smythe; Washington, D.C.: Catholic Univ. Press), appeared in 1992.

2. "See final paragraph above," Gallagher.

3. *New York Times*, 25 Sept. 1967, 58.

4. See below, p. 154.

5. Leonard mentions short stories by, of course, Irish writers Sean O'Faolain (1900–1991) and Frank O'Connor (1903–1966), and English author H. E. Bates (1905–1974).

6. U. S. dramatist George Simon Kaufman (1889–1961) and American librettist Moss Hart (1904–1961).

7. That is, Irish dramatists Brian Friel (b. 1929) and Thomas Murphy (b. 1935).

8. Leonard Alfred George Strong (1896–1958), writer born of Irish parents in England and raised there but characterized by a strong love of the Irish countryside.

9. English humorist Alan Coren (b. 1938).

10. English dramatist Alan Ayckbourn (b. 1939).

11. John Boynton Priestly (1894–1984), British novelist.

12. French dramatist Georges Feydeau (1862–1921).

13. American librettist Stephen Sondheim (b. 1930).

14. British dramatist John Arden (b. 1930).

15. British dramatist Harold Pinter (b. 1930).

16. *Out after Dark* was published in 1989 (London).

17. Published in 1988 (Gerrards Cross, Eng.).

18. The American author Thornton Wilder's *Our Town* was first performed in 1938, and Welsh writer Dylan Thomas's radio play *Under Milkwood* was first read in 1954.

19. *Moving* was published in 1994 (London).

Medbh McGuckian

1. See the interview with Paul Muldoon.

2. See the interviews with Eiléan Ní Chuilleanáin and Eavan Boland.

3. See the interview with Nuala Ní Dhomnaill.

4. An illusion to the first scene of Sean O'Casey's *The Plough and the Stars*, where Mrs. Gogan remarks to Fluther on "the mysthery of havin' a woman's a mysthery no longer."

5. An allusion to Keats's sonnet "Bright Star": "Bright star . . . Like Nature's patient, sleepless Eremite."

6. Probably an allusion to either or both of Chaucer's two nuns: the Second Nun with her humorless prologue and heavily moralizing story of St. Cecilia's martyrdom, and the Prioress who narrates the brutal murder of the young Hugh of Lincoln by members of the Jewish community and then details the savage retribution meted out to them.

7. Among his marginalia on William Wordsworth's *Poems* William Blake wrote, "There is no such Thing as natural Piety Because The Natural Man is at Enmity with God" (Annotations to Wordsworth's *Poems* [London, 1815], *The Poetry and Prose of William Blake*, ed. David V. Erdman [Garden City, N.Y.: Doubleday, 1965], 654).

8. Jan Toorop (1858–1928), Dutch artist associated with the art nouveau movement and influenced by Celtic art.

9. Simone de Beauvoir (1908–1986), French feminist writer.

10. In the Fenian, or Ossianic, cycle of ancient Irish tales the poet Oisín was the son of Finn mac Cumaill (McCool) and Blaí. Líadan was a seventh-century Munster poet who sacrificed her love to become a nun. She is the fictional speaker of the ninth-century poem "Líadan and Cuirithir."

11. Granuaile, or Grace, O'Malley (c. 1530–1603), was a powerful "queen" whose principal castle was Carrickahowley in Clew Bay, County Mayo. McGuckian's forename also recalls the ancient queen of Connaught, Medhbh or Maeve, whose exploits constitute part of the ancient Irish epic, the *Táin Bó Cuailnge* or *Cattle Raid of Cooley.*

12. Eva Gore-Booth (1870–1926), Irish suffragette and poet. Katharine Tynan (1861–1931), Irish poet closely associated with William Butler Yeats and the Irish literary revival.

13. Maire Devenport O'Neill (1879–1967), Irish poet closely associated with Yeats and the Irish literary revival.

14. McGuckian alludes to chapter 5 of James Joyce's *Portrait of the Artist as a Young Man* where Stephen employs the image of nets to suggest social and intellectual constraint, repression: "When the soul of a man is born in this country there are nets flung to hold it back from flight. You talk to me of nationality, language, religion. I shall try to fly those nets" (*A Portrait of the Artist as a Young Man*, ed. Chester G. Anderson [New York, 1964], 203).

15. See the interviews with Michael Longley, Derek Mahon, and Paul Muldoon.

16. W. B. Yeats served six years as a senator in the Irish Parliament, or Dail, 1922–28.

Eavan Boland

1. Among Boland's other principal works are the following: *The War Horse* (Dublin: Arlen House; London: Gollancz, 1975); *In Her Own Image* (Dublin: Arlen House, 1980); *Introducing Eavan Boland: Poems* (Princeton, N.J.: Ontario Review Press, 1981); *Night Feed*

(Dublin: Arlen House, 1982); *The Journey and Other Poems* (Manchester, Eng.: Carcanet, 1987); *Selected Poems* (Manchester, Eng.: Carcanet, 1989); *Outside History: Poems 1980–90* (Manchester, Eng.: Carcanet; New York: W. W. Norton, 1990); and *An Origin Like Water: Collected Poems* (New York: W. W. Norton, 1996).

2. "The Achill Woman & Other Poems: A Special *APR* Supplement," *American Poetry Review*, 19, no. 2 (1990).

3. Two particularly critical reviews illustrate this Irish patriarchal gender prejudice: William Logan, "Animal Instincts and Natural Powers," *New York Times Book Review*, 22 Apr. 1991; and Denis Donoghue, "The Delirium of the Brave," *New York Times Book Review*, 26 May 1994.

4. 19 (1990).

5. See n. 4, above.

6. *New Territory*.

7. *Irish Poetry after Joyce*, 1st ed. (Notre Dame, Ind.: Univ. of Notre Dame Press, 1985).

Derek Mahon

1. Possibly refers to *Journalism: Selected Prose Pieces, 1970–1995*, eventually published in 1996 (Oldcastle, Ireland: Gallery Books; Winston-Salem, N.C.: Wake Forest Univ. Press). Other more recent works include *Selected Poems* (Oldcastle, Ireland: Gallery Books, 1990) and *The Hudson Letter* (Oldcastle, Ireland: Gallery Books; Winston-Salem, N.C.: Wake Forest Univ. Press, 1995).

2. British poet and colonist in Ireland, Edmund Spenser (1552?–1599) in his *Short View of the Present State of Ireland* (1596) criticizes the Old English landowners for "going native," becoming in effect "more Irish than the Irish," which is how one may translate the Latin phrase with which Mahon ends this response.

3. In 1601 the Irish rebel leader Hugh O'Neill, earl of Tyrone, led an Irish army to the southern coastal town of Kinsale where the English general Charles Blount, Lord Mountjoy, was besieging a Spanish expeditionary force sent to assist the Irish. The disastrous defeat that befell the Irish occurred on 24 December.

4. Belfast's prestigious Linen Hall Library was founded in 1788 by the Belfast Society for Promoting Knowledge.

5. Thomas Russell (1767–1803) and Henry Joy McCracken (1767–1798) were prominent leaders in the Society of United Irishmen.

6. Dubliner Theobald Wolfe Tone (1763–1798) was perhaps the most influential of the United Irishmen.

7. The Royal Ulster Constabulary.

8. Basil Brooke (1888–1974), viscount Brookeborough, was Unionist prime minister of Northern Ireland 1943–63. For Stormont see n. 2, p. 219.

9. For Philip Hobsbaum see n. 3, p. 217.

10. F. R. Leavis (1895–1978), British literary critic and educator known for his position that literary criticism must discriminate and offer moral judgments on works of literature.

11. See the interview with Michael Longley.

12. See the interviews with Brendan Kennelly and Eavan Boland.

13. Myles na Gopaleen is the journalistic pen name of satirist and Irish language scholar Brian O'Nolan (1911–1966).

14. Edward Dowden (1843–1913) was professor of English literature at Trinity College, Dublin.

15. John Charles McQuaid (1895–1973), Roman Catholic archbishop of Dublin and primate of Ireland, 1940–72, was noted for his ultraconservative policies.

16. In the historical event on which Mahon elaborates, Owen's father, radical socialist and pacificist Francis Sheehy-Skeffington (1878–1916), tried to prevent looting during the Easter Rising of 1916. Captain J. C. Bowen-Colthurst arrested and executed him.

17. That is, Lucy McDiarmid.

18. Ironically, Louis MacNeice (1907–1963), William Robert Rodgers (1909–1969), and John Harold Hewitt (1907–1987) are all "Northern"

writers.

19. Fred Hanna's is a well-known Dublin bookstore.

20. Francis Stuart (b. 1902), Irish writer remembered particularly for his fiction and his support for Germany during World War II. *The High Consistory* was published in 1981 (London: Martin Brian and O'Keefe).

Eiléan Ní Chuilleanáin

1. Space does not permit inclusion of the full text of Deborah McWilliams's original headnote, which also includes critical discussions of several poems by Ní Chuilleanáin.

Suggested Readings

General Works and Collections of Essays

Brophy, James D., and Eamon Grennan, eds. *New Irish Writing: Essays in Memory of Raymond J. Porter.* Boston: Iona College Press, 1989.

Byrne, John M. *The Significance of Landscape in the Poetry of Seamus Heaney, Derek Mahon and John Montague.* Newcastle-upon-Tyne: University of Newcastle-upon-Tyne, 1984.

Corcoran, Neil, ed. *The Chosen Ground.* Bridgen, Wales: Poetry Wales; Chester Springs, Pa.: Dufour Editions, 1992.

Deane, Seamus. *Celtic Revivals: Essays in Modern Irish Literature.* Winston-Salem, N.C.: Wake Forest Univ. Press, 1985.

Field Day Theatre Company. *Ireland's Field Day.* London: Hutchinson, 1985.

Garratt, Robert F. *Modern Irish Poetry: Tradition and Continuity from Yeats to Heaney.* Berkeley and Los Angeles: Univ. of California Press, 1986.

Genet, Jacqueline, and Wynne Hellegouarc'h, eds. *Irish Writers and Their Creative Process.* Gerrards Cross, Eng.: Colin Smythe, 1996.

Haberstroh, Patricia Boyle. *Women Creating Women: Contemporary Irish Women Poets.* Syracuse, N.Y.: Syracuse Univ. Press, 1996.

Imhof, Rüdiger. *Contemporary Irish Novelists.* Tübingen, Germany: G. Narr, 1990.

Johnston, Dillon. *Irish Poetry after Joyce.* 2d ed. Syracuse, N.Y.: Syracuse Univ. Press, 1997.

Kenneally, Michael, ed. *Cultural Contexts and Literary Idioms in Contemporary Irish Literature.* Totowa, N.J.: Barnes and Noble, 1988.

Longley, Edna. *Poetry in the Wars.* Newark, N.J.: Univ. of Delaware Press, 1987.

Rickard, John S., ed. *Irishness and (Post) Modernism*. Lewisburg, Pa.: Bucknell Univ. Press, 1994.

Weekes, Ann Owens. *Irish Women Writers: An Uncharted Tradition*. Lexington, Ky.: Univ. of Kentucky Press, 1990.

Wills, Clair. *Improprieties: Politics and Sexuality in Northern Irish Poetry*. Oxford: Oxford Univ. Press, 1993.

John Banville

Banville, John. "The Personae of Summer." In *Irish Writers and Their Creative Process*. edited by Jacqueline Genet and Wynne Hellegouarc'h,118–22. Gerrards Cross, Eng.: Colin Smythe, 1996.

Imhof, Rüdiger. "In Search of the Rosy Grail: The Creative Process in the Novels of John Banville." In *Irish Writers and Their Creative Process*. edited by Jacqueline Genet and Wynne Hellegouarc'h, 123–36. Gerrards Cross, Eng.: Colin Smythe, 1996.

———. *John Banville: A Critical Introduction*. Dublin: Wolfhound Press, 1989.

McMinn, Joseph. *John Banville: A Critical Study*. Dublin: Gill and Macmillan, 1991.

———. "Stereotypical Images of Ireland in John Banville's Fiction." *Éire-Ireland* 23, no. 3 (1988): 94–102.

O'Brien, George. "John Banville: Portraits of the Artist." In *New Irish Writing: Essays in Memory of Raymond J. Porter,* edited by James D. Brophy and Eamon Grennan, 161–73. Boston: Iona College Press, 1989.

Eavan Boland

Brother, Laura Lee. *Eavan Boland's Repossession of a Silenced Literary History*. Lexington: Univ. of Kentucky Press, 1993.

Conboy, Shiela C. "Eavan Boland's Topography of Displacement." *Éire-Ireland* 29, no. 3 (1994): 137–46.

Consalvo, Deborah McWilliams. "In Common Usage: Eavan Boland's Poetic Voice." *Éire-Ireland* 28, no. 2 (1993): 98–115.

Haberstroh, Patricia Boyle. "Eavan Boland." In *Women Creating Women: Contemporary Irish Women Poets*, 59–90. Syracuse, N.Y.: Syracuse Univ. Press, 1996.

Johnston, Dillon. "Afterword." In *Irish Poetry after Joyce*. 2d ed., 273–342, passim. Syracuse, N.Y.: Syracuse Univ. Press, 1997.

Weekes, Ann Owens. "'An Origin Like Water': The Poetry of Eavan Boland and Modernist Critiques of Irish Literature." In *Irishness and (Post) Modernism*, edited by John S. Rickard, 159–76. Lewisburg, Pa.: Bucknell Univ. Press, 1994.

Jennifer Johnston

Connelly, Joseph. "Legend and Lyric as Structure in the Selected Fiction of Jennifer Johnston." *Éire-Ireland* 21, no. 3 (1986): 119–24.

McMahon, Sean. "Anglo-Irish Attitudes: The Novels of Jennifer Johnston." *Éire-Ireland* 10, no. 3 (1975): 137–41.

Weekes, Ann Owens. "Jennifer Johnston: From Gortnaree to Knappogue." In *Irish Women Writers: An Uncharted Tradition*, 191–211. Lexington, Ky.: Univ. of Kentucky Press, 1990.

Brendan Kennelly

McDonald, Marianne. "'A Bomb at the Door': Kennelly's *Medea*." *Éire-Ireland* 28, no. 2 (1993): 129–37.

Pine, Richard, ed. *Dark Fathers into Light: Brendan Kennelly*. Newcastle-upon-Tyne: Bloodaxe Books, 1994.

This Fellow with the Fabulous Smile: A Tribute to Brendan Kennelly. Newcastle-upon-Tyne: Bloodaxe Books, 1996.

Benedict Kiely

Casey, Daniel J. *Benedict Kiely*. Lewisburg, Pa.: Bucknell Univ. Press, 1974.

Eckley, Grace. *Benedict Kiely*. New York: Twayne Publishers, 1972.

———. "The Fiction of Benedict Kiely." *Éire-Ireland* 3, no. 4 (1968): 55–65.

Ward, Catherine. "Land and Landscape in Novels by McLaverty, Kiely, and Leland." *Éire-Ireland* 23, no. 3 (1988): 68–78.

Hugh Leonard

Gallagher, S. F., ed. "Introduction." In *Selected Plays of Hugh Leonard*. Gerards Cross, Eng.: Colin Smythe; Washington D.C.: Catholic Univ. Press, 1992.

Michael Longley

Allen, Michael. "Options: The Poetry of Michael Longley." *Éire-Ireland* 10, no. 4 (1975): 129–36.

Johnston, Dillon. "Afterword." In *Irish Poetry after Joyce.* 2d ed., 308–12. Syracuse, N.Y.: Syracuse Univ. Press, 1997.

Longley, Michael. "Memory as Acknowledgement." *Irish Review*, nos. 17/18 (1995): 153–59.

McDonald, Peter. "Michael Longley's Homes." In *The Chosen Ground*, edited by Neil Corcoran, 65–83. Bridgen, Wales: Poetry Wales; Chester Springs, Pa.: Dufour Editions, 1992.

Peacock, Alan J. "Prolegomena to Michael Longley's Peace Poem." *Éire-Ireland*, 23, no. 1 (1988): 60–74.

Derek Mahon

Deane, Seamus. "Derek Mahon." In *Celtic Revivals: Essays in Modern Irish Literature*, 156–73. Winston-Salem, N.C.: Wake Forest Univ. Press, 1985.

Frazier, Adrian. "Proper Portion: Derek Mahon's *The Hunt by Night*." *Éire-Ireland*, 18, no. 4 (1983): 136–43.

Haughton, Hugh. "'Even now there are places where a thought might grow': Place and Displacement in the Poetry of Derek Mahon." In *The Chosen Ground*, edited by Neil Corcoran, 87–120. Bridgen, Wales: Poetry Wales; Chester Springs, Pa.: Dufour Editions, 1992.

Johnston, Dillon. "MacNeice and Montague." In *Irish Poetry after Joyce.* 2d ed., 204–46. Syracuse, N.Y.: Syracuse Univ. Press, 1997.

Kennedy, Brian P. "A Theoptic Eye: Derek Mahon's *The Hunt by Night*." *Éire-Ireland*, 25, no. 4 (1990): 120–31.

Longley, Edna. "The Singing Line: Form in Derek Mahon's Poetry." In *Poetry in the Wars*, 170–84. Newark, N.J.: Univ. of Delaware Press, 1987.

John McGahern

Brown, Terence. "John McGahern's *Nightlines*: Tone, Technique and Symbolism." In *The Irish Short Story*, ed. Patrick Rafroidi and Terence Brown, 289–301. Gerrards Cross, Eng.: Colin Smythe; Atlantic Highlands, N.J.: Humanities Press, 1979.

The Canadian Association for Irish Studies 17, no. 1 (1991). Special McGahern issue.

Cronin, John. "John McGahern: A New Image?" In *Irish Writers and Their Creative Process.* edited by Jacqueline Genet and Wynne Hellegouarc'h, 110–17. Gerrards Cross, Eng.: Colin Smythe, 1996.

Fournier, Suzanne J. "Structure and Theme in John McGahern's *The Pornographer.*" *Éire-Ireland* 22, no. 1 (1987): 139–50.

Kennedy, Eileen. "Sons and Fathers in John McGahern's Short Stories." In *New Irish Writing: Essays in Memory of Raymond J. Porter,* edited by James D. Brophy and Eamon Grennan, 65–74. Boston: Iona College Press, 1989.

Lloyd, Richard Burr. *The Symbolic Mass: Thematic Resolution in the Irish Novels of John McGahern.* Emporia, Kans.: Emporia State Univ., 1987.

McGahern, John. "Reading and Writing." In *Irish Writers and Their Creative Process.* edited by Jacqueline Genet and Wynne Hellegouarc'h, 103–9. Gerrards Cross, Eng.: Colin Smythe, 1996.

Samson, Denis. *Outstaring Nature's Eye: The Fiction of John McGahern.* Dublin: Lilliput Press, 1993.

Schwartz, Karlheinz. "John McGahern's Point of View." *Éire-Ireland* 19, no. 3 (1984): 92–110.

Medbh McGuckian

Docherty, Thomas. "Initiations, Tempers, Seduction: Postmodern McGuckian." In *The Chosen Ground,* edited by Neil Corcoran, 191–210. Bridgen, Wales: Poetry Wales; Chester Springs, Pa.: Dufour Editions, 1992.

Haberstroh, Patricia Boyle. "Medbh McGuckian." In *Women Creating Women: Contemporary Irish Women Poets,* 123–58. Syracuse, N.Y.: Syracuse Univ. Press, 1996.

Johnston, Dillon. "Afterword." In *Irish Poetry after Joyce.* 2d ed., 276–81, 293–98. Syracuse, N.Y.: Syracuse Univ. Press, 1997.

McGuckian, Medbh. "Visiting Poet." *Irish Review* no. 11 (1991–92): 47–49.

O'Connor, Mary. "'Rising Out': Medbh McGuckian's Destabilizing Poetic." *Éire-Ireland* 30, no. 4 (1996): 154–72.

Wills, Clair. "Medbh McGuckian: The Intimate Sphere." In *Improprieties: Politics and Sexuality in Northern Irish Poetry,* 158–93. Oxford: Oxford Univ. Press, 1993.

John Montague

Bizot, Richard. "A Sense of Places: The Homing Instinct in the Poetry of John Montague." *Éire-Ireland* 30, no. 1 (1995): 167–76.

Dawe, Gerald. "Invocation of Powers: John Montague." In *The Chosen Ground*, edited by Neil Corcoran, 15–32. Bridgen, Wales: Poetry Wales; Chester Springs, Pa.: Dufour Editions, 1992.

Deane, Seamus. "John Montague: The Kingdom of the Dead." In *Celtic Revivals: Essays in Modern Irish Literature*, 146–55. Winston-Salem, N.C.: Wake Forest Univ. Press, 1985.

Frazier, Adrian. "Pilgrim Haunts: Montague's *The Dead Kingdom* and Heaney's *Station Island*." *Éire-Ireland* 20, no. 4 (1985): 134–43.

Garratt, Robert F. "Poetry at Mid-Century II: John Montague." In *Modern Irish Poetry: Tradition and Continuity from Yeats to Heaney*, 198–229. Berkeley and Los Angeles: Univ. of California Press, 1986.

Irish University Review 19, no. 1 (1989). Special John Montague issue.

Johnston, Dillon. "Devil and Montague." In *Irish Poetry after Joyce*. 2d ed., 167–203. Syracuse, N.Y.: Syracuse Univ. Press, 1997.

Kersnowski, Frank L. *John Montague*. Lewisburg, Pa.: Bucknell Univ. Press, 1975.

Martin, Augustine. "John Montague: Passionate Contemplative." In *Irish Writers and Their Creative Process*. edited by Jacqueline Genet and Wynne Hellegouarc'h, 37–51. Gerrards Cross, Eng.: Colin Smythe, 1996.

Montague, John. "The Sweet Way." In *Irish Writers and Their Creative Process*. edited by Jacqueline Genet and Wynne Hellegouarc'h, 30–36. Gerrards Cross, Eng.: Colin Smythe, 1996.

Poger, Sidney. "Crane and Montague: The Pattern History Weaves." *Éire-Ireland* 16, no. 4 (1981): 114–24.

Redshaw, Thomas Dillon. "John Montague." *Éire-Ireland* 11, no. 4 (1976): 122–33.

———. "Ri, as in Regional." *Éire-Ireland* 9, no. 2 (1974): 41–64.

Skelton, Robin. "John Montague and the Divided Inheritance." In *Celtic Contraries*, 225–46. Syracuse, N. Y.: Syracuse Univ. Press, 1990.

Paul Muldoon

Brown, Richard. "Bog Poems and Book Poems: Doubleness, Self-Translation and Pun in Seamus Heaney and Paul Muldoon." In *The Chosen Ground*, edited by

Neil Corcoran, 153–67. Bridgen, Wales: Poetry Wales; Chester Springs, Pa.: Dufour Editions, 1992.

Frazier, Adrian. "Juniper, Otherwise Known: Poems by Paulin and Muldoon." *Éire-Ireland* 19, no. 1 (1984): 123–33.

Grennan, Eamon. "Two-Part Invention: Reading into Durcan and Muldoon." In *New Irish Writing: Essays in Memory of Raymond J. Porter,* edited by James D. Brophy and Eamon Grennan, 203–31. Boston: Iona College Press, 1989.

Johnston, Dillon. "Toward 'A Broader and More Comprehensive Irish Identity'"; "Afterword." In *Irish Poetry after Joyce.* 2d ed., 263–72, 289–91. Syracuse, N.Y.: Syracuse Univ. Press, 1997.

Kendall, Tim. *Paul Muldoon.* Bridgend, Wales: Poetry Wales, 1996.

Longley, Edna. "'Varieties of Parable': Louis MacNeice and Paul Muldoon." In *Poetry in the Wars,* 211–43. Newark, N.J.: Univ. of Delaware Press, 1987.

Marken, Ronald. "Paul Muldoon's 'Juggling a Red-Hot Half-Brick in an Old Sock': Poets in Ireland Renovate the English-Language Sonnet." *Éire-Ireland* 24, no. 1 (1989), 79–91.

McCurry, Jacqueline. "'Scrap': Colonialism Indicted in the Poetry of Paul Muldoon." *Éire-Ireland* 27, no. 3 (1992): 92–109.

Wills, Clair. "The Lie of the Land: Language, Imperialism and Trade in Paul Muldoon's *Meeting the British.*" In *The Chosen Ground,* edited by Neil Corcoran, 123–49. Bridgen, Wales: Poetry Wales; Chester Springs, Pa.: Dufour Editions, 1992.

———. "Paul Muldoon: Dubious Origins." In *Improprieties: Politics and Sexuality in Northern Irish Poetry,* 194–235. Oxford: Oxford Univ. Press, 1993.

Eileán Ní Chuilleanáin

Haberstroh, Patricia Boyle. "Eiléan Ní Chuilleanáin." In *Women Creating Women: Contemporary Irish Women Poets,* 93–120. Syracuse, N.Y.: Syracuse Univ. Press, 1996.

Johnston, Dillon. "Afterword." In *Irish Poetry after Joyce.* 2d ed., 281–86, 291–93. Syracuse, N.Y.: Syracuse Univ. Press, 1997.

McWilliams, Deborah H. Headnote to "Interview with Eiléan Ní Chuilleanáin." *Irish Literary Supplement,* 12 (spring 1993): 15–16.

Nuala Ní Dhomhnaill

Consalvo, Deborah McWilliams. "The Lingual Ideal in the Poetry of Nuala Ní Dhomhnaill." *Éire-Ireland* 30, no. 2 (1995): 148–61.

Haberstroh, Patricia Boyle. "Nuala Ní Dhomhnaill." In *Women Creating Women: Contemporary Irish Women Poets*, 161–95. Syracuse, N.Y.: Syracuse Univ. Press, 1996.

Johnston, Dillon. "Afterword." In *Irish Poetry after Joyce*. 2d ed., 288–91. Syracuse, N.Y.: Syracuse Univ. Press, 1997.

O'Connor, Mary. *Sex, Lies, and Sovereignty: Nuala Ní Dhomhnaill's Revision of "The Táin."* Boston: Northeastern Univ., 1992.

Ó Tuama, Sean. "'The Loving and Terrible Mother' in the Early Poetry of Nuala Ní Dhomhnaill." In *Repossessions: Selected Essays on the Irish Literary Heritage*, 35–53. Cork: Cork Univ. Press, 1995.

Tom Paulin

Frazier, Adrian. "Juniper, Otherwise Known: Poems by Paulin and Muldoon." *Éire-Ireland* 19, no. 1 (1984): 123–33.

O'Donoghue, Bernard. "Involved Imaginings: Tom Paulin." In *The Chosen Ground*, edited by Neil Corcoran, 171–88. Bridgen, Wales: Poetry Wales; Chester Springs, Pa.: Dufour Editions, 1992.

Wills, Clair. "Tom Paulin: Enlightening the Tribe." In *Improprieties: Politics and Sexuality in Northern Irish Poetry*, 121–57. Oxford: Oxford Univ. Press, 1993.

William Trevor

Hildebidle, John. "Kilneagh and Challacombe: William Trevor's Two Nations." *Éire-Ireland* 28, no. 3 (1993): 114–29.

Loughman, Celeste. "The Mercy of Silence: William Trevor's *Fools of Fortune*." *Éire-Ireland* 28, no. 1 (1993): 87–96.

Morrison, Kristin. *William Trevor*. New York: Twayne Publishers, 1993.

Paulson, Suzanne Morrow. *William Trevor: A Study of the Short Fiction*. New York: Twayne Publishers, 1993.

Ponsford, Michael. "'Only the Truth': The Short Stories of William Trevor." *Éire-Ireland* 23, no. 1 (1988): 75–86.

Rhodes, Robert E. "'The Rest Is Silence': Secrets in Some William Trevor Short Stories." In *New Irish Writing: Essays in Memory of Raymond J. Porter*, edited by James D. Brophy and Eamon Grennan, 35–53. Boston: Iona College Press, 1989.

Schirmer, Gregory A. *William Trevor: A Study of His Fiction*. London: Routledge, 1990.

Index

James P. Myers, Jr., professor of English literature at Gettysburg College, teaches Shakespeare, early seventeenth-century, and Irish literature. His earlier published work explored the Elizabethan reconquest of Ireland (*Elizabethan Ireland: A Selection of Writings by Elizabethan Writers on Ireland*, 1983) and the Jacobean settlement (a critical edition of Sir John Davies's *A Discovery of the True Causes Why Ireland Was Never Entirely Subdued . . .* , 1988). He is now writing on Irish and Scots participation in the French and Indian War, particularly on the 1758 expedition of John Forbes against Fort Duquesne and the settlement of, and ethnic conflict on, the Pennsylvania frontier.